'For actors, actor-trainers and directors, it is a must-have for understanding Stanislavky's practices and spirit, and a complement to any other system being taught.' *Tanya Moodie, actor and associate teacher at RADA*

'This may be the only acting handbook you'll ever need . . . meticulously organised, well-written, and a pleasurable read.' *Back Stage East*

'A great achievement . . . a serious, no-nonsense interpretation of Stanislavsky's thinking written by an actor-teacher with considerable experience . . . I shall be going back to this *Toolkit* again and again.' *Reviews Gate*

'This is a book to be loved, treasured and thumbed through by both the teacher and student.' *Word Matters*

'Drawing from recent Stanislavsky scholarship and her rich experience as an actor, director, teacher and scholar, Bella Merlin magically converts her extensive knowledge into real-world practice and on-the-floor technique. This new edition is a necessary and lively resource for any theatre practitioner.' *David Chambers, Professor of Directing, Yale School of Drama*

'One of the essential books about acting for both professionals and students. This revised edition brings new clarity to unlocking what Stanislavsky means for actors today.' *Michael Earley, Principal, Rose Bruford College of Theatre and Performance*

'The ultimate "all in one" panacea for drama teachers struggling to make Stanislavsky's teachings understandable for students.' *Teaching Drama*

'Erudite but very accessible . . . a brilliantly researched study.' *Amateur Stage*

Bella Merlin

Bella Merlin is an actor, writer, and actor-trainer, acclaimed internationally as a practice-as-researcher and for her work on Stanislavsky.

She appears regularly on stage and screen, including seasons at the Colorado Shakespeare Festival; her original one-woman play, *Tilly No-Body: Catastrophes of Love*; a number of productions for Max Stafford-Clark's Out of Joint, the National Theatre, Andy Lavender's Lightwork Theatre Company, and BBC Television and Radio. Her training at the State Institute of Cinematography in Moscow resulted in a renegotiation of Stanislavsky's acting principles. Her account of the training – *Beyond Stanislavsky: The Psycho-Physical Approach to Actor Training* (Nick Hern Books, 2001) – is the first English-language book to detail Stanislavsky's rehearsal practice, Active Analysis, from the actor's perspective. She has directed a number of theatre productions exclusively using Active Analysis.

As an actor-trainer, Merlin has led workshops in Japan, France, Poland, Australia, Colombia, North America, and across the UK. She was a key contributor to Derek Paget's 'Acting with Facts' project (University of Reading), and Nick Kaye and Gabriella Giannacci's 'Performing Presence' project (Universities of Exeter, Stamford and London). With a PhD from the University of Birmingham, UK, she is currently Professor of Acting and Directing at the University of California, Riverside.

Merlin has published widely, with books including *Acting: The Basics* (Routledge); *With the Rogue's Company: Henry IV at the National Theatre* (Oberon/National Theatre); *Konstantin Stanislavsky* (Routledge Performance Practitioners); and the co-editing with Andrei Kirillov of Michael Chekhov's autobiographies, *The Path of the Actor* (Routledge). Her work is featured in the online Routledge Performance Archive, and in 2012 she recorded an album of original songs, *Scenes Through the Tenement Windows*.

More details can be found at www.bellamerlin.com

The Complete Stanislavsky Toolkit

BELLA MERLIN

NICK HERN BOOKS
London
www.nickhernbooks.co.uk

A Nick Hern Book

The Complete Stanislavsky Toolkit
first published in Great Britain in 2007
by Nick Hern Books Limited
The Glasshouse, 49a Goldhawk Road, London W12 8QP

This revised edition published in 2014

Copyright © 2007, 2014 Bella Merlin

Bella Merlin has asserted her moral right
to be identified as the author of this work

Cover designed by Ned Hoste, 2H
Typeset by Country Setting,
Kingsdown, Kent, CT14 8ES
Printed and bound in Great Britain by
Ashford Colour Press Ltd, Gosport, Hampshire

A CIP catalogue record for this book
is available from the British Library

ISBN   978 1 84842 406 7

For Margaret, Michael and Miles

Contents

Preface to New Edition

2013 marked one hundred and fifty years since Konstantin Stanislavsky was born. Across the theatre world, there were celebrations and salutations for the man who catapulted acting from stereotypes to subtleties, from imitation to embodiment, and from stock theatricality to the 'inner life' that resonates on stage and screen today.

This book – *The Complete Stanislavsky Toolkit* – was first published in 2007 by Nick Hern Books. Nick had also published my first book, *Beyond Stanislavsky*, and in subsequent conversations I'd frequently talked about 'tools' and 'toolkit' – terms that I'd coined from my Russian Scenic Movement director, Vladimir Ananyev. I didn't really like 'system' or 'method' to describe Stanislavsky's work, and I was excited when Nick gave me the charge to write a 'toolkit', a book that made readily accessible an array of Stanislavsky's acting strategies. Little did we realise, as we sat in our favourite Italian haunt near Shepherd's Bush Underground, what an egg we were hatching – and my gratitude to Nick is immense.

One of my main resources for *The Toolkit* was Elizabeth Reynolds Hapgood's 1936 translation of *An Actor Prepares*. Although this is a seminal text for actors and directors across the English-speaking world, it's actually a highly abridged version of Stanislavsky's original tome. So I was very intrigued when, in 2008, Jean Benedetti's translation of the full version, *An Actor's Work*, appeared in print. Here, Benedetti introduced new translations of the Hapgood terms, and these translations were closer to the Russian originals and often more actor-friendly. Although *The Complete Stanislavsky Toolkit* had already been on the market for a year, Benedetti's changes set me thinking about the ways in which actors and directors use terminology. What works for an actor? What alienates an actor? Which word is best – 'objective', 'task', 'desire' or 'need'? Is 'unit' a useful name for a chunk of text, or is 'bit' more appropriate (especially as it's closer to the original Russian word, *kusok*)? Does it even matter what terms you use as long as you get the results?

In April 2012, I was invited to give the Annual Stanislavski Centre/Routledge Lecture at the Stanislavski Centre, UK, so I set some gentle cats among some gentle pigeons by posing these questions. I began to wonder if there was a gap between theatre scholars (who advocate absolute fidelity to Stanislavsky's originals) and practitioners like myself (who aspire to acting excellence whatever the specifics of terminology). Given this fascination with acting vocab, I was delighted when Nick Hern agreed to publish a revised edition of *The Toolkit*. Here was an opportunity to update the first edition, in light of both Benedetti's 2008 translation and my own experimentations as an actor and a trainer.

The main terms that I've adopted from Benedetti's *An Actor's Work* are: 'inner psychological drives' (rather than Hapgood's 'inner motive forces') and 'logic and sequence' (rather than 'logic and coherence'). The reason I've chosen 'inner psychological drives' is essentially instinctive. As an actor, I find the focus on 'drives' more helpful than 'forces': 'What is *driving* my character to do this?' yields me more imaginative fruit than 'What is *forcing* my character to do this?' Although personally I'd rather they were called '*psycho-physical* drives', 'psychological' is arguably a more accessible adjective than 'motive' in this particular context.

My choice for 'logic and sequence' over 'logic and coherence' is quite simple. I've found that the more we understand as actors the ways in which one action leads to the next action, to the next, to the next, to the next – in a *logical sequence* – the more precise our process becomes. (I learned this very much from working with my own acting coach, Katya Kamotskaya, when she directed me in *The Seagull* in 2010.) I write in *The Toolkit* about the 'Action-Reaction-Decision' sequence that underpins all human discourse. If you can genuinely open yourself up to all the nuances of this sequence and if you listen to your onstage partner, something really dynamic can happen between you. You no longer have to fake it and force it: instead, you can feel the electric way in which you're dependent on each other's actions, reactions and decisions. And this process can occur regardless of genre or style – be it vampires and wolves, or doctors and nurses. Each character in each context will have a particular logic underpinning their choices, and that logic moves them sequentially from one action to the next to the next.

The main (somewhat radical) adaptation that I've made concerns 'communication', which is the title of Chapter 10 in *An Actor's Work*. This is Jean Benedetti's translation of Elizabeth Hapgood's 'communion'. For many years I used the term 'communion', fully aware that it had an esoteric, almost religious overtone. Yet I enjoyed the unseen qualities implicit in the idea of 'communing' with something – be it God or Man or Nature. After all, Stanislavsky was very intrigued by yoga and *prana* energy, and certainly the word 'communion' implies some silent connection, in which the tiny nuances of energetic changes, facial expressions and body positions give as much information as any spoken word. That said, I can't deny that on a couple of occasions I've had workshop participants show a little resistance to the term 'communion'. So I was more than happy to look for an alternative. However, Benedetti's 'communication' didn't work for me either. In our technological age, the word 'communication' comes with a heap of digital and electronic overtones, and seems to reduce the intangible, intuitive aspects of human intercourse. Since neither term seems to be entirely serviceable, I've adapted them in my own practice to the word 'connection', since 'connection' allows for both physical and energetic contact. And that's the term that I've used here in *The Toolkit*.

There are a handful of terms that I've left in *The Toolkit*, although I don't really use them any more: they include 'mental reconnaissance' and 'concentration of attention'. 'Mental reconnaissance' no longer resonates for me. As an actor-trainer, I tend to avoid any direct reference to 'mental' processes or anything that separates the actor's thinking mind from their imaginative body. Since writing *The Complete Stanislavsky Toolkit*, I've come to understand much more fully the term 'bodymind' (a concept that I didn't wholly embrace five years ago: see pp. 255–6). The whole idea of psycho-physicality means that it's almost impossible to separate your brain from your body. And neuroscience categorically endorses that fact. So I now refer to detailed text analysis or 'mental reconnaissance' as 'forensic detective work'. To me, that sounds less cerebral and more imaginative. As someone hooked on the television documentary *Forensic Files* and real-life crime, it feeds my imagination to think about scraping away at the skeleton of the black-and-white text to trace back to the flesh-and-blood character. 'Text analysis' sounds a bit dull. 'Mental reconnaissance' sounds like a general poring over battle plans. 'Forensic detective work' brings with it the excitement of uncovering something that may never have been discovered before. Therefore, it gives space for the actor's imagination and unique interpretation. So, although I've kept 'mental reconnaissance' in this book, I frequently use an alternative.

One of the nitty-gritty terms with which Benedetti and his Russian-language consultant, Katya Kamotskaya, wrestled in *An Actor's Work* was 'concentration and attention'. Hapgood uses 'concentration of attention'. Benedetti wanted to use 'concentration'. At last he and Kamotskaya settled on 'concentration and attention'. I write in *The Toolkit* about the difficulties surrounding the word 'concentration', and in recent years I've found myself adopting the word 'focus'. To focus on something has a clarity, an uncomplicatedness – like a camera lens focusing on an object. The process is direct and doesn't require unnecessary brain power, just as our eyes usually focus without us thinking about it too much. I do still use the term 'attention' (particularly with exercises like the one described in this book: 'Circles of attention'). However, I rarely use 'concentration' and almost always use 'focus'. That said, I've adopted 'concentration and attention' in this second edition of *The Toolkit* to remain connected to both the Hapgood and Benedetti translations.

*

Since the first publication of *The Complete Stanislavsky Toolkit*, I've significantly streamlined my own use of Stanislavsky's ideas, and I offer in this Preface a kind of roadmap for how you can concisely integrate his principles into your own acting practices.

1. Guiding principles

First of all, I have Four Principles that underpin my work as an actor and a teacher:

1. *Dynamic listening* (obviously this means listening to our partners and the audience, etc., but it actually begins with an ability to listen to all the minute changes that occur within ourselves each day – physically, emotionally and experientially. After all, we're both the materials and the instruments with which we create);

2. *Willing vulnerability* (a playfulness to take risks and not to be afraid to look 'foolish' in rehearsal. If the director doesn't like the choices we offer, we know that our imaginations are so fertile, we have plenty of other ideas from where that first choice came);

3. *Psycho-physical co-ordination* (whatever is going on inside us impacts on our physical expression, and whatever input we receive from the outside world impacts

on our inner life. The membrane between *inner* world and *outer* expression is very porous, as we try to remain 'thin-skinned');

4. *A constant state of inner improvisation* (this entails always saying 'yes' to whatever our partner or director offers us; we're able to remain within a tight staging when necessary and with a dead-letter-perfect delivery of text, yet we're always imaginatively alive and playful, even in the darkest tragedy).

2. Preparing for creative work

Then there are the Four Pillars on which Stanislavsky built his 'system' and which help me as an actor to prepare an appropriate INNER CREATIVE STATE before I start work:

i.   RELAXATION (and for me, this means psycho-physical relaxation, not just bodily relaxation. It's like Michael Chekhov's 'quality of ease': relaxation is imaginative playfulness, as much as physical release);

ii. FOCUS (or 'concentration of attention': i.e. the ability to home in on a task, a person, an object, and to let the imagination connect with it playfully);

iii. OBSERVATION (i.e. curiosity about the world, not seeking all our imaginative stimuli from our smartphones, but returning to such old-fashioned pastimes as people-watching and live engagement with the world around us);

iv. IMAGINATION (and knowing that we are bound by nothing but our own imaginations, in terms of the world views that we can adopt and the realms that we can inhabit).

3. Specific work on building a character

As I begin work on a character, I allow Stanislavsky's Three Levels of Research to guide me:

a. Detailed work on the *text* (this will unlock the specifics of language, syntax, POV, etc. and ties in with the first four FUNDAMENTAL QUESTIONS below);

b. Research on the *realm of the play and the playwright* (this will reveal some useful historical, cultural, social details to inform my choices as I build the character);

c. Research on the *self* (this will help me find the LURE or bait to connect my own imagination, body, emotional repertoire and creative juices with the world opened up to me by the playwright).

Working with these three levels of research, I rely heavily on the SIX FUNDAMENTAL QUESTIONS:

The first three (Who? Where? When?) relate to Level [a] of research, and they bed me in my thorough, forensic detective work on the text. This text analysis helps me define the GIVEN CIRCUMSTANCES; locate the BITS of action; and unlock the atmosphere and TEMPO-RHYTHM of the playwright's style and world;

The fourth question (Why?) reveals my OBJECTIVES and my SUPEROBJECTIVES, and why the playwright wrote each scene. (This links Levels [a] and [b] of the research);

The fifth question (For What Reason?) stimulates my imagination, as I combine Level [b] with Level [c] to make a lively connection with the play, a connection that ignites my desire to embody the character;

And the sixth question, 'How?', will access my ACTIONS and my constant state of inner improvisation (see above), as I adapt to my partner's moves, intonations and gestures.

These main strategies form the bedrock of my work on a role. All the other wonderful tools, such as INNER PSYCHOLOGICAL DRIVES, MOMENTS OF ORIENTATION and HEROIC TENSION are applied within this main structure as appropriate.

*

So Stanislavsky was born over one hundred and fifty years ago, and his ideas about acting endure from generation to generation. Every time I return to his toolkit and 'system', a new idea leaps off the page, a new tool presents itself as invaluable, or a particular acting challenge is resolved by applying an obvious tool that I'd forgotten all about.

Stanislavsky receives some bad press from those who are determined to lock him in the closets of realism/emotion memory/dry-and-boring. I would urge them to look at the playfulness, the anarchy, the endless curiosity that he brought to the world of acting. The fact that he ended his life creating an *opera* studio goes to prove just how little he confined himself to realism! As part of the centenary celebrations, I was invited in October 2012 to the Moscow Art Theatre's 'Open Class: Stanislavsky Continues: An International Festival of Acting Schools'. It was my first return to Russia after nearly twenty years, and I took myself back to Stanislavsky's House Museum. When I'd been there two decades ago, I was a very young and inexperienced actor. I'd written nothing about Stanislavsky. I had no ambitions to be an acolyte of his practices or a torch-bearer for his toolkit. Nonetheless, that first visit to his house was still very moving.

Returning twenty years later, I found myself endlessly smiling. Playfulness hung in the air. Strange furniture from motley productions. Set models and stained glass. Photographs of Stanislavsky in various costumes and productions – including some in which he looked decidedly ham! One of the little curator ladies told me an amusing tale: one day, some visitors had called upon Stanislavsky to find him (tall, aristocratic, shock of grey hair) crouching beneath the piano.

'What are you doing?' they asked. 'Finding out what it's like to be a mouse,' he replied (no doubt those bright eyes twinkling from beneath his heavy brows). This was a man who knew that being an actor was to be a perpetual child, always playing, always curious, always allowing the body and the imagination to guide the heart. And in this book are some of the tools he offered to help us all achieve that state.

Bella Merlin
Los Angeles, 2014

Acknowledgements

The Complete Stanislavsky Toolkit owes much to many. Every effort has been made to contact copyright holders and obtain permissions, and thanks go to A&C Black for permission to quote from Stanislavsky's *An Actor Prepares*, *Building a Character*, *Creating a Role* and *My Life in Art*, as well as extracts from David Mamet's *American Buffalo* and Mark Ravenhill's *Shopping and Fucking*. To Faber and Faber for permission to quote from Harold Pinter's *The Lover*, David Hare's *The Permanent Way*, and Stanislavsky's *On the Art of the Stage*. To Farrar, Straus and Giroux for US permission to quote from the *On the Art of the Stage*. To Nick Hern Books for permission to quote from Helen Edmundson's *Anna Karenina* and Stephen Mulrine's translations of Chekhov's *The Seagull*, *Three Sisters* and *The Cherry Orchard*. To Mike Pushkin for his terrific translation of Maria Knebel's *On the Active Analysis of Plays and Roles*, along with Professor Maggie Gale and the University of Birmingham who helped towards the commissioning of the translation.

Without the brilliant contributions of various actors, directors, writers and teachers including Max Stafford-Clark, David Hare, Vladimir Ananyev, Albert Filozov, Katya Kamotskaya, Alex Delamere, Flaminia Cinque, Matthew Dunster, Richard Cottrell, Edward Baker-Duly, Joe Anderson, Terry Johnson, John Lyons, the late Fritha Goodey with whom I thrashed out many an idea over a Starbucks Americana, Matthew Lloyd at the Actors Centre London and numerous workshop participants there, along with Professors Phillip

Zarrilli and Chris McCullough and the gifted students of the University of Exeter, there simply would have been no book. The ongoing research of scholars and practitioners including Sharon M. Carnicke, Jean Benedetti, Robert Leach, Robert Ellerman, Jonathan Pitches and Rose Whyman, among many others in the research community, is a continual and vital resource and provocation: my thanks to them, whether they've been directly quoted or indirectly turned to. And special thanks to my agent, Natasha Stevenson, for her perpetual patience, to Linda di Lieto for her generosity and brave story, to Jane Wilson for a blessed haven in which to write, and my parents Margaret and Michael for their unflinching support.

Last but very far from least, mighty gratitude is owed to the ever-incisive and supportive Nick Hern, and his meticulous colleagues Claire Grady, Caroline Downing, Nick de Somogyi and Simon Trussler. And above all to Miles Anderson, who not only furnished me with countless wisdoms and witticisms, but also passionately and indomitably slashed through various drafts with me late into the night with a carving knife and a Chianti. God bless.

The Complete Stanislavsky Toolkit

Introduction

Konstantin Stanislavsky was without question the father of contemporary acting practice, particularly when it comes to the kind of realism which dominates Western theatre and screen today. He was the inspiration behind what became known as the American 'Method', and he was arguably the first acting practitioner to look at what human beings do naturally in their everyday lives and turn it into something systematic for the stage.

The study of his ideas is on almost every acting academy timetable, every drama degree syllabus, every theatre studies exam, and – be it implicitly or explicitly – his terms and theories are on the lips of most Western acting practitioners.

And yet, bizarrely, he's often dismissed. Why so?

Is it due to poor translations? Misdirected editors? Vainglorious gurus who clamour to 'claim' him? Post-modern performers who consider psychology obsolete? Could it even be due to his own inability from time to time to express his emerging ideas succinctly, with the result that his writings sometimes seem to go round in circles and muddy his practical propositions?

Whatever the reason, his highly hands-on notions have frequently become distorted into something academic and atrophied. And let's face it, the alternatives are very attractive: David Mamet is muscular; Ivana Chubbuck is chic; Suzuki is sexy. Yet all of them use Stanislavsky, whether they know it or not. So it's time to look beneath the bad translations and the cranky turns of phrase, and reappraise what Stanislavsky really had to offer.

As a key for opening *The Complete Stanislavsky Toolkit*, I'm going to use one of the tools described in *An Actor Prepares* as the Six Fundamental Questions. Those six questions are: 'Who?', 'When?', 'Where?', 'Why?', 'For what reason?', and 'How?'[1] (all of which are examined in detail in Chapter 2 below). Stanislavsky believed that the information contained in your answers to these questions could save you as an actor from floundering in a quagmire of generalisation once you greeted the audience or stood in front of the camera.

Putting the questions simply in the context of this book:

- Who was Stanislavsky?

- When was he working?

- Where was he working?

- Why might we as twenty-first-century actors need this book?

- For what reason has it been written?

- How does it go about setting out the tools for the actor?

Here are some possible answers to these questions:

Who was Stanislavsky?

He was a Russian. Born in 1863. And he was arguably the first person to systematise natural (and often *unconscious*) human responses and organise them into something which could be *consciously* applied to the artifice of acting.

Whether we call it a 'system' or a 'method' – two terms which Stanislavsky used, yet simultaneously resisted – his acting principles emerged from a whole lifetime of practical exploration. As an ardent adolescent, he devised plays with his siblings for their family's entertainment. By the age of twenty-two, he was probing his own acting experience, asking himself questions not just about the broad brushstrokes of a character but about its *physiological* qualities and its *psychic* aspect:[2] thus, even at this early stage as a young amateur actor, he was eager to negotiate the profound and nuanced dialogue between our *bodies* and our *psychologies*. In fact, the relationship between our physical lives and our psychological experiences underpinned Stanislavsky's investigations throughout the whole of his life: little by little, he developed his understanding of the human being (and, therefore, the actor) as what he called a 'psycho-physical' instrument. (This phrase forms the bedrock of much of this book's terrain.)

After setting up the Moscow Art Theatre in 1897 with the professional writer-producer, Vladimir Nemirovich-Danchenko, Stanislavsky pursued his investigations into acting processes till the day he died in 1938.

When was he working?

Stanislavsky's investigations into performance exploded into the international arena at a very timely point. It coincided with the climax to a debate which had been bubbling for centuries. The debate concerned the idea of what at various stages had been termed 'truthful' acting, 'authentic emotion' and 'natural behaviour' on the stage. Hamlet's 'Speak the speech' words to the players reveal it was a sixteenth-century preoccupation. Then in the eighteenth century, the British actor David Garrick shocked his public with realistic portrayals of swooning and sweating, before passing the dramatic baton to Edmund Kean as the eighteenth century drew to a close; while across the sea in France, Constant Coquelin declared that 'Everything must spring from truth',[3] so that by the end of the nineteenth century when Stanislavsky appeared on the stage, the whole of Europe could be seen to be at it. The arts were truly evolving.

And not just the arts: in the sciences too evolution was reaching a new peak with the publication of Charles Darwin's *The Origin of Species* (1859) and *The Expression of the Emotions in Man and Animals* (1873). Not to mention Pavlov and his incredible drooling dogs. Stanislavsky's emergence as a theatre pioneer was a timely marriage of science and arts and it's highly likely that if *he* hadn't created a 'system', it wouldn't have been long before somebody else did. Would it have been a Briton or a German? A Gaul or a Swede? Who knows? But there's something to be said for the significance of Stanislavsky's geographical placement in the development of his ideas.

Where was he working?

There are two reasons why it's relevant that Stanislavsky was working in Russia. First of all, the *state of the art* as he began life as an actor and director. And secondly, the *state of the state* as he developed his acting theories.

As far as *the state of the art* was concerned, Russian theatre at the end of the nineteenth century was in a tawdry condition. Morals were low, ethics were shabby, and acting was little more than a poorly paid means to a poorly valued end. The repertoire was uninspiring. The performances were dissolute. And actors staggered drunkenly through performances, relying on the prompter to haul them through to the curtain call.

Out of the midst of this mediocrity rose Stanislavsky, a lover of acting and, in all senses of the word, a true *amateur*. For him:

> The theatre is one large family where you live together in closest harmony or where you engage in mortal quarrels.

> The theatre is a beloved woman, sometimes capricious, ill-tempered, ugly and selfish; sometimes fascinating, tender, generous and beautiful.

> The theatre is an adored child, unconsciously cruel and artlessly charming. His whims demand everything and you cannot refuse him anything.

> The theatre is your second home, it nourishes you and drains all your forces.

> The theatre is a source of heartaches and immeasurable joys.

The theatre is air and wine, which we must breathe in frequently and be intoxicated by.[4]

And for a lifetime, he was intoxicated by it.

As for *the state of the state*, the Soviet regime of the early twentieth century rejected personal emotion and championed rock-solid action. In this political climate, Stanislavsky had no choice but to veer away from his own early fascination with emotion and turn his attention towards that all-important action. And thus he created the 'Method of Physical Action' and 'Active Analysis' – his two powerful legacies (described in detail in Chapter 2).

Why do we need this book?

Because his ideas became fractured.

Stanislavsky never wanted his 'system' to be considered gospel. That's why he resisted committing it to print. But after a tour to the States in the early 1920s raised his international profile, the American public grew hungry. The pressure was on, and he finally began work on a written version in 1925. His intention was to publish all the psychological and the physical aspects of actor-training together in one volume. Yet what began to emerge was a tome of such gargantuan proportions that no serious publisher could accept it. Against his better judgement, he was persuaded to produce two books: the first was to be called *An Actor's Work on Himself in the Creative Process of Experience* and the second was to be called *An Actor's Work on Himself in the Creative Process of Physical Characterisation*. He agreed to this – on the condition that he also wrote an overview, alerting his readers to the fact that the two strands of acting (as presented in the two books) were two halves of the same whole.

Sadly, the overview never appeared. Even today most readers consider *An Actor Prepares* (the published English-language name of the first volume) to be the main stay of the 'system' with its emphasis on the *psychological* perspectives.

And many never even go near *Building a Character* (the published English-language name of the second volume), which includes many of the *physical* perspectives.

Curiously, the third book in what might be called Stanislavsky's English-language 'trilogy' – *Creating a Role* – contains some of his most revealing ideas, and yet it remains elusive. Maybe because it's an amalgam of various writings, rather than a complete book in its own right. As a result, few readers fully fathom its practicability – which is a shame, because it's gold-dust.

The aim of *The Complete Stanislavsky Toolkit* is to take the basic elements of each of the three books and re-integrate them into one user-friendly volume. Beyond the 'trilogy', *The Toolkit* draws together many of his other writings, so that we have the *psychological* elements together with the *physical* aspects, as well as the rehearsal practices from *Creating a Role*, all meshed into one unified whole.

For what reason?

It's curious that although Stanislavsky's legacies have been impacting on global acting practice for well over a century, they still remain shrouded in mystery. I regularly encounter actors who have rejected his ideas, because at some point they've been at the mercy of a teacher or a director who has mystified everything for them.

But why anyone would want to mystify the practical? In Peter Brook's words, 'There are no secrets'. By referring here to a 'toolkit', rather than a 'system' or a 'method', anyone can pick it up and use it. It doesn't take a specialist to ask: 'Do I need a hammer for this job? A saw? Or a plane? Can I unlock this particular role with the "inner psychological drives"? Or "emotion memory"? Or "grasp"?' A toolkit can be accessed by both the apprentice and the master craftsman. Each role will require different tools and a different application. And we can begin to understand which options are available to us without any mystification.

How are the tools made accessible?

The *Complete Stanislavsky Toolkit* has two strands:

First of all, each tool is defined. Those definitions come from Stanislavsky's own writings, as well as those of his pupils and protégés. One of these protégés is a practitioner less well-known in the West, Maria Knebel, who was one of Stanislavsky's assistant directors at the time of his death in 1938. Her book *On the Active Analysis of Plays and Roles* (*O deistvennom analize p'esy i roli*) is a seminal text in Russia though it has yet to appear in English translation. Until now. *The Toolkit* contains several examples from her book to access deeper aspects of some familiar tools, as well as to introduce some new ones.

Within the definitions of each tool are illustrations. They come from Stanislavsky, from his acolytes including Knebel, and from my own working practice as an Anglo-Russian-trained performance practitioner. The illustrations place the definitions in concrete, practical examples, so you can understand how the tools impact on an actor, a director and a writer.

The second strand of *The Toolkit* consists of exercises, contained in Chapter 4: these give you direct means to use the particular tool-in-hand. Sometimes various tools are clustered together, when it would be unhelpful to separate the different components or it would fracture too significantly the holistic kit. And not every tool has an exercise, as sometimes they're most effectively used as part of a cumulative process. Basically, the exercises in Chapter 4 are just starting points for you to develop your own working strategies.

The book as a whole falls into four main chapters. The division of the first three chapters is something of a construct, given the integrated nature of Stanislavsky's work. But the idea is to tease out the various aspects of acting – just as an artist might set out the primary colours in order to mix them into a whole palette of possible shades.

CHAPTER 1, 'Actor-Training', looks at a number of the basic ideas and philosophies included in Stanislavsky's 'trilogy', as well as his other writings: it serves as a foundation for the rest of the book. 'Actor-Training' needn't be confined to the eighteen-year-old student. Since our raw materials as actors – i.e. our bodies, imaginations, voices and emotions – change every day according to our life experiences, we can never really afford to stop training. We need to return constantly to the toolkit just to keep up with our own ever-changing instrument. So don't be fooled by the term 'Actor-Training': there should be elements of Chapter 1 which appeal to the seasoned Shakespearean or the celebrated soap star, as much as to the beginner at drama school.

CHAPTER 2, 'Rehearsal Processes', forms the kernel of the book, and it focuses on three main areas of Stanislavsky's work on a role. The first section, 'Mining the Text', covers the kind of detective analysis you might embark upon (either on your own or with the whole company) before putting a play on its feet. The second section, 'Embodying the Role', considers issues of building a character in rehearsal. The final section of Chapter 2, 'Approaches to Rehearsal', looks at Stanislavsky's legacies of the Method of Physical Actions and Active Analysis. To some extent, Chapter 2 moves from *cerebral* work on a text, through *physical* work on a character, to *ensemble interaction* on a scene.

CHAPTER 3, 'Performance Practices', addresses some of the issues which arise when you step out in front of an audience or camera. What happens to your creative processes when your work goes public? And which tools are available to you to keep your performance on course?

Drawing out the three prongs of 'Actor-Training', 'Rehearsal Processes', and 'Performances Practices' highlights the different strategies that we adopt as actors at various stages in our creative process. Of course, the cross-over points between all three

prongs are numerous, since so many of the tools in the kit combine our logic with our imagination, our bodies with our psychologies, and our conscious technique with our subconscious
inspiration. Nonetheless, we can begin to see how our processes develop as we move from the intimacy of our own
training, into the working environment of a rehearsal room,
and from there into the public arena of live or recorded
performance. And time and again we'll see that at the heart of
it all lies action.

CHAPTER 4 provides 'An Overview of the Toolkit', along with
the various exercises proposed.

The Complete Stanislavsky Toolkit adopts the metaphor of a
real-life toolkit with its various metal trays and compartments.
Particular tools are collected together in specific 'trays' when
their application can be seen to share similar ends. Whenever a
tool is mentioned, it appears in small capitals but if, however,
it's not the tool being described in that particular section, it
will be detailed elsewhere in the book and the index at the back
will guide you to the appropriate 'tray'. On occasion, a tool
such as 'imagination' or 'emotion' does *not* appear in capitals,
because there's no need at that moment to draw specific
attention to it; for example, where it forms part of a list of the
actor's raw materials including, say, body, imagination, emotions and psyche.

One of the tricky things about Stanislavsky's writings is that
he only discusses theatre. At the time when he was working,
film was still in its infancy and the very first television
experiments didn't happen until 1924 when Logie Baird 'hit
the screen'. So Stanislavsky simply didn't have the reference
points. That doesn't mean that the basic tools aren't transferable from one medium to another. Usually when he refers to
'on stage', he could just as easily have written 'in front of the
camera'. Wherever possible, I've drawn parallels. Even in radio
where you seemingly don't 'have a body', you can use many of

these psycho-physical tools as you approach a character. Admittedly, it's hard to transfer the extended work on rehearsals featured in Chapter 2 completely to television, film or radio, where rehearsal is a financial luxury and not an accepted norm. And obviously, any illustrations which rely on the nightly responses of an audience can only be applied to theatre or live broadcasts. However, when it comes to building a character and turning the black-and-white pages of a script into a flesh-and-blood living creation, medium is irrelevant. You'll take whatever you need from *The Toolkit*, depending on the character you're playing, the director, the medium and a whole range of other production challenges.

My own illustrations throughout the book come from my eclectic experiences of acting, directing and teaching. In terms of performance, I draw heavily on the original production of David Hare's *The Permanent Way* (2003) directed by Max Stafford-Clark as a co-production between his own company Out of Joint, the National Theatre, London, and ultimately the Sydney Theatre, Australia. Because the production run was long and the material was emotionally charged, the experience of performing *The Permanent Way* threw up all sorts of challenges that have impacted hugely on my understanding of acting. Elsewhere in the book I've been a complete magpie and collected anecdotes and examples from the actors, directors, writers and students, whom I've had the fortune to encounter in the course of compiling *The Toolkit*. Their hands-on experiences are invaluable and I'm immensely grateful to them for their honesty, insights, talent and wit.

Throughout *The Toolkit*, we must remain absolutely clear about something: Stanislavsky never intended his 'system' to be gospel. If your process ain't broken, there's no need to fix it. If the Muse descends upon you, celebrate that visitation, and don't overlay it with conscious intervention. But if you do need a mole-grip or a monkey-wrench, then use them – from any source: it doesn't have to be from Stanislavsky. It's vital that each actor's unique and idiosyncratic toolkit should include fretsaws, hacksaws, chisels and hammers from Meisner, Brecht, Lecoq, Hagen, Chubbuck, or any number of other practitioners. It all depends on your own personality and training, as well as the task-in-hand and the character and the director. My personal favourites include David Mamet's 'terrifying unforeseen'[5] (where you just get out there and see what happens), Michael Chekhov's 'quality of ease'[6] (where you perform even the darkest tragedy with a lightness of touch), and Jerzy Grotowski's *via negativa*[7] (where you eliminate the blocks between your inner impulse and your outer expression). All of these (in their own ways) are permutations of tools from Stanislavsky's original 'system'. At the end of the day, it doesn't really matter whether you use a Swiss Army knife or a Leatherman, as long as you get the job done effectively, creatively and, above all, inspirationally.

I

Actor-Training

I

Actor-Training

The art of true listening

Stanislavsky's 'big thing' was 'truthful' acting. That doesn't mean his toolkit is great for realism and hopeless for anything else. He started his career in Gilbert and Sullivan and ended his life with opera students. How much more non-naturalistic and highly theatrical can you get than *The Mikado* or *Rigoletto*?

That said, most of us as actors in the West are going to spend our time performing scripts (for film or stage) where the genre is essentially 'psychological realism', i.e. what the viewer sees is pretty close to life as we know it. Even if we're on the planet Mars, the characters' behaviour will have a certain psychological dimension to which we can relate as twenty-first-century human beings. That doesn't necessarily mean we *believe* in what we're seeing: rather, we believe in its *possibility*. This is a subtle but important difference, to which we shall return.

There's an inherent paradox in good acting, particularly when it comes to psychological realism. You create the illusion of absolute 'truth' and naturalness, as if you're really 'living in the moment' and conjuring up those particular words in that particular moment of performance. (Stanislavsky called this process 'the creation of the living word'.)[8] Yet, in most cases, you can only seem that spontaneous if your *technique* is finely honed. Stanislavsky maintained that the greater your talent, the more refined your technique should be if you really want to reach the heights of virtuosity. But how many of us want to hear this truism? Since realistic acting is basically about replicating something that everyone does quite naturally every single day of their lives – i.e. living – it's easy to assume that anyone can act. And this assumption is bolstered when you see a TV personality or a *Big Brother* finalist becoming a Hollywood star or a West End attraction. Furthermore there's the curious phenomenon of people playing themselves with brilliance and conviction in Paul Greengrass's 2006 film, *United 93*. So if anyone can act, why bother with technique?

Actually, the art of repeatedly 'living naturally' – either within the artificial conditions of the stage or the technical demands of the film-set – is bizarrely difficult and requires real skill. For Stanislavsky, we block our chances of developing that skill when we assume we have great talent:

> Because they are lazy or stupid these actors of 'genius' convince themselves that all they have to do is 'feel' something . . . in order to have the rest take care of itself.[9]

As all actors know from experience, 'feeling something' is a capricious and unsustainable activity. For 'the rest to take care of itself', you need a disciplined actor-training.

The foundation of a decent actor-training as far as Stanislavsky was concerned was PSYCHO-PHYSICALITY. Although we'll come back to this tool in detail, PSYCHO-PHYSICALITY basically alludes to the fact that your body and your psyche are trained together to achieve a sense of inner-outer co-ordination. This means that what you experience *internally* is immediately translated into an *outer* expression, and (conversely) what your body manifests *physically* has a direct and acknowledged affect on your *psychological* landscape. So, I bury my head in my hands: before long, my muscular memory and my imagination kick in, and I start to feel despair. Or maybe I'm feeling buoyantly happy: without me consciously contriving it, my shoulders relax and my chest expands and there's a Puckish spring in my step. The membrane between what's going on inside me and my body's expression of that inner information is delicate and porous.

But why does an actor need a specifically 'psycho-physical' training? The art of great acting is the art of true listening. Listening operates on two levels: you have to listen to yourself in terms of your own inner activity ('What's this sensation I'm experiencing?') and at the same time you have to listen to your performance partners ('What's she saying? What's he doing? And how do their words and deeds affect me?'). This level of listening can only exist when you're in a particular state of receptivity: rather than fixing your performance to be exactly the same every time you do it, you have the confidence on stage or in front of the camera to respond playfully to the ever-changing nuances of each moment. If you can be this responsive, then the opportunities for stimulating INSPIRATION may come thick and fast. And ultimately we all long to be inspired actors, so anything we can do *consciously* to prepare the ground for the possibility of being inspired is surely a positive thing.

Basically, that's what Stanislavsky's actor-training is geared towards: putting you in the strongest possible place – physically, imaginatively, emotionally and vocally – to listen, listen, listen, and from that true listening will rise INSPIRATION. And here's where *The Toolkit* comes in.

All the tools in this chapter can be used for pretty much every kind of theatre or screen preparation, as they can assist you in developing a basic actor-training. They're fundamentally tools for establishing an INNER CREATIVE STATE. If you can establish an appropriate INNER CREATIVE STATE, you can begin to listen *internally* to your body and *externally* to your fellow actors, and from there you can enhance your sense of playfulness and spontaneity.

Of course, Stanislavsky's full actor-training programme in the Moscow Art Theatre included physical disciplines such as ballet, stage-fighting and acrobatics, as well as vocal training in diction and scenic speech, though I don't detail these disciplines in this chapter. That's partly because Stanislavsky himself doesn't describe exactly what the classes entailed, as he had specialist teachers to lead them. It's also partly because today there are plenty of books and workshops available for actors of all ages and stages, who want to learn or improve on these particular skills. And it's partly because Stanislavsky's own specialism as an actor, director and teacher was his 'psycho-physical' approach, so that's the main emphasis of *The Toolkit*.

This chapter isn't intended as a rule-by-rule guide to actor-training. It simply provides a chance for you to understand what works for you personally, and from there you can build your own technique. It falls into three sections:

First of all, we look at three 'attitudes' towards the art of acting, which can put you in a strong place to begin your creative work:

- psycho-physicality
- discipline
- stage ethics

We then pick up the first three hands-on tools in the kit:

- relaxation
- breathing (to prepare your body)
- concentration and attention (to prepare your psyche)

Finally, we look at four 'conditions' of creativity, which the toolkit aims to develop:

- inspiration
- spirituality
- the inner creative state
- creative atmosphere

TRAY I

THREE 'ATTITUDES' TOWARDS THE ART OF ACTING

Essentially, these three 'attitudes' underpin any basic actor-training, as well as any performance environment, and they're really perspectives from which you might approach your acting work.

Psycho-physicality

We should be absolutely clear what we mean by PSYCHO-PHYSICALITY, as it informs everything else that follows in *The Toolkit*.

Basically, PSYCHO-PHYSICALITY refers to the dialogue between your body and your psyche. Your body can give you as much information about the character as your brain does, and your psychology inevitably affects how you use your body. It's an inner – outer transference.

So how does that impact on acting?

The main vehicle you have for communicating to the audience the world that the writer has invented is your body, in that the *physical* form you present on stage or screen conveys your *psychological* interpretation of a character. And by 'body', I also mean your vocal apparatus, from your lungs to your lips. If you didn't have a body, how could you give shape to your thoughts, feelings and fantasies?

Because your body is the interface between your inner land-scape and the world-at-large, the more expressive your body can be, the more variations of character you can portray. You don't necessarily have to be gymnastically nimble or acrobatic-ally versatile – though of course the more supple and adroit you are, the greater the reach of your physical vocabulary. But it's more a question of being aware that each of your *physical* actions holds within it a *psychological* resonance, and, conversely, your *psychological* state impacts on your *physical* expression.

So, developing a psycho-physical technique has two aspects. First of all, you have to increase your ability to listen to your internal dialogue between what you feel *inside* and how you express it *externally*. Secondly, you need to become sufficiently physically versatile to convey to your audience the whole gamut of complex responses whizzing around your psyche. If you can begin to achieve these two things – making of yourself a subtle flute upon which the range of your humanity can play – you can access a multitude of nuances to your characterisations and then present those nuances to the receiving audience through the apparatus of your physical body.

This all sounds great, but once you get out into the big, wide world of the twenty-first-century 'industry', the process ain't so easy. The short-cuts demanded of you in the brief rehearsal schedules of theatre or the next-to-no-rehearsal times of television can dull your inner listening. You stop *hearing* the dialogue between body and psyche, and – worse still – you can actually *forget* that the dialogue exists. The characterisations you come up with may be very beautiful in their physical forms, but they'll be lifeless re-creations of effects you achieved in some quite different context. So when you strike the metaphorical tuning-fork, there's no resonance, no reverberation between what you're doing and your present circumstances. If you get caught in this trap, it's hard to excite yourself, let alone transport your audience.

However . . .

You have the capability as an actor to develop a sense of your own inner-outer co-ordination. If you prepare yourself appropriately, you find that each of your *physical* gestures can instantly open up an *inner* landscape for you, and each *inner* impulse translates itself effortlessly into something *physical*. Once this inner-outer co-ordination kicks in, you start to replicate in your creative work the process that spontaneously and naturally unfolds in everyday life. As Stanislavsky says in *Creating a Role*:

Our deep spiritual well springs open wide *only when the inner and outer feelings of an actor flow in accordance with the laws fixed for them, when there is absolutely no forcing, or deviation from the norm, when there is no cliché or conventional acting of any kind.*[10]

Being psycho-physically aware is much closer to our natural state as human beings than is often the case in many training spheres and performance situations. We frequently find ourselves as actors in rather formal and inflexible circumstances: 'Go there! Do that! Speak this! Make me laugh! Make me cry! Hit that mark! Miss that microphone!' As Stanislavsky notes:

> In the vast majority of theatres the actors and producers are constantly violating nature in the most shameless manner.[11]

So how do you prevent yourself as an actor from 'violating nature'?

One of the easiest ways is to appeal directly to your body, rather than to your emotions or intellect. And Stanislavsky was very clear that a human being's muscular memory (especially when a certain sensitivity has been awakened through a thorough actor-training) is very well-developed – unlike many memories of emotions and sensations which can be unreliable and fragile. Your body is biddable, your feelings are capricious. So why not consciously construct a role through its physical dimensions? This doesn't mean slapping on a latex nose or adopting a limp, and lo and behold! – the character is formed. Far from it. But all you have to do is remind yourself of the basic tenet of PSYCHO-PHYSICALITY: that *physical action* has an inherent *psychological resonance*. As long as you're psycho-physically open and listening out for that resonance, the physical dimensions of your characters will never just be empty forms, they'll actually stir within you genuine inner sensations.

One inner sensation we should note at this stage is the experience of the vital energy produced by the actual act of acting itself. Stanislavsky suggests that if you simply feel this energy coursing through your veins, it arouses a particular creative pleasure. This pleasure can even be powerful enough to lure you into an appropriate INNER CREATIVE STATE, in which you can produce truly compelling performances. How fantastic is this! It means you don't have to chase the emotions of the role. You don't have to crank yourself up into some kind of performative state. You can simply use your natural, creative energy – or your performance-related adrenalin – to springboard into the character's inner life; there, you can feed off your creative energy's own peculiar psycho-physical openness and aesthetic playfulness to stimulate your performance. (We'll return to this idea with various other tools, including EMOTION MEMORY and EMOTION.)

There's one final – and huge – advantage to being psycho-physically trained. Because you're more 'resonant' as a performer, you're also far more useful as a resource to your director. Since a director's means of tangibly expressing his artistic vision of a play is predominantly through the actors' bodies, the more psycho-physically responsive you are, the greater the palette of colours you can offer him. With a psycho-physically fine-tuned acting troupe, rehearsals can be quicker, easier and infinitely more textured. You never know – having a psycho-physical 'attitude' could get you more work!

In brief:

- PSYCHO-PHYSICALITY means training your body to be receptive to your psyche, and vice versa. Through this training, you can start to listen to your acting instrument and hear the range of its possibilities.

- A psycho-physical process is much closer to the way you respond in everyday life than the strategies of many training environments and performance situations.

- The emotional energy of acting itself can be a fertile starting point for your psycho-physical voyage into the heart of a character.

- The more psycho-physically adept you are, the more resources you can offer your director.

The panacea inherent in all these ideas begs the question: why aren't all training systems and schools more overtly 'psycho-physical' in their ethos?

Possibly because the Western tendency is to segregate disciplines: 'Now we're doing tap, now we're doing Shakespeare, now we're doing accents and dialects'. My own experience in the Russian tradition of actor-training was that every discipline employed very similar vocabulary, so that the holistic nature of psycho-physical acting was always in evidence. Whether we were dubbing voice-overs onto animations or preparing *ports de bras*, our tutors constantly alluded to the integration of body, voice, soul and psyche. Each discipline reflected the others.

And DISCIPLINE is a crucial word. Becoming psycho-physically fine-tuned may present you with a panorama of creativity drawing upon a very natural state of being, but it's no doddle. Whether it's the first day of training or the hundred-and-fifth performance, it requires an incredible amount of DISCIPLINE.

Discipline

DISCIPLINE can sound like an oppressive term. We like acting because it's childlike, challenging, playful, and immensely pleasurable: we don't want to hear that it involves a heap of hard work.

But how can an activity, which demands that at a specified time on a specific day you should go through a predetermined series of actions, deliver words not of your own spontaneous choosing, and conjure up powerful emotions at the flick of a spotlight or the click of a clapper-board, require anything *but* DISCIPLINE of the highest order?

For Stanislavsky, DISCIPLINE had a particular resonance. Not only was he fighting against a profession which was in a fairly shabby state of disrepair at that time in Russia, but he also believed that, if it was properly used, theatre had an incredible potential to influence and reflect social change. (This is just before Brecht, don't forget):

> If an actor does not possess complete self-control, if his inner self-discipline is not strong enough to produce creative discipline or an ability to disregard everything of a personal nature, how can he be expected to find the necessary powers to reflect the highest achievements of the social life of his time?[12]

To a twenty-first-century liberal ear, this may sound seriously Soviet and self-righteous: 'self-discipline', 'creative discipline', 'the highest achievements of the social life'. And let's be honest, most of us have probably turned up late to a class, or staggered blearily to a rehearsal, or even done a matinee after a rather boozy lunch. But there's another connotation to DISCIP-LINE, aside from carrying out your job professionally. It concerns your ability to discern between your own personal 'baggage' and your creative raw material: i.e. DISCIPLINE is your 'ability to disregard everything of a personal nature'.

Discriminating between your personal 'shit' and your imaginative resources is vital when you're training psycho-physically. If all you have to work with is yourself – your own body, imagination, emotions and psyche – it can be all too easy to blur the boundaries between your creative 'self' and your personal 'cargo'. It's an incredibly delicate process, extricating yourself from your own baggage. You have to be able to forget the row you had with your boyfriend over breakfast this morning, or the fact that your mobile phone was nicked last night: you have to know how to leave your metaphorical dirty boots at the door. And there's no denying, it takes a curious amount of inner DISCIPLINE to keep the work creative and not allow a training environment or a rehearsal room – or even a film-set – to become a therapeutic chamber. Good training is, therefore, largely about developing the appropriate self-awareness to understand how the raw materials that you bring into the working environment – i.e. your own body, imagination, emotions and psyche – can be constructively fashioned into something relevant to the script and the character.

Once again, your first inroad into developing this awareness is through your body, as it's tangible, touchable and therefore directly trainable. In Stanislavsky's words:

> Your immediate objective . . . has to be to train your physical apparatus to the limits of your natural, inborn capacity. You must . . . go on developing, correcting, tuning your bodies until every part of them will respond to the predestined and complex task . . . of presenting in external form your invisible feelings. You must educate your bodies according to the laws of nature. That means a lot of complicated work and perseverance![13]

This 'complicated work and perseverance' needn't be a chore. In fact it *shouldn't* be a chore. If every aspect of your physical training is invested with an imaginative core, then very quickly it becomes a pleasurable and thought-provoking psycho-physical experience, and not a dull discipline.

I discovered this to my great delight at the State Institute of Cinematography in Russia (where I studied acting in the 1990s) during my Mime training with Scenic Movement teacher, Vladimir Ananyev. I'd previously 'done time' at a British drama school lined up in a row on a Friday afternoon with seventeen other students, pretending to place our hands on an invisible wall by repeatedly tensing and relaxing our fingers and palms. It was a dull discipline to say the least, and I can't say I was inspired by the prospect of more Mime in Russia. But Ananyev's training was heavily steeped in Stanislavsky (and Michael Chekhov), and suddenly I found we were exploring invisible caves, shimmying through underground tunnels, flinging open imaginary treasure chests, and plunging our hands into pools of pretend mud. The training was still all about relaxing and tensing our palms and fingers, but our ATTENTION was switched from the taxing technical specifics to the challenges of the imaginary journey. A physical and precise DISCIPLINE was effortlessly transformed into a fun, psycho-physical experience.

Of course, DISCIPLINE carries through from actor-training into performance practice, especially when it comes to the precision of film. An actor friend of mine was once filming a very emotional scene for a BBC drama not far from Uxbridge on the flight path to Heathrow airport, so that every time an aeroplane flew over, the filming had to grind to a halt. Added to which, there was a clay pigeon shoot taking place not far away. Whenever the cry 'Cut!' went up, the actors had to be able to hold on to all the appropriate inner sensations without going emotionally cold. 'Could you weep between that clay pigeon and that Boeing 747, please?' Now *that* requires real psycho-physical DISCIPLINE.

But DISCIPLINE doesn't stop with your body and psyche. For Stanislavsky, DISCIPLINE was also an attitude towards your fellow performers. It's astonishing how many actors don't learn their lines dead-letter-perfectly – even with classical texts, even with Shakespeare, even at the National Theatre, London! And I used to be as guilty as the next actor. As long as I got the gist of a line, I thought that was kind of okay. Heck, doesn't a certain amount of improvisation keep you on your toes and enhance your sense of being 'in the moment'? Stanislavsky would certainly say no! He's absolutely clear about why an acute sense of DISCIPLINE towards learning lines is not only fundamental to serving the writer, but also vital to developing a truly collaborative ensemble:

> When they do not get the right cues, the conscientious
> actors make violent efforts to stir the initiative of the

sluggish actors, thereby impairing the true quality of
their own acting.[14]

In other words, it's the generous actor who suffers at the hands
of the others' deficit of DISCIPLINE. DISCIPLINE is, therefore,
right at the heart of a psycho-physical ensemble. If you find
yourself making adjustments primarily to accommodate your
partner's 'sluggishness', you're neither honouring your own
skills as an actor nor serving the true dynamic of the play. So
hey, sluggards – don't pass the buck!

In brief:

• You need *psychological* DISCIPLINE to distinguish
between what's *your* baggage and what's useful for the
character.

• You need *physical* DISCIPLINE to train your body
rigorously.

• You need *imaginative* DISCIPLINE to invest any technical
training with a colourful, playful backdrop.

• You need a sense of *collective responsibility* towards your
fellow actors, which you can go a long way towards
developing by simply knowing your lines properly.

Springboarding directly from DISCIPLINE is Stanislavsky's
notion of STAGE ETHICS – the third 'attitude' to underpin most
acting environments. Although he calls it '*stage* ethics', the
chief principles are just as relevant to film, television and radio.

Stage ethics

Stanislavsky looked at STAGE ETHICS from three angles:

• how the actor behaved *inside* the theatre;

• how the actor behaved *outside* the theatre;

- the *working relationship* in a theatre-building between the artistic employees and the administrative staff.

All three aspects were geared towards one basic ethos: to celebrate and elevate the art of acting. Because Stanislavsky felt so passionately that theatre could be an instrument of radical, social reform, he saw acting as a calling which shouldn't be taken lightly:

> Unless the theatre can ennoble you, make you a better person, you should flee from it.[15]

And he truly believed that you couldn't abuse your body and psyche *offstage* without it impacting on your work *onstage*.

His passion for STAGE ETHICS grew out of his desire to prepare the best conditions within which an actor's INNER CREATIVE STATE could flourish. To this end, he pounced on any behaviour that might disrupt the working environment. Lateness, for example, was a particular bug-bear:

> If even one person is late, it upsets all the others. And if all are late your working hours will be frittered away in waiting instead of being applied to your job. That makes an actor wild and puts him in a condition where he is incapable of work.[16]

Although Stanislavsky's words are nearly a century old, there's something curiously familiar about them:

> The struggle for priority among actors, directors, jealousy of each other's success, divisions caused by differences in salaries and types of parts – all this is strongly developed in our line of work and constitutes its greatest evil. We cloak our ambition, jealousy, intrigues, with all kinds of fine-sounding phrases such as 'enlight-ened competition', but all the time the atmosphere is filled with the poison gases of backstage backbiting.[17]

Each of these 'poisons' – ambition, jealousy, intrigue and backbiting – can all too easily become part of your inner fabric if you're not very careful. One of our difficulties as actors is that, unlike a painter with his blank canvas, a sculptor with her block of marble, a potter with his lump of clay, or a composer with her fresh page of manuscript paper, we begin each new work with a 'canvas' already marred by 18 or 29 or 41 or 63 years of graffiti, with tucks, tears and tatters, blotches, blobs and splodges. Somehow we have to prepare a blank canvas within ourselves so that we can start the work on each new character from a place of artistic neutrality. Only then do we give ourselves the best opportunities to be creatively vivid and unexpected, rather than falling into the clichés of our everyday habits.

To prepare our own personal blank canvas before setting to work on it with our metaphorical oils or charcoal or water-colours or pastels, we can draw upon a number of basic tools in the kit.

At this stage in our actor-training, there are four very simple tools with which we can begin: the first two of them are RELAXATION and BREATHING.

TRAY 2

FOUR BASIC TOOLS FOR
PREPARING THE 'BLANK CANVAS'

Relaxation

Challenge Number One: How do you create a blank canvas of yourself on which you can start to create?

Time and again in *The Toolkit*, we'll return to the notion that *the body* is the most biddable of tools and is, therefore, often the most useful starting point. So we'll begin with the body.

As I've already suggested, part of the difficulty as an actor is that every time you start work on a character – even if you're an eighteen-year-old drama student, let alone a sixty-year-old pro – your 'canvas' is already riddled with various idiosyncrasies.

These are a combination of whatever nature has bestowed upon you, along with a whole host of tensions which have embedded themselves in your body throughout the course of your life. Your first task is to recognise these tensions and then begin to ease them away. And the tool for the job is physical RELAXATION.

Stanislavsky saw unnecessary physical tensions as 'the most substantial obstacles to creative activity'.[18] Which makes sense really: we know that the principle of psycho-physical co-ordination is that your inner antennae become receptive to your physical expressions (and *vice versa*). So if you've got the constant white noise of physical tensions blasting around your psyche, the signal of communication between your inner life and your outer body will be endlessly distorted. It'll be impossible for you to 'hear' the most useful information for creating exciting and idiosyncratic characterisations: instead, you'll simply lock onto your own habits and shortcuts.

Furthermore . . .

If your *physical* body is tense, it's quite likely that your *psychological* apparatus is also tense. It's curious how easily we think we can just get up and play Hedda or Hamlet or Henry V: we leap blindly into the complex task of tackling immense psychological problems when our physical bodies are creaky and out-of-condition. Or we're muscle-bound and pumped up, which is equally unhelpful.

An actor is like a sculptor: before you can start shaping an expressive figurine, you need to soften the clay – which, in this case, is your body. Once you're in a state of RELAXATION, your body is much more likely to be at your creative beck and call, and (looking at it from the other way round) if you're physically relaxed, you'll probably be psychologically open. Which is why Stanislavsky placed RELAXATION at the foundation of his 'system'. He believed that if you could free your body of every sort of tension, your inner life would respond accordingly, and then you could more readily and accurately 'reflect the life of the play in which [you're] appearing'.[19]

There's another crucial reason for relaxing your body: tension can be the fast-track to stage-fright.

Stage-fright usually occurs when you become dislocated from the onstage action. This dislocation might be the result of a momentary lapse in your focus and you suddenly find yourself rocket-propelled out of the world of the play and hurled into a vortex of 'What happens next? *What am I doing? what do i say?*' It can also occur when you become more bothered about what's going on in the auditorium than what's going on onstage. Crises of confidence hurtle round your head: 'Do they like me? Am I interesting enough? Is my agent impressed? Am I good enough? Do I sound convincing? Will that critic slate or rave?' Because you're a psycho-physical being, these mental tensions inevitably cause a ripple effect of physical tensions, and a dam is suddenly erected in the flow of your creative juices.

However . . .

If your body is relaxed, your mind usually opens, and then you can lock your focus into the onstage action without any effort whatsoever. Then your juices can generously flow. And when those creative juices are flowing, you no longer judge your own performance. You simply get on with the action and allow yourself to exist honestly and naturally in the performance space. Your sense of playfulness is acute and your emotions are increasingly accessible to you. Which is what I discovered when I played a bereaved mother in David Hare's *The Permanent Way*, a role which required me to break down in mid-sentence twice in twenty minutes. The challenge in performance was not only how to tap into my emotions, but how to sustain that emotional accessibility over the course of a run totalling 10½ months. During this time, I discovered that the less I worried about whether or not the tears would actually flow, the more readily they did. If I went on stage with the relaxed attitude of, 'Well, maybe I'll cry tonight, maybe I won't,' then – no problem: the tears sprung forth. If I wound myself up into a physical and mental knot, fretting, 'Oh, Christ, I've got to cry in ten minutes!', I was emotionally as dry as a bone. Each night, I had to allow myself to be an empty vessel into which the words of the play could pour and, in that state of psycho-physical RELAXATION, my experience of the character's journey was far more pleasurable and psychologically fleshy.

So . . . psycho-physical RELAXATION is the first step in prepping yourself to receive all manner of creative impulses. If you're sufficiently relaxed, you'll be playful and inventive in your decisions. And if you can knead yourself like clay into this open INNER CREATIVE STATE, you make room for INSPIRATION to come flooding in.

With this in mind, we'll turn to the second basic tool for preparing the blank canvas: BREATHING.

Breathing

You have no choice – you've got to breathe. And, as most meditational practices reveal, BREATHING is closely allied to RELAXATION.

BREATHING (or 'respiration') is the rhythm of life, the sustainer of the human body, and a fundamental tool for Stanislavsky in terms of acting processes:

> Till you realise that the whole basis of your life –
> respiration – is not only the basis of your physical
> existence, but that *respiration plus rhythm forms the*
> *foundations of all your creative work*, your work on
> rhythm and breathing will never be carried out in full
> consciousness, that is to say, as it should be carried
> out, in a state of such complete concentration as to
> turn your creative work into 'inspiration'.[20]

Part of the reason that 'respiration plus rhythm forms the foundations of all your creative work' is that *Breath + Rhythm = Emotion*.

I came to understand this equation fully when I was again working with my Russian Scenic Movement tutor, Vladimir Ananyev:

'Breathe out three times, and breathe in once,' he instructed one day. 'And repeat that sequence three times. So: out-out-out-in, out-out-out-in, out-out-out-in, out-out-out-in.'

This I did.

'Now do the opposite,' he continued, 'breathe in three times and out once. In-in-in-out, in-in-in-out, in-in-in-out, in-in-in-out.'

I did this too.

What I discovered was that the first breathing pattern provoked a sense of well-being and jolliness, whereas the second breathing pattern made me feel anxious and tense. The first pattern felt expansive and natural; the second pattern felt shallow and grasping. Ananyev then pointed out that the first pattern was that of laughter, and the second pattern was that of tears. As you'll discover if you try it for yourself, repeating either pattern a few times – without hyperventilating, of course – quickly induces a state in which you genuinely start to feel either positive or perturbed. Your muscular memory ignites your emotions purely from the alterations you make to your breathing pattern. It's not a trick: it's just another way of working psycho-physically, this time from the outside in. (See EMOTION.)

Perhaps a more obvious use of breath is in voice production, and herein lies a curious challenge for an actor: what happens if the amount of breath required for certain *performance situations* isn't the same as the amount of breath required for *the character's emotional rhythm*? Again, this was brought to the fore for me with *The Permanent Way* and the two moments when my character, the Second Bereaved Mother, broke down into tears. As Ananyev's 'in-in-in-out' exercise reveals, the breathing pattern of sorrow is quite shallow. And yet often with *The Permanent Way*, we were touring to large venues which required a huge amount of breath and breath-control simply to fill the space. I found myself making quite significant adjustments in performance to accommodate both the breath-ing pattern of my *character* and my own breathing pattern as a *vocal technician* in order that I could reach the back row of the gods while remaining true to the character's emotional state. The result was that when we were performing in larger spaces, I had to invest more energy into the character's EMOTIONS than I did when we were in studio spaces. It wasn't a question of being vocally louder, but rather of turning up the temperature on the character's feelings: if I increased the intensity of the Mother's sorrow, I could fill the space vocally without having to shout her intimate confessions. In this way, I consciously combined BREATHING and emotional energy to marry the technical challenges of the performance space with the TRUTH of the dramatic action.

So you see, BREATHING and EMOTION are intricately interwoven when you start working psycho-physically. You don't have to squeeze your emotions like a tube of toothpaste: you can simply hook into a particular physical breathing pattern and trust your muscular memory.

RELAXATION and BREATHING are the first two hands-on physical tools in *The Toolkit*. Having relaxed the body and activated the breath, it's time to warm up our inner apparatus with the last of the four basic tools for preparing the blank canvas: CONCENTRATION AND ATTENTION.

Concentration and attention

CONCENTRATION AND ATTENTION were very important tools for Stanislavsky, as revealed by the fact that his writings are riddled with references to them. *An Actor Prepares* has a whole chapter devoted to them. Elsewhere, he describes 'concentration' as 'the first of the steps common to all creative artists' and suggests that it's actually the most difficult step.[21] As early as 1908, it was one of the key terms he used in his first tentative documentations of his 'system',[22] and later, RELAXATION and 'concentration' formed part of the primary phases of the actor-training programme which he devised and put into practice between 1929 and his death in 1938. All in all, 'concentration' was a crucial tool in the kit right from its formative stages.

Why so? Let's go back to the artistic climate in which Stanislavsky formulated his 'system'.

It was common practice in nineteenth-century Russian theatre for the stars of a play to make their entrance and head straight to the front of the stage. There they took a number of bows, while the supporting cast froze in mid-action. Having received their due adulation, the celebs returned to the drama of the play, at which point the supporting cast unfroze and the performance could continue. Stanislavsky wanted to get away from this star system, away from the convention that the actors play to the audience rather than to each other, away from a style of theatre which he felt lacked artistic integrity and inner substance. His idea with CONCENTRATION AND ATTENTION was that:

> In order to get away from the auditorium you must be interested in something on the stage.[23]

To this end, he invented the idea of the 'fourth wall',[24] an idea discussed in Chapter 5 of *An Actor Prepares* (a chapter which happens to be called 'Concentration of Attention', see Preface): the 'fourth wall' was an imaginary wall between the actor and the audience designed to keep the actor's ATTENTION on the stage.

Being 'interested in something on the stage' may seem obvious enough today, but it was a bizarrely pioneering proposition at the time. And surprisingly it's a far more significant directive than it at first appears . . .

The American writer and director David Mamet is very dismissive of the notion of 'concentration':

> Acting has nothing to do with the ability to
> concentrate. It has to do with the ability to imagine.
> For concentration, like emotion, like belief, cannot be
> forced. It cannot be controlled.[25]

However, if we focus on the term CONCENTRATION AND ATTEN-
TION rather than 'concentration', *per se*, we suddenly find there's
actually very little disparity between what Mamet proposes and
Stanislavsky's own suggestions. When Mamet says –

> The ability to concentrate flows naturally from the
> ability to *choose something interesting*. Choose some-
> thing legitimately interesting to do and concentration
> is not a problem. Choose something less than inter-
> esting and concentration is impossible.[26]

– he's talking the same talk as Stanislavsky. Like Mamet,
Stanislavsky advocates that you begin by guiding your
'concentration' towards what your character really *wants* in a
scene, towards his or her driving desire or what Stanislavsky
calls an OBJECTIVE. If you find something that truly interests
you, your powers of 'concentration' are effortlessly harnessed
and deliciously directed towards actions relevant to the script,
and then the audience no longer preoccupies you. Or as Mamet
writes, cutting to the chase:

> The teenager who wants the car, the child who wants
> to stay up an extra half an hour, the young person
> who wants to have sex with his or her date, the
> gambler at the race-track – these individuals have no
> problem concentrating. Elect something to do which
> is *physical and fun* to do, and concentration ceases to
> be an issue.[27]

Physical and fun: that's the key. CONCENTRATION AND ATTENTION
are about finding something physical and doing it with a sense
of fun.

As we compare and contrast nineteenth-century Russian
Stanislavsky with twenty-first-century American Mamet, we
see that CONCENTRATION may begin as a kind of inner process –
be it OBSERVATION of a person or thing, or a thought about
your OBJECTIVE – but with the appropriately directed ATTEN-
TION, it quickly prompts you towards ACTION. In fact, we soon

begin to see that everything is about ACTION - even *thought*, which you might have 'thought' was static: as Stanislavsky himself puts it:

> What is it that acts? Thought. So . . . concentration is an inner active action of thought.[28]

So CONCENTRATION is extremely active. And it's outward-flowing. You don't need to turn your ATTENTION *inwards* towards your *emotions*. Instead, you should turn it *outwards* towards your ACTIONS and OBJECTIVES.

What emerges from all these ideas is that if we keep adding the notion of ATTENTION, then CONCENTRATION becomes a remarkably dynamic activity, and not a mental tension.

In brief:

- CONCENTRATION AND ATTENTION is arguably a more creatively useful phrase than 'concentration' on its own.

- CONCENTRATION AND ATTENTION keep your focus geared towards the onstage action by finding ACTIONS and OBJECTIVES, which interest you and draw you towards something physical and fun.

Having unlocked some of the ideas behind CONCENTRATION AND ATTENTION, let's clarify what exactly Stanislavsky means by the word ATTENTION on its own.

Stanislavsky had three clear uses for ATTENTION:

- to find your initial 'lure' into a role;

- to begin the delicate merger of yourself as an actor with the writer's character in your early stages of working on a role;

- to attend to your own 'mental health'.

Let's take each of these in turn.

1. The 'lure'

When you approach a scripted role, your primary task as an actor is to prise that part off the page and plunge it into your pores. So how are you going to do that? Stanislavsky suggests that the tool of ATTENTION can help you out significantly, if you

concentrate your attention on the most effective lure
for [your artistic emotions] . . . The bond between the
lure and the feeling is natural and normal and one
that should be extensively employed.[29]

The 'lure' into the character – i.e. something in the character which naturally draws your ATTENTION – will be your initial trigger into the role. As you get to know the play and the role better, you'll probably refine or adjust that connection. But the great thing about the 'lure' is that it sets those all-important creative juices flowing pretty quickly.

I once asked a seasoned classical actor which Shakespearean part he would play if the whole gamut of roles were at his fingertips. 'Richard III,' he replied. When I asked what 'lured' him towards that character, he described how Richard's *humour* really excited him. He liked the fact that, after Richard has wooed and won Anne, he turns to the audience and basically says: 'Look how powerful I am now: I can have anyone I want, even though I'm an ugly bastard!'

And I no friends to back my suit withal,
But the plain devil, and dissembling looks,
And yet to win her, – all the world to nothing!
Ha! [30]

The actor's ATTENTION to the role quickly accessed a trigger for him to knead his imaginative clay.

2. The merger

Once you've identified your 'lure' into a character, you need to find a way to *merge with the role*. Stanislavsky suggests the best way to do this is to convert your 'lure' into an OBJECTIVE. The most user-friendly way to use an OBJECTIVE is to sum it up in a phrase which begins, 'I want to . . . ', followed by a goal or ambition towards which you can then strive. Using Mamet's quotation above, your OBJECTIVE might be: 'I want to own that car', 'I want to stay up late', 'I want to screw that guy', 'I want to back the winning horse'.

For the actor playing Richard III, it's very easy to convert his initial 'lure' into a useable OBJECTIVE. Instead of saying, 'Look how powerful I am: I can have anyone I want', he could simply adjust the words to something like: 'I want to prove my power to everyone'.

To merge even more closely with the character, the next task for our classical actor would be to road-test his initial OBJECTIVE. This involves giving his IMAGINATION a bit of a work-out, because he has to concentrate on his OBJECTIVE and use his ATTENTION to fine-tune his choice.

To do this fine-tuning, he thinks through the various aspects of the play, constantly changing his points of ATTENTION. So sometimes he might turn his ATTENTION to the other characters. Sometimes to particular scenes in the play. Sometimes to the specific psycho-physical facts we have about Richard, such as his hump or his ambition. Basically, our actor uses his ATTENTION to train his IMAGINATION, so that it responds to his initial 'lure'.

Once our actor has presented himself with a host of options, Stanislavsky would then invite him to

> choose only those problems you need and endow
> them with your own individual qualities by merging
> them with those given you by your part.[31]

And this is the important bit. The reason that our actor allows his IMAGINATION to flit from one point of ATTENTION to another is to enable his inner tuning-fork to sound the TRUTH of what he has chosen. All the time, he balances whatever activates his *personal creative juices* with whatever is accurate to *the playwright's script*, as both of these points of ATTENTION will develop his inner sense of TRUTH. As a result of this imaginative flitting, our actor may then want to fine-tune his original OBJECTIVE, which was 'I want to prove my power to everyone'. He might now find that the verb 'flaunt' or 'celebrate' is more provocative than 'prove', as in 'I want to flaunt my power' or 'I want to celebrate my power'. He might find that either of these verbs draws out more vigorously the initial sense of ironic *humour*, which 'lured' our actor so fervently towards the role of Richard in the first place, thereby strengthening his inner sense of TRUTH.

In effect, what our actor is doing is using his ATTENTION to merge himself organically with the role. If he locates any fractures between himself and the character, he'll need to fill them in at some stage; otherwise they'll hold him at one remove from the character. If there's too much 'writer' and not enough 'him', his characterisation will be formal and empty. If there's too much 'him' and not enough 'writer', the story will be off-kilter.

3. Your 'mental health'

Because psycho-physical actor-training is very intensive and draws on all your resources of body, imagination, emotion and psyche, you need to monitor how each of these is affected by your creative work. Stanislavsky is very clear about your emotional responsibility to yourself:

> Remember to devote the greatest possible attention to
> the slightest sign of depression in yourself! For if you
> let despondency steal into your heart today, you can
> be sure that your work will never thrive, either today,
> or tomorrow or the day after.[32]

This is important. CONCENTRATION AND ATTENTION aren't tools you need to labour with too ardently. The more effortless you can be in your actor-training, the more pleasure you'll take in your creative process.

In brief:

- ATTENTION is the 'lure' of your actor's nature – your trigger – into the heart of the character.

- ATTENTION can be used in the early stages of merging with your character, as you transform your 'lure' into an OBJECTIVE and imaginatively investigate the play.

- ATTENTION is your means of monitoring your mind so that you can maintain the right level of 'mental hygiene'.

You can use your ATTENTION with a lightness and brightness to ensure that your training (and, ultimately, your performance) proceeds with ease and joy.

*

The four tools we've looked at so far – RELAXATION, BREATHING, and CONCENTRATION AND ATTENTION – have a simple purpose: to prepare and lay the basic foundations for our personal blank canvas. Each one is also geared towards developing our inner listening skills: the first tool (RELAXATION) focuses on the body, the second (BREATHING) on the emotional rhythm of the body, and the third and fourth (CONCENTRATION AND ATTENTION) on our imaginative resources.

Once we've put the first four tools to use, the remaining ideas in this chapter –

- inspiration
- spirituality
- creative atmosphere
- the inner creative state

– constitute 'conditions' within which we should ideally find ourselves working. They're the means by which we can begin to paint the most aesthetically vibrant picture on our newly-prepared psycho-physical blank canvas.

TRAY 3

FOUR 'CONDITIONS' OF ACTING PRACTICE

Inspiration

What do we mean by INSPIRATION?
The spontaneous.
The instantaneous.
The creatively exciting.
It arises when (in that much used, but frustratingly imprecise, phrase) you're 'living in the moment'. You create fantastic dialogues 'in the moment' of improvisation or you execute extraordinary actions 'in the moment' of performance. All these moments are totally unexpected, yet utterly in keeping with the character you're playing and the action of the writer's script. That's when you know you're inspired.

Stanislavsky began to elucidate his ideas about INSPIRATION in 1906. His early years as an actor-director at the Moscow Art Theatre had been extremely challenging to him personally, so he took a holiday to Finland. There he found the space and time to formulate the basics of what would later became known as his 'system'. The more he thought about the state of mind in which you find yourself as an actor when you're in performance, the more he knew that the INNER CREATIVE STATE of mind was the ideal one. A nervous state of mind, a fractured state of mind, a preoccupied state of mind – none of these does anything but interfere with your process. But if there was a way of guaranteeing that as an actor you were always in an INNER CREATIVE STATE of mind, then maybe this would be the first step towards accessing a direct path to INSPIRATION. As he sat in his study in Finland, Stanislavsky asked himself some questions (as summed up here by David Magarshack):

Could [a creative state of mind] be achieved at will?
And if not, could this creative state of mind be produced bit by bit, put together from different elements
after a series of carefully devised exercises? An
ordinary actor would of course never become a genius
[simply] because he knew how to achieve the creative
state of mind on the stage, but might he not come
very close to the thing that distinguished a genius?[33]

That distinguishing 'thing' is INSPIRATION. Behind all Stanislavsky's questions was an unavoidable and creatively exasper-
ating fact: INSPIRATION cannot be summoned at will. And yet
the nature of our profession almost demands it. Unlike an
artist or a poet or a songwriter or a sculptor, we can't wait until
we feel inspired. Our creative work has to happen at 7.30 on a
Tuesday evening, or at 6 a.m. or at midnight or at whatever
ungodly hour appears on our filming call-sheet. Who gives a
tuppenny fig whether we're in an INNER CREATIVE STATE or
not? It's our job to come up with the artistic goods.

This is the very reason why Stanislavsky formulated his
'system'. Looking at the vagaries of INSPIRATION and the
uncompromising DISCIPLINE demanded of actors to create to
order, he set about devising some *conscious* means through
which the SUBCONSCIOUS (the twin sister of INSPIRATION)
might be aroused. His belief was:

The more you have of *conscious* creative moments
in your role the more chance you will have of a flow of
inspiration.[34]

Of course he was perfectly well aware that:

My 'system' will never manufacture inspiration. It
can only prepare a favourable ground for it.[35]

And he's right. However prepared you are, however rigorously
you've warmed up, however thoroughly you've researched
your part and learned your lines, sometimes your creativity will
work for you and sometimes it won't. But at least if your actor-

training provides you with the right tools to prepare consciously the INNER CREATIVE STATE of your body and mind, then you give yourself the best possible chance to tap into the kind of INSPIRATION that over the centuries has fuelled the greatest artists in the world. Alternatively, you can just end up going through the motions of a well-worn rehearsal choreography, and that gives little pleasure to anyone.

The paradoxical joy of a *conscious* and well-founded technique is that once it's fully embedded in your body, you can forget all about it. You don't go out on the stage or in front of the camera to show the audience how conscientiously you've developed your technique. You go out on the stage or in front of the camera to tell the writer's story and lead the spectator towards a particular experience. As Stanislavsky incited his actors:

> If today you are in good form and are blessed with
> inspiration, forget about technique and abandon
> yourself to your feelings.[36]

And how fantastic such moments of abandonment are!

And yet, we mustn't become too idealistic or evangelical about our mission. We needn't punish ourselves if our creative work is occasionally pedestrian. Stanislavsky gives us a timely reminder that, however prepared we may be, we're only human after all. So:

> An actor should remember that inspirations appear
> only on holidays.[37]

The challenge is to try and create a sense that every day's training or rehearsal or performance could be a 'holiday'. Or, to pick up a term from Peter Brook – a 'holy' day. Which leads us to our next 'condition' of performance: SPIRITUALITY.

Spirituality

A close partner to INSPIRATION, SPIRITUALITY crops up in Stanislavsky's work with astonishing regularity. Especially when we consider that he was writing in Soviet Russia at a time when anything esoteric was heavily suppressed. Here are just a handful of the references to SPIRITUALITY harvested from *An Actor Prepares*:

> The essence of art is not in its external forms but in its spiritual content.[38]

> The main purpose of our art [is] to create the life of a human soul and render it in artistic form.[39]

> Your own physical and spiritual state will tell you what is right.[40]

> An artist must have full use of his own spiritual, human material because that is the only stuff from which he can fashion a living soul for his part.[41]

There are nigh on fifty other references to 'spirit' or 'soul' throughout *An Actor Prepares*, and yet how often do you hear the term used in most Western performance circles?

We shouldn't fight shy of the term 'spirit' in acting. It's no coincidence that early theatre came out of the church and that ancient rituals involved mask, costume, impersonation and transformation. Sadly, there's not much time for the 'spirit' in the cut-and-thrust of the twenty-first-century acting industry. We're often judged at castings by our height, weight, looks and physiognomy, as much as by our acting acumen, let alone any 'spiritual' connection we might have with our art. One year, I walked into three consecutive auditions and, even before I'd opened my mouth, I heard the words, 'You're too short!' So I left. It's quite hard to be spiritual in those situations.

You might think it's quite hard to be 'spiritual' when you're blasting the shit out of some villain in a cops-and-robbers movie, but that would be slightly missing the point. If you genuinely tap into your resources of body, imagination, intellect and emotion, then you'll almost inevitably unlock in your work a much deeper resonance, which could be called your 'spirit', regardless of how mindless or otherwise the GIVEN CIRCUMSTANCES of the script might seem.

In terms of acting processes *per se*, Stanislavsky is quite specific about the significance of 'spirit'. He suggests that when there's

> an organic connection of the *spiritual aspec*t of the actor with his *personal technical* equipment [42]

then you can access a direct avenue to INSPIRATION. How so? According to Stanislavsky, if you open yourself up as an actor to the possible existence of your 'spirit' and combine that belief with your 'personal technical equipment', you unavoidably call into action all aspects of your acting instrument:

> not only sight and hearing, but all human emotions, body, thought, the will, memory and imagination.[43]

This unavoidable interaction between the components of your psycho-physical being puts you in a very strong position to enhance your inner-outer coordination. You could even say that true psycho-physical co-ordination *is* the creation of a 'spiritual' life. And this 'spiritual' life is manifested

> only when an actor feels that his inner and outer life on the stage is flowing naturally and normally . . . [Then] the deeper sources of his subconscious gently open, and from them come feelings . . .[44]

We see here how closely Stanislavsky's terminology connects SPIRITUALITY and INSPIRATION. His suggestion is that when you're creatively open (through RELAXATION, BREATHING and CONCENTRATION AND ATTENTION) and you can put yourself in a natural, childlike state of play, then – *sans* coercion – your deeper, less conscious resources come bubbling to the surface.

If this seems a little obscure at the moment, the practical use of 'spirit' becomes much more accessible in Chapter 2, when we come to the tools of CONNECTION and GRASP. For now, let's just be clear that any mention of SPIRITUALITY in acting in no way interferes with your own religious or personal beliefs.

What we're looking at really is the idea of some powerful, but invisible affectivity, which can springboard us as actors into all sorts of creative experiences. These experiences might otherwise be suppressed if we were to lock actor-training into nothing but the body, the emotions and the head.

We've talked about creative openness and playfulness and about having physical fun. Everything we've looked at so far – whether in terms of the 'attitudes' towards our profession, or the three basic tools for preparing our metaphorical blank canvas, or our striving for INSPIRATION through opening ourselves 'spiritually' – is leading towards the development of an INNER CREATIVE STATE which tends to flourish in a CREATIVE ATMOSPHERE.

Inner creative state and Creative atmosphere

The INNER CREATIVE STATE is one in which anything is possible, where your sense of play and spontaneity is at your finger tips. You're so physically relaxed and psychologically warmed-up that you're open to every changing nuance in your fellow actors, your audience and yourself. In this state, you really *are* listening.

Stanislavsky's response to the significance of the INNER CREATIVE STATE in his own 'system' was quite clear:

> In my involvement with the new methods of inner technique, I sincerely believed that to express the *experience* [i.e. what the character goes through in the course of the play], the actor need only master the *creative state*, and that all the rest will follow.[45]

Which implies that the INNER CREATIVE STATE is a powerful state. And the best seedbed in which it can flourish is a CREATIVE ATMOSPHERE.

A CREATIVE ATMOSPHERE is one in which everyone is utterly attentive to everyone else's artistry. In which there's absolutely no judgement of anyone's process, since that would only lead to the inhibition of your own INNER CREATIVE STATE, as well as that of your fellow-actors.

CREATIVE ATMOSPHERE and the INNER CREATIVE STATE are, therefore, mutually interdependent.

A CREATIVE ATMOSPHERE is safe. It's trusting and nurturing. At the same time, it's bold. It's dangerous and daring. It's playful – yet serious. It's sincere – yet mischievous. To exist in it is joyous. To create it is damn hard. To destroy it is dead easy:

> Creative atmosphere is one of the powerful factors in our art and we must remember it is extraordinarily difficult to create a working atmosphere. The director is in no position to create it on his own, only the collective can create it. But it can be destroyed unfortunately by any person.[46]

The responsibility for nurturing a CREATIVE ATMOSPHERE percolates far beyond the actors. As we saw with STAGE ETHICS, everyone in the building – be it the Royal Academy of Dramatic Art, the National Theatre or Universal Studios – is responsible for the overall CREATIVE ATMOSPHERE. A CREATIVE ATMOSPHERE requires an unspoken contract on everyone's part: it can't be assumed or taken for granted. As Stanislavsky's assistant director, Maria Knebel, writes in *On the Active Analysis of Plays and Roles*:

> Art doesn't come to us straight away. It demands an enormous effort. 'The work of the theatre,' wrote Nemirovich-Danchenko [Stanislavsky's co-founder of the Moscow Art Theatre] . . . [is] a dogged, persistent, many-faced kind of work which fills the whole backstage, from top to bottom. From the flies above the stage to the traps under the stage; there lies the actor's work on the role. But what does that mean? It means work on yourself, what you've been given, on your nerves, on your memory, on your habits.[47]

Stanislavsky's own preoccupation with the INNER CREATIVE STATE follows the same concerns and adopts the same vocabulary as those which he uses for both PSYCHO-PHYSICALITY and INSPIRATION. He believed that the INNER CREATIVE STATE actually mirrors your normal state in everyday life. The paradox is that – just as with psycho-physical acting – you need great patience to develop it, despite its naturalness and normality.

During his vital time in Finland in 1906, Stanislavsky beavered away to fathom some techniques to create it. Eventually he came up with four steps into the INNER CREATIVE STATE, stemming from the tools of RELAXATION and ATTENTION. He proposed that as an actor, you needed:

1 to be physically free, yet in control of your relaxed muscles;

2 to be infinitely alert in your ATTENTION;

3 to observe and listen to what's going on around you – just as you would in real life – so that your onstage contact is as plugged in as it is in real life;

4 to believe in the EVENTS on stage.

Step 4 might sound a little troublesome at first but, as we've already touched upon, you don't have to believe you really are Lavinia in *Titus Andronicus*, having every unmentionable abuse enacted upon your body: you simply have to believe in the *possibility* of the events. (See THE MAGIC 'IF'.)

Were you to distil the basic learning outcome of Stanislavsky's actor-training down to one particular element, it would probably be this: to encourage you as an actor to develop an INNER CREATIVE STATE of body and mind, a state in which you almost don't give a damn. You're not censoring yourself. You're not judging yourself. You're not worried about whether or not you're giving the director what he or she wants. You're just responding and playing. And when you're in an INNER CREATIVE STATE, your inner–outer listening is sharpened and your opportunities for inspired acting are increased. Which is why actor-training is as relevant for the proven professional as it is for the student actor, because accessing an INNER CREATIVE STATE remains an ongoing concern for you from your first day at drama school to the last night of your retirement run. The INNER CREATIVE STATE is a healthy state. And it's a playful state. Above all, it's a listening state. It's physical, emotional, intellectual and spiritual. What more could you want? Bring it on.

Overview

So far, we've established some fundamental ground rules by looking at the appropriate 'attitudes' towards acting (PSYCHO-PHYSICALITY, DISCIPLINE and STAGE ETHICS).

We've begun to prepare the blank canvas with some basic tools (RELAXATION, BREATHING and CONCENTRATION AND ATTENTION).

We've seen the goals or 'conditions' of performance towards which we're aiming (INSPIRATION, SPIRITUALITY and the existence of an INNER CREATIVE STATE and a CREATIVE ATMOSPHERE).

It's time now to walk into the rehearsal room and set to work on a script.

Once you get into the rehearsal room, the director will usually assume that you've done all the necessary preparation on yourself and your psycho-physical instrument, and that your actor-training is readily serving you. Therefore, the work inside the rehearsal room will inevitably springboard off your own particular acting tools. That doesn't mean that your actor-training stops: you're simply shifting into a different creative gear.

2

Rehearsal Processes

2

Rehearsal Processes

Diving in

So you're in rehearsal, with all the trepidation and excitement that that entails. Ahead of you may be eight weeks before opening in a big commercial show, four weeks before filming a feature, or a five-minute line-run before the television camera rolls. Whatever the scenario, it's time to start showing your true creative colours, as you begin to incarnate a role and assure the director that casting you was the best decision she ever could have made.

In this chapter, we look at a host of tools which can help you in a multitude of circumstances. Its contents fall into three key areas:

- Mining the Text
- Embodying the Role
- Approaches to Rehearsal

The first section, 'Mining the Text', looks at the kind of analysis you might apply to a script, either collectively with the director or independently as part of your own detective work. Although it's essentially head-led work, we'll see how its reverberations are profoundly psycho-physical.

The second section, 'Embodying the Role', moves on to issues of physically building a character, again either collectively as a company or independently, according to the director and the medium. As well as physical 'tools', we'll also assess some imaginative, emotional and psychological options.

The third section, 'Approaches to Rehearsal', is the meat of *The Complete Stanislavsky Toolkit*, and here we look specifically at Stanislavsky's later rehearsal practices, the METHOD OF PHYSICAL ACTIONS and ACTIVE ANALYSIS. The exciting element in both these rehearsal processes is that, right from the word go, they offer you the chance to build your character *in relation to other actors*. The work is collective and collaborative, and creatively very sexy.

As with all the chapters in this book, the divisions I've made are to simplify presentation on the page. In reality, there are endless cross-overs between these divisions, some of which I allude to explicitly, and some of which you'll note from your own experience and practice. The paradox of compiling *The Complete Stanislavsky Toolkit* is that I've had to fragment something which is inherently holistic. But then if Stanislavsky can do it – as he does throughout his writings – then I'm in good company.

Section 1
Mining the Text

TRAY 4

FOUR GENERAL TOOLS
FOR BEGINNING TEXTUAL ANALYSIS

Continuing the image of the trays in a metal toolkit, the tools in this section are divided into small groups. The initial four are:

- the first reading
- the text
- mental reconnaissance
- given circumstances

These are big tools for general usage, like a hammer, a saw, a spirit-level and a spanner. They provide some broad introductions to pretty much any kind of script.

The first reading

Getting a new script is very exciting: it's like a blind date with a new lover. Seeing and feeling that big, chunky wad of paper, containing the map of the journey on which your whole creative life is about to embark, is immensely provocative. And just as you'll have a powerful immediate response the moment you clap eyes on your blind date, so the importance of your first impression of a script shouldn't be underestimated. It harnesses your instinct and your intuition, both of which are potent creative energies. Even if your immediate response is, 'I don't like this character' – that in itself can yield a rich harvest of ideas about empathy and understanding. No first impression is a bad impression.

However . . .

Unless you're forewarned, it's hard to appreciate just how vital and fecund these first impressions can be. So Stanislavsky suggests that, before you pick up a script to read it for the first time, you should prepare an environment which is as conducive as possible for you to receive those invaluable first responses. The bus-stop is out. The quick hop on the underground is a no-no. Reading Act 1 in the bath, Act 2 in Starbucks and Act 3 in the supermarket checkout queue is definitely out of the question. After all, as Stanislavsky warns:

> This moment of your first meeting with a part should
> be unforgettable . . . The loss of this moment is
> irreparable because a second reading no longer
> contains the element of surprise so potent in the
> realm of intuitive creativeness.[48]

Obviously if we're talking Shakespeare or Chekhov or Ibsen, for example, you may well be familiar with the play already. Yet, regardless of how well you may know a text, that first encounter – when you know you're going to be playing a specific part in a specific production for a specific director – will have a particular frisson which can still be relished.

To feel the full value of your immediate impressions, Stanislavsky proposes that you create something of a ritual for your FIRST READING, where there will be no interruptions and where an appropriate INNER CREATIVE STATE of mind can be tapped into straight away:

> One must know how to choose the time and the place. The occasion should be accompanied with certain cere-moniousness; if one is to invite one's soul to buoy-ancy, one must be spiritually and physically buoyant.[49]

Part of being 'spiritually and physically buoyant' is being utterly open-hearted to the words that you're reading, and Stanislavsky is particularly ardent about this:

> Since, in the language of the actor, *to know* is synonymous with *to feel*, [the actor] should give free rein, at a first reading of a play, to his creative emotions. The more warmth of feeling and throbbing, living emotion he can put into a play at first acquaintance, the greater will be the appeal of the dry words of the text to his senses, his creative will, mind, [and] emotion memory, [and] the greater will be the suggestiveness of this first reading to the creative imagination of his visual, auditory, and other faculties, of images, pictures, sensation memories.[50]

All too often we forget how profoundly a FIRST READING can impact on us, as we stuff the script into our rucksack to be flicked through at some opportune moment. Stanislavsky's gripe with this 'unceremonious' attitude is that it hints at a certain hubris:

> We do it not so much because we want to come to know the play but because we want to imagine ourselves in some fat part or other.[51]

How many of us have rifled through the pages of a new script to find our scenes, count our lines, and only then decide whether to go to the casting or not? Of course, if you're a very successful actor with a mound of scripts on your desk, the ongoing process of 'ceremonious' readings might be just too daunting, and then the 'fat part' will unashamedly be the likeliest lure. However, if 'some fat part' were determined solely by the number of lines, then Kattrin in *Mother Courage* could easily be given the cold shoulder . . . But a blind date, who doesn't say much, may pack a few punches in other ways.

The blind date is of course the TEXT itself, and in relation to a FIRST READING, Stanislavsky has some very specific suggestions.

The text

Your first point of negotiation with a TEXT – if it's a conventionally written piece – is the black-and-white words on the page. Your task as an actor is to convert those words into living, breathing ACTIONS.

This can be something of a challenge if the TEXT is no great work of literature. The onus is then on you as an actor to find its hidden reverberations. That means looking for the script's *emotional content* along with its *literary texture*, as according to Stanislavsky, the latter will give you the former:

> A subtle understanding of the *literary texture* of the
> play is one of the most important conditions for an
> actor to be able to render these *feelings* on the stage.[52]

I'd suggest that the 'literary texture' comprises the script's structure, language and TEMPO-RHYTHM. Every TEXT, whether it's the well-fashioned work of a literary giant or the tentative scribblings of a first-time playwright, will inevitably have some kind of literary texture, since no TEXT can help but have a combination of language, structure and TEMPO-RHYTHM. There's no point in us saying, 'This script's no good; this part's unintelligible': it's our job to get inside the writer's words, to find the literary texture, and to breathe life into it, whether we're talking a box-office blockbuster, an episode of *EastEnders* or a Maeterlinck masterpiece.

You have to 'Treasure the spoken word'.[53] And certainly no word should be uttered unless you're crystal clear about *why* you're saying it:

> It is absolutely wrong to speak your words to no
> purpose. You must acquire the habit of putting the
> greatest possible meaning into every word you utter.
> You must be fully aware of the value of every word.[54]

But perhaps we're putting the cart before the horse. Can we really think about 'valuing every word' until we've understood the underlying thoughts and their accompanying ACTIONS? And acquiring that understanding requires a certain amount of detective work, otherwise known as 'round-the-table analysis' or MENTAL RECONNAISSANCE.

Mental reconnaissance

Stanislavsky's emphasis on 'round-the-table analysis' – or MENTAL RECONNAISSANCE – evolved around 1904, as he began to move away from an extremely dictatorial way of directing (in which he told his actors exactly what to do and where to go) towards a highly collaborative rehearsal practice (in which he invited his actors to pool all their ideas). The whole cast would sit together around a table, animatedly studying and nimbly dissecting a TEXT, so that everyone shared an understanding of the play. Decisions about the artistic direction of the production arose from their collaborative process of discovery, rather than from the single-minded vision of a dictatorial director. After all, if the actor is to be the main avenue through which the play's content is communicated to the audience, then the director needs to nurture a process in which the actor is placed right at the centre of any creative discovery. So significant was this shift in Stanislavsky's rehearsal ethos –

from dictating every move to assessing every contribution –
that, by the 1930s, MENTAL RECONNAISSANCE (or 'the logical
investigation of the play')[55] had become a formal part of the
rehearsal process for all theatrical organisations right across
Russia. The idea behind MENTAL RECONNAISSANCE was to
obliterate what Stanislavsky called 'the seamier side'[56] of his
actors: i.e. their passivity. He wanted to endow them with a
sense of genuine responsibility towards creating their roles
from the very first moment of rehearsal. To this end, it was
vital that the MENTAL RECONNAISSANCE of a script wasn't a
dry and cerebral activity; it was about stimulating emotional
responses:

> The analysis made by an artist is quite different from
> one made by a scholar or a critic. If the result of
> scholarly analysis is thought, the result of an artistic
> analysis is *feeling*.[57]

This is important, and it takes us back to the notion of being
utterly open-hearted during your FIRST READING of a TEXT.
Through your MENTAL RECONNAISSANCE you open yourself
up to your *visceral* and *intuitive* impressions of the script, you
don't accumulate *intellectual* facts. You're not swotting for an
exam, you're preparing yourself for a full-blown one-to-one
with the character you're playing. It's a significant relationship:
it's going to haunt you, hunt you, excite you and preoccupy
you for a good few weeks. So you might as well enjoy it and let
those creative juices flow.

Of course, MENTAL RECONNAISSANCE doesn't have to be
undertaken collectively 'round a table': it's the sort of work you
can do quite easily on your own. One of the ways in which
Stanislavsky suggests you might carry out your analytic detective work is by looking at seven 'planes' of a TEXT.[58] These
'planes' are extremely useful and comprise:

1. THE EXTERNAL PLANE, which is basically the dramatic
structure of the script, its events, plot-devices and form.

Through the 'external plane', you can see the writer's *architectural* perspective, and this can be a very handy way of understanding the script's *rhythmic composition* as much as its *structure*. So, with Chekhov's *Three Sisters*, for example, we know the action takes place over four acts, chronologically spaced out over nearly five years, with 21 months between Acts 1 and 2, and 2¾ years between Acts 2 and 3, and a matter of months between Acts 3 and 4: this information in itself gives us a feel for the play's overall TEMPO-RHYTHM and relation to time. The main events are 1) a name-day party; 2) a cancelled shrove-tide party; 3) a fire in the town; and 4) the departure of the soldiers: given these events, each act has a very distinctive atmosphere pervading it. By looking at the 'external plane', we get a clear sense of Chekhov's architecture in terms of time, EVENTS and emotional temperature.

2. THE PLANE OF THE SOCIAL SITUATION, which includes details such as the characters' class and nationality, and the historical setting, etc. Assessing the script through this plane involves gleaning all the GIVEN CIRCUMSTANCES, and it provides us with clear, skeletal facts onto which the flesh and blood of the characters can then be grafted. So with *Three Sisters*, we know the girls are Russian; they're the daughters of a general; two out of three of them have jobs; and it's the end of the nineteenth century. Sometimes the writer consciously chooses *not* to give us those specifics. In Beckett's *Waiting for Godot*, we intuit that the characters are working-class; their nationality could be anything, though the names Vladimir, Estragon and Pozzo give a European flavour; and the historical setting is fairly non-specific. All we know is that it's a country road, there's a tree and it's evening. The lack of 'social situation' provides us with information in an impressionistic, rather than a literal way.

3. THE LITERARY PLANE, which incorporates the ideas and style of the writing. The kinds of language that the writer uses in general, as well as the different types of dialogue that are

specific to each character, give us nuances of characterisation, as well as dictating the overall genre and emotional pitch of the script. So in *Three Sisters*, we have Vershinin's philosophising, Kulygin's Latin phrases and his various schoolmasterly references such as 'C-minus for conduct',[59] and Solyony's quotings of strange Russian poetry. With *Henry IV Part 1*, we have the blood-thirsty rhetoric of Hotspur, the folksy speech of Mistress Quickly with her ur-Malapropisms, Falstaff's relishing of language, and the measured, military tones of the King. Certain characters speak in prose, others in poetry: the language tends to be very muscular, and – as is the case with most Shakespearean characters – they all enjoy words, taking a distinct pleasure in the sound of their own voices. In the world of TV, a hospital drama adopts a vocabulary quite distinct from a sitcom or a domestic soap opera. And similarly a Quentin Tarantino movie uses language in a strikingly different way from a chick-flick.

4. THE AESTHETIC PLANE, which addresses the theatrical devices adopted by the writer, and the scenic and artistic choices. Chekhov has chosen to enfold most of the action in *Three Sisters* on an internal level, with very little plot development revealed explicitly. And we have only to compare *Jack and the Beanstalk* with *The Mousetrap* with *Carousel* with *Death of a Salesman* with the direct address of David Hare's *The Permanent Way* to gain an instant impression of the impact the aesthetic plane makes upon a TEXT. In some ways, the choice the writer makes about the 'aesthetic plane' tells you something about the relationship between the audience and the stage, and the kind of journey on which the writer wants to take the audience. With most Chekhov plays, the audience has to work quite hard to piece together the various characters' THROUGH-LINES, whereas Brecht hands on a plate to the audience the contents of a scene by virtue of placards such as:

> Three years later Mother Courage is taken prisoner
> along with elements of a Finnish regiment. She

manages to save her daughter, likewise her covered
cart, but her honest son is killed.[60]

5. THE PSYCHOLOGICAL PLANE, which considers the inner
workings of the characters and their underlying feelings and
OBJECTIVES. Here we definitely move from the writer's
perspective (which largely dictates planes 1 – 4) to that of the
actor (which largely dominates planes 5 – 7). Although a writer
will give you huge clues as to the character's psychological
make-up, your way of manifesting it in dramatic terms will be
filtered through your own individual life experience,
professional technique, and imaginative interpretation. How I
choose to incarnate Masha in *Three Sisters* might be quite
different from another actress: I might pursue Masha's
romantic restlessness, and therefore I might consider her
OBJECTIVE to be 'I want to fall in love with the ideal man'.
Another actress might choose to emphasise Masha's need for
intellectual compatibility, and therefore might describe her
OBJECTIVE as 'I want to quench my thirst for knowledge and
understanding through a knowledgeable man understanding
my needs'. Yet another actress might focus on the role Masha's
father clearly had in her life and how that might then impact
on her connection with both her husband, Kulygin, and her
lover, Vershinin – both of whom are older and both of whom
are in professional positions of authority. For this third actress,
Masha's OBJECTIVE might be expressed as simply as 'I want a
father figure'.

6. THE PHYSICAL PLANE, which can be defined in terms of the
ACTIONS that the characters execute and the *external characterisations* which the author provides (such as Epikhodov's
squeaking shoes in *The Cherry Orchard* or the King's deformity
in *Richard III*). Again, your choices as an actor merge with the
details provided in the script: some physical activities will be
specified – such as Chebutykin's constant beard-combing in
Three Sisters; others will be supplemented by the actors – such
as any clowning tricks which the actors playing Estragon and

Vladimir in *Waiting for Godot* may wish to add to those Beckett suggests in the text.

7. THE PLANE OF PERSONAL CREATIVE FEELINGS, which belong to you as an actor and which will be aroused through your process of analysing the text. This plane really involves many of the tools discussed so far: the process begins with your 'lure' into the character, your connection with the role and with the script, and those aspects of the script which may begin to get your creative juices flowing. From that point of departure, all manner of ideas and desires may occur to you. As you investigate the 'plane of personal creative feelings', you're actually engaging in a process of fully merging yourself with the character, allowing your imaginative connection and your emotional connection and your empathic connection with the TEXT to propel you into the heart of the character, so that the join between the two (self and character) becomes seamless. We can begin to see this emerging in the example above concerning the three actresses' OBJECTIVES for Masha on the 'psychological plane': I would suggest that the 'psychological plane' and the 'plane of personal creative feelings' inform each other quite significantly. As we work our way through the toolkit, the implications of the 'plane of personal creative feelings' will become increasingly evident.

These seven planes are an incredibly useful way of analysing a TEXT – partly because they present a gradual movement from the writer to the actor, but also because we start at the 'periphery' of our creative journey (i.e. the TEXT) and step by step move towards the 'centre' of our creative journey (i.e. the way in which the details of the TEXT touch and inspire us as actors and directors).

And this is the general process behind MENTAL RECONNAIS-SANCE as a whole. Whether the process is engaged in collectively by the whole company or independently on your own, you're not trying to become an encyclopaedia; you're hunting for the 'lures' into the character. You do it in such a way that the process – of examining, weighing, recognising, of rejecting some ideas and confirming others – engages your IMAGINA- TION, your EMOTIONS, your thoughts and physical impulses, so that you're inspired to get up on your feet and act, act, act! MENTAL RECONNAISSANCE is not pure head work; it's another step along the path of finding *conscious* means to activate *un- conscious, inspirational* and *spontaneous* processes. Which means that if the process is adopted by the director and the company collectively, your round-the-table discussions shouldn't become too protracted; otherwise you'll kill stone-dead your desire to act. After all, you want to dive into the very heart of the script, you don't want to become a fact-accumulator.

However . . .

Although the intention is not to accumulate facts intel- lectually, there are some facts which are vital: Stanislavsky called them GIVEN CIRCUMSTANCES, and to a large degree they also constitute the various elements that you draw from the seven 'planes' of MENTAL RECONNAISSANCE.

Given circumstances

The early round-the-table MENTAL RECONNAISSANCE is great for clarifying the GIVEN CIRCUMSTANCES, which Stanislavsky describes as being:

- the story of the play [*e.g. is it linear or fragmented? Chronological or kaleidoscopic? This may draw upon ideas from the 'aesthetic plane'*];

- the facts, events, epoch, time and place of action [*this connects in many ways with the* SIX FUNDAMENTAL QUESTIONS];

- the conditions of life for the character [*this will probably incorporate the 'plane of the social situation'*];

- the actors' and directors' interpretation [*this will probably incorporate the 'plane of personal creative feelings'*];

- the MISE-EN-SCÈNE, or stage pictures [*this will probably incorporate the 'aesthetic plane' to some extent*];

- the details of production, including the sets, the costumes, properties, lighting and sound effects [*again this may draw upon the 'aesthetic plane'*].[61]

Then there are other GIVEN CIRCUMSTANCES to consider, as we're not just talking 'Female, aged 26, one-legged, of Egyptian extraction'. Suppose you're involved in an outdoor production of *The Merchant of Venice*: the particular technical and geographical circumstances will affect your artistic decisions. Likewise with an 'in-the-round' Ionesco, or a filmed-on-location Lorca, or Sophocles for school kids, or Racine on the radio. Basically, the GIVEN CIRCUMSTANCES consist of all the data you can glean from the script *plus* the physical conditions of the actual production as determined by the director and the medium (stage, screen, radio, etc.).

GIVEN CIRCUMSTANCES are essentially the springboards for your IMAGINATION to propel you towards what Stanislavsky calls THE MAGIC 'IF': 'What would I do *if* I suspected my uncle had murdered my father?' (*Hamlet*) 'What would I do *if* my wife was accused of witchcraft and I knew she was innocent?' (*The Crucible*) As with all aspects of MENTAL RECONNAISSANCE the process of assembling the GIVEN CIRCUMSTANCES is not about acquiring a whole list of facts and figures; it's about appealing to your IMAGINATION, to your 'personal creative feelings' and then stimulating your desire to get up and act out the script's drama.

What you're doing is seeking physical ACTIONS and feeling their impact on your inner landscape. Which gives us another equation: *Given Circumstances + Actions = Powerful Emotions*. Stanislavsky himself is keen to emphasise this.

> We artists must realise the truth that even small physical movements, when injected into given circumstances, acquire great significance through their influence on emotion.[62]

MENTAL RECONNAISSANCE addresses character and psychology: you're not researching how your character might have lived in a particular epoch simply to patch fascinating historical details onto your characterisation. You're unpacking the GIVEN CIRCUMSTANCES – be they historical, social, or economic – so you can understand what kinds of dreams and ambitions your character might have, and the constraints under which they might suffer. If it's winter in nineteenth-century Russia and you come back from working in the post office saying, 'I'm so tired,' the chances are your fatigue and general *Weltschmerz* will have been exacerbated by your wearisome journey. If it's a twenty-first-century Hollywood movie and you come back from the office saying, 'I'm so tired,' you've probably just driven home in an air-conditioned car, so your preoccupations and expectations will be quite different from the nineteenth-century Russian post-mistress. The GIVEN CIRCUMSTANCES surrounding geographical place, historical setting, weather, life-style, material conditions, are there to fuel your imaginative ideas about your character.

And the most astonishing details can crop up when you start researching the GIVEN CIRCUMSTANCES, details which can flesh out your characterisations in quite idiosyncratic ways. I once played Masha in Chekhov's *The Seagull*, and during my investigation into the 'plane of the social situation', I discovered that, in the late nineteenth century, people in Russia used to mix cocaine into their snuff. *Eureka*! What a fabulous 'lure' into the character! 'Maybe that's why Masha is forever pinching snuff . . . maybe she's a coke addict!' The snippet of historical information instantly gave me a new and intriguing way to play the character, one which both tickled my imaginative fancy and stirred my CREATIVE INDIVIDUALITY.

I then read of the plight of many intelligent middle-class women in Russia at the time, women who, for various economic and political reasons, hadn't been able to fulfil their educational potential – so maybe that might be true for Masha, too. Maybe she's intellectually bored and she's educationally unfulfilled, so she's clutching at romantic straws to give her life a certain substance. With details like this, I was beginning to create a dynamic PERSPECTIVE for Masha. Through a comparatively small amount of research into the GIVEN CIRCUMSTANCES of the time, my IMAGINATION had been prompted to build up a possible past and future for her, and as Stanislavsky writes:

> The present cannot exist not only without a past but also without a future. People will say that we can never know it or predict it. However, we not only can but we must desire it and have perspectives on it. If in life there can be no present without a past or without a future, then on the stage too, which reflects life, how can it be otherwise?[63]

As I worked on Masha, I found that my creative juices had been stimulated enormously by the research. The playwright had provided me with a particular GIVEN CIRCUMSTANCE – Masha '*Takes a pinch of snuff*'[64] – and I'd fleshed it out with other historical details to give myself a sense of creative volume. (See the SIX FUNDAMENTAL QUESTIONS.)

There's one final point to make about being psychophysically open to the GIVEN CIRCUMSTANCES of a script. With television in particular, character descriptions can sometimes change quite radically once you get to the casting – or even as late as the costume fitting. At the snap of a finger or the change of a T-shirt, the 'attractive parent from Surbiton' can become the 'single mum from Clerkenwell'. If you're psychophysically relaxed and happy to be playful, you can adapt and adjust to most GIVEN CIRCUMSTANCES with comparative ease and a lot of pleasure. If scenes are cut or added, and vital information about your character is consequently lost or inserted, you're happy to adapt to those huge shifts in the GIVEN CIRCUMSTANCES while still bedding your creation in a sense of TRUTH.

*

So far, we've noted our instantaneous responses – the 'lures' – towards the script and we've trawled the TEXT for various GIVEN CIRCUMSTANCES. Time now in our 'mining of the text' to look at the actual, detailed, structural mechanisms that the writer has put in place: What happens when? Which EVENT precedes or succeeds which other dramatic EVENT? And why has the author put the EVENTS in this order? The tools for looking at scenic structure are:

- bits
- objectives and counter-objectives
- subtext
- punctuation
- the Six Fundamental Questions

TRAY 5

FIVE TOOLS FOR BREAKING
DOWN THE STRUCTURE OF A SCENE

Bits

When you first read a play, you naturally assume that the order of the scenes is the order in which the author always intended them to flow. As any dramaturg or script editor knows, it ain't necessarily so. Not only can the order change, but sometimes whole chunks of text are ditched or added. Sometimes lines are reallocated to different characters, as the writer herself gets to know the terrain of her own creation.

Once the script hits the rehearsal-room floor, the task of the actors and director is then to reverse that whole process – to unpick the structure blow by blow, or as Stanislavsky might put it, BIT by BIT. By doing this, you can unlock the characters' psychological OBJECTIVES and you can begin to understand how the writer constructed them. In other words, you can re-create the writer's original process.

What exactly is a BIT of action? (Note here that 'action' is used to refer to the dramatist's structuring of dramatic action – i.e., which event follows or precedes another – rather than the tool of ACTION – see page 132 – which refers to the choices made by the actor in the playing of a particular moment.)

A BIT is simply a piece of text lasting anything from about six lines to maybe a page. A typical 3-page piece of dialogue may consist of between two and five BITS of action depending on what's going on in the scene and what kind of tactics each character is using. In her translation of *An Actor Prepares*, Elizabeth Reynolds Hapgood uses the word 'unit' of action, though Stanislavsky's original Russian word for BIT (*kusok*) was totally non-scientific-sounding and arguably less alienating. Although the term 'unit' is commonly used in rehearsal practices, there's something more pliant about the term BIT: often the divisions in a piece of dialogue are not entirely clear-cut, so the word BIT reflects that essential blurriness. In fact, more and more practitioners are using BIT as the accepted terminology, so I'd advocate adopting it here, while simul-taneously remaining open to the interchangeability of BIT and 'unit' according to your director's predilections in the rehearsal room.

So . . .

When it comes to breaking down a piece of text into BITS, the decision about where one BIT ends and another BIT starts is very much up for grabs, and it could shift slightly depending on which character's PERSPECTIVE you take. Chopping up the chamber scene in *Hamlet* might involve slightly different divisions if you see it through Gertrude's eyes rather than Hamlet's. That said, I think the process is far less complicated than it can sometimes seem in a rehearsal when you've got ten actors around a table all chipping in their penn'orth.

Here are some basic guidelines:

The simplest demarcation of a BIT usually occurs where one character exits the action or another enters; the dramatic arc of the scene will inevitably be affected by Character A's departure or Character B's arrival, and this will provoke a change in dynamic, however subtle that change may be.

You can also determine the movement in a scene from one BIT to another when the subject-matter of the dialogue changes, or where one character who was rather reactive in a scene begins to become particularly proactive.

Be warned, though: in the early stages of breaking down a scene into its composite BITS, it's not very helpful to have too many divisions. While your urge may be to mark every single change in the subject-matter, these changes may simply be little diversions in a larger current which is surging the action forward, rather than a complete break in the flow of the scene. You're really looking to see where the entire course of the stream alters – not where there's a kink in the banks. Stanislavsky urged:

> Do not break up a play more than is necessary, do not use details to guide you. Create a channel outlined by large divisions . . .[65]

Of course, it depends on the length of the script and the complexity of its content, but try not to over-fragment the text and keep your life easy in the early stages.

Paradoxically, the process of breaking down a text into BITS of action is to ensure that once you put all the BITS back together again into a 'score', the flow of the script is much more articulate and precise than it was before. The 'score' of BITS becomes a kind of blueprint, guaranteeing that a production retains its shape throughout its run and doesn't become aesthetically flabby. As Stanislavsky puts it:

> When they are gathered up and grow together, these separate ['bits'] form the *score of the role*; the scores of separate roles, after constant work together during

rehearsals, and after the necessary adjustments . . .
have been made by the actors, finally merge into the
score of the whole performance.[66]

When we come to the METHOD OF PHYSICAL ACTIONS and
ACTIVE ANALYSIS, we'll look in more detail at the 'score of the
role'. Both of these rehearsal approaches are built on
improvisation, which is why it's helpful not to have too many
BITS of action through which you then have to navigate in your
improvisations. At this early stage, stick to the main channel,
and try to avoid letting the details misdirect you.

As well as ensuring a flow to the script by drawing together
every character's 'score', there's another vital reason for
breaking a scene into BITS of action: it becomes much easier to
identify what exactly it is that your character *wants* from the
other characters. This 'want' – as we've touched upon already
– is known as an OBJECTIVE, and as David Mamet and Ivana
Chubbuck would endorse full-bloodedly, OBJECTIVES and
COUNTER-OBJECTIVES lie at the heart of all impactful drama.

Objectives and counter-objectives

You could almost say there's only one basic purpose behind the
process of accumulating the GIVEN CIRCUMSTANCES and
breaking down the text into BITS of action: it's to unlock *why*
the character does what he or she does in the course of the
dramatic action. You can't really go on stage or in front of the
camera unless you know what it is you're *doing* – and it's hard
to do anything if you don't really know *why* it is you're doing
it. What do you want? What's your desire? What do you want
to achieve? Who do I want to influence and persuade? Such a
desire or a drive or an impulse is what Stanislavsky called a
'goal' or a 'task' (*zadacha*), a word which then became translated in *An Actor Prepares* as the somewhat more scientific-
sounding OBJECTIVE. This term has come into common
parlance all over the Western performance world and is sometimes expressed by actors, when confronted with a line or an

ACTION in the script that they don't immediately understand, as 'What's my motivation?'

OBJECTIVES and BITS of action are very closely interconnected: you can't really have one without the other. Or as Stanislavsky puts it:

> At the heart of every ['bit'] lies a creative objective . . .
> Each objective is an organic part of the ['bit'], or,
> conversely, it creates the ['bit'] which surrounds it.[67]

He maintains that the method of drawing an OBJECTIVE from a 'bit' is extremely simple:

> It consists of finding the most appropriate name for
> the ['bit'], one which characterises its inner essence . . .
> The right name which crystallises the essence of a
> ['bit'] discovers its fundamental objective.[68]

If the naming of one tool leads to the naming of the other, then we need to clarify the whole labelling process before we go any further.

Over the years – as I've kneaded Stanislavsky's 'system' to my own practical use – I've found that the name you give to a BIT can be anything that helps you in any way. It can be a noun, a catch-phrase, a complete sentence. Here are some that I've used at various times: 'The Catalyst', 'Setting the Record Straight', 'His Last Chance', 'Casing the Joint', 'Her Burgeoning Love', 'Going their Separate Ways', 'Her Perspective' and 'His Perspective'. In labelling a BIT, you can use absolutely anything as long as it engages your feelings, as well as your analytical thoughts. You want a phrase which ignites you on both an imaginative and a visceral level, something that sparks your fantasy and kindles your passions. And as Stanislavsky suggests, you're searching for something which

> will embrace the innermost meaning of the whole
> ['bit']. *This word will spell your objective.*[69]

However . . .

There's an important difference between the labelling of an OBJECTIVE and the labelling of a BIT. While I'd suggest you can express the name of the BIT in any way that works for you, Stanislavsky insists that:

> *You should not try to express the meaning of your objectives in terms of a noun.* That can be used for a ['bit'] but the objective must always be a *verb* . . . This is because a noun calls forth an intellectual concept of a state of mind, a form, a phenomenon, but can only define what is presented by an image without indicating motion or action. *Every objective must carry in itself the germ of action.*[70]

This is the crux of the matter: 'Every objective must carry in itself the germ of action.' ACTION is at the heart of everything. Why?

Because essentially an OBJECTIVE is both psychological and physical. It's *psychological* in that it sums up something without which your character cannot exist (their emotional drive, the *need* within the character). And it's *physical* in that the character is compelled to execute a series of ACTIONS in order to try and obtain whatever their OBJECTIVE might be. That's why the OBJECTIVE must be expressed as a verb, as verbs conjure up ACTIONS. Verbs are *doing* words, and it's the impulse to act which is the vital touch-paper in your acting process. The best way to express an OBJECTIVE, therefore (as I've already mentioned), is to start by saying, 'I want to . . . [*do* something]'.

It's all common-sense really: if you *want* something, you have to *do* something to get it. Let's take the notion of success and the ways in which 'being successful' might manifest itself:

'I want to live in a bigger house.' What do I have to do to make it happen? 'I have to go to work and earn more money.'

'I want to star in a major role in that movie.' What do I have to do to make it happen? 'I have to phone my agent

and make sure she's put me up for it. Then I have to perform well at the casting.'

Inherent in these transitive verbs are feelings – the desire to
work and earn, the drive to phone and perform. These feelings
in turn are my 'inner challenges to action'.[71] In other words, I
can't just *be* successful: I have to do something to create a
circumstance or situation or relationship, which leads to me
being successful.

Of course I might not achieve my OBJECTIVE, because someone else's COUNTER-OBJECTIVE (sometimes known as an 'obstacle') might block it. I might not earn more money because
maybe my boss has embezzled the funds and the firm goes
bankrupt. My agent might not have put me up for the role
because she doesn't see me as a tall, buxom, blonde Bond girl.
I might not perform very well at the casting because maybe the
director took a call on his mobile in the middle of the audition
and disrupted the whole proceedings. Even if I do perform
well, I might not clinch the movie anyway, as the director
planned to cast his wife in the role all along.

Whatever the outcome, my desire to achieve my OBJECTIVE
must be passionate. So finding the right name for the
OBJECTIVE is very important. It can't be cold and intellectual.
It must be precise and emotive. You need to find something so
magnetic that it draws you onto the stage or in front of the
camera with such creative compulsion you simply can't wait to
get out there and fulfil that action. Your OBJECTIVE burns –
and so do you.

Let's see how to make them burn. Using the tools of BITS,
OBJECTIVES and COUNTER-OBJECTIVES (or 'obstacles'), let's
look at an extract from Helen Edmundson's adaptation of
Tolstoy's *Anna Karenina* and understand how the labels you
choose both for the BIT of action and for the OBJECTIVES and
COUNTER-OBJECTIVES interconnect.

In this scene, Anna is at home, pregnant, awaiting the arrival
of her lover, Count Vronsky, who is also the father of her
forthcoming child. She's still living with her husband, who for

the time being is tolerating the affair. Rather unfortunately, Vronsky has just bumped into Anna's husband at the front door:

ANNA: You met him?

VRONSKY: Yes. At the door.

ANNA: It serves you right for being late.

VRONSKY: Your note said he would be at the Council; I would never have come otherwise.

ANNA: Where have you been, Alexei?

VRONSKY: I'm sorry my darling. It's been a busy week.

ANNA: Really? Busy? Betsy came to see me this morning. I heard all about your Athenian evening. How disgusting.

VRONSKY: It was disgusting but I had to go. The Colonel asked me to entertain a foreign dignitary.

ANNA: Oh – you mean that little French girl you used to see. I believe she was there.

VRONSKY: Anna, you don't understand . . .

ANNA: No, I don't. What do I know – a woman who can't even share your life? I only know what you tell me and how do I know whether you tell me the truth?

VRONSKY: Anna, don't you trust me?

ANNA: Yes, yes. You just don't understand what it's like for me. How can I go out like this and with the way people are talking? I don't think I'm jealous, I'm not jealous – I trust you when you're here but when you're away leading your own life . . . oh, I believe you, I do believe you. Alexei, I've stopped now. The demon has gone.

VRONSKY: I don't enjoy that kind of life anymore. I thought you understood that.

ANNA: I do, I do. I'm sorry.

She kisses him.[72]

As I've said, the breaking-down of a piece of text into BITS of action is never set in stone: one person may think that a BIT ends at a very different point from another, though it's important to come to some sort of collective agreement. On some occasions, you may even find that a director comes to a rehearsal with the BITS (or 'units') already determined; on other occasions, you may all sit 'round the table' and work them out together. What I offer below in the case of the *Anna Karenina* extract is far from gospel, but we're looking to see where the stream changes course, rather than where the banks slightly kink. That said, you'll see that I've marked the kinks with ▼ to indicate where a character's tactic changes, even though the general thrust of the scene remains more or less the same. Likewise with the titles I offer for each BIT: they're only springboards into further creative possibilities:

Bit 1: Tit-for-tat

ANNA: You met him?

VRONSKY: Yes. At the door.

ANNA: It serves you right for being late.

VRONSKY: Your note said he would be at the Council; I would never have come otherwise.

We see in BIT 1 how Anna is slightly getting her own back on Vronsky. Although she didn't intend for him to run slap-bang into her husband, she's got issues with Vronsky at the moment and she probably quite enjoys the discomfort he must have endured having to exchange pleasantries at the front door with the cuckolded husband.

Bit 2: Anna cuts to the chase

ANNA: Where have you been, Alexei?

VRONSKY: I'm sorry my darling. It's been a busy week.

ANNA: Really? Busy? ▼ Betsy came to see me this morning.
I heard all about your Athenian evening. How disgusting.

VRONSKY: It was disgusting but I had to go. The Colonel asked
me to entertain a foreign dignitary.

ANNA: Oh – you mean that little French girl you used to see.
I believe she was there.

VRONSKY: Anna, you don't understand . . .

Anna isn't going to waste time now. Ever since Princess Betsy,
the renowned society gossip, turned up at the Karenins' house
this morning, Anna has been seething with anxious thoughts
about what Vronsky has been up to while she's stuck at home
heavily pregnant with his illegitimate child. The thought of
an 'Athenian evening' and all the lewdness inherent in togas
and French girls and free-flowing wine must surely have
provoked the green-headed Envy-monster. Her insecurities,
her jealousies and inadequacies all come surging to the fore,
and she's not going to hang about making small talk with him.
Her preoccupation with the Athenian evening is what we
might call her PRESSING ISSUE.

PRESSING ISSUE is not necessarily a Stanislavsky phrase, but
it's a useful tool, nonetheless. It's the subject that underlies a
dialogue, propelling it – either secretly or explicitly – in a
particular direction and (see SUBTEXT) it's the preoccupation
which can drive a character's OBJECTIVE. Indeed, it may have
echoes with a character's SUPER-OBJECTIVE (discussed in
detail below), though it's not the same. A SUPER-OBJECTIVE
will usually underpin a character's action throughout the
whole play, whereas here, for example, Anna's PRESSING ISSUE
has been sparked by the conversation with Princess Betsy
which only took place that very morning: its history is recent.
A character may actually have a series of PRESSING ISSUES
throughout a play, a new one sparking each particular scene,
but there will only be one SUPER-OBJECTIVE driving the
character throughout the whole play.

The PRESSING ISSUE is also tied in with TEMPO-RHYTHM, in that if we choose to suppress our PRESSING ISSUE and not let anyone know what it is that's preoccupying us, we often find that our inner TEMPO-RHYTHM is at odds with our outer TEMPO-RHYTHM. Conversely, if we bring our PRESSING ISSUE right to the fore, as indeed Anna does here, our inner and outer TEMPO-RHYTHMS will tend to synchronise, as the amount of SUBTEXT is reduced: i.e. there's little disparity between what we think and what we say, everything's on the surface. If, for example, I meet some friends for a drink to celebrate a birthday and I've just landed a fantastic television role and I'm feeling really terrific, then my inner TEMPO-RHYTHM of jubilation will be in synchrony with my outer TEMPO-RHYTHM of *bonhomie*. If, however, I've just received a whacking great tax bill for which I've not saved a bean, my PRESSING ISSUE will resonate at a very different inner TEMPO-RHYTHM from my outer show of hilarity, which I feel bound to maintain so as not to sabotage the celebrations.

I've marked a ▼ sign in BIT 2, at the point in which we see that Anna has a very clear MOMENT OF DECISION (see SUBTEXT and ACTION). She could choose to let Vronsky convince her that he *has* been very busy; instead, she takes the moment to raise the issue of the Athenian evening, possibly haunted by the thought of him watching scantily clad *tableaux vivants* of Athenian-dressed beauties.

MOMENTS OF DECISION (also not absolutely pure Stanislavsky tools, but useful nonetheless) are vital, and all too easily rushed over in a piece of drama. In real life, MOMENTS OF DECISION have a distinct danger to them as we can never truly predict what another person's reaction may be to what we say or do; regardless of how well or little we know them, they might still surprise us with their response. I might decide to say to my boyfriend, 'I've been thinking: things haven't been going too well lately and perhaps we need a break from each other', my OBJECTIVE being that 'I want to test my partner's love for me and hopefully elicit the response, "Nonsense, darling, we just haven't spent enough time together: let's go to Paris for a romantic weekend".' And yet, for all I know, he might come out with the words, 'You're absolutely right – I've been thinking the same, so let's call it a day, yeah?' In my MOMENT OF DECISION, I have to be prepared to take the consequences of whatever response or outcome might be elicited by my words.

I've marked Anna's second speech with ▼ because there's a definite MOMENT OF DECISION here, which indicates a slight kink in the bank of the stream rather than a complete change of BIT.

Bit 3: Anna's explosion

> ANNA: No, I don't. What do I know – a woman who can't even share your life? I only know what you tell me and how do I know whether you tell me the truth?
>
> VRONSKY: Anna, don't you trust me?
>
> ANNA: ▼ Yes, yes. You just don't understand what it's like for me. How can I go out like this and with the way people are talking? ▼ I don't think I'm jealous, I'm not jealous – I trust you when you're here but when you're away leading your own life . . .

Here we see the emotional consequence of the PRESSING ISSUE. A volatile back-pressure has been building up within Anna at the end of BIT 2, and Vronsky's words, 'you don't understand', are like a red rag to a bull, because – from her PERSPECTIVE – it's *him* who doesn't understand *her*, not the other way round. Now her guard is completely down: her reaction is instinctive and, as a result, her emotions pour out uncensored.

Within this explosive BIT, I've suggested there are two MOMENTS OF DECISION: in the first ▼ Anna chooses to lie to Vronsky and tell him she trusts him, when clearly everything in the previous BIT illustrates that she doesn't. In the second ▼

she chooses to address her own inner machinations, and try to understand whether or not she *is* jealous, before going on to qualify the extent of her trust: 'I trust you when you're here but when you're away leading your own life . . . '. Which is the whole point, isn't it? If you don't trust someone when they're not around, then you don't really trust them, period.

Bit 4: Anna digs herself out of a hole

ANNA: . . . oh, I believe you, I do believe you. Alexei, I've stopped now. The demon has gone.

VRONSKY: I don't enjoy that kind of life anymore. I thought you understood that.

ANNA: I do, I do. I'm sorry.

She kisses him.

By this time – possibly in response to Vronsky's silent reaction embedded in the '. . .' of Anna's speech – she realises that she's rapidly alienating him and she needs to draw him back to her. Mercifully, she has enough self-awareness to hear the sound of her own demons and to attempt to reduce their impact. She seals the deal with a kiss, papering over the emotional distance between herself and Vronsky with a sign of physical intimacy.

My division of this dialogue into these four particular BITS is partly led by viewing the action from Anna's PERSPECTIVE, as she seems to be driving the scene in the *proactive* (or 'major' role) with Vronsky in the *reactive* (or 'minor' role). If we were to look at the dialogue more specifically from Vronsky's PERSPECTIVE, we might slightly alter the division of the BITS to something like this:

Bit 1: Tit-for-tat

ANNA: You met him?

VRONSKY: Yes. At the door.

ANNA: It serves you right for being late.

VRONSKY: Your note said he would be at the Council; I would never have come otherwise.

Bit 2: Vronsky defends himself

ANNA: Where have you been, Alexei?

VRONSKY: I'm sorry my darling. It's been a busy week.

ANNA: Really? Busy? Betsy came to see me this morning. I heard all about your Athenian evening. How disgusting.

VRONSKY: It was disgusting but I had to go. The Colonel asked me to entertain a foreign dignitary.

ANNA: Oh – you mean that little French girl you used to see. I believe she was there.

Bit 3: Vronsky corrects Anna

VRONSKY: Anna, you don't understand . . .

ANNA: No, I don't. What do I know – a woman who can't even share your life? I only know what you tell me and how do I know whether you tell me the truth?

By marking a BIT here, we see how Vronsky starts to take control, a stance which he continues into the next proposed BIT.

Bit 4: Vronsky challenges Anna

VRONSKY: Anna, don't you trust me?

ANNA: Yes, yes. You just don't understand what it's like for me. How can I go out like this and with the way people are talking? I don't think I'm jealous, I'm not jealous – I trust you when you're here but when you're away leading your own life . . .

Again, we see how his leading question places him in the 'major' position, even though Anna speaks far more text than he does. Silence can be eloquent.

Bit 5: Vronsky straightens the situation (perhaps by making as if to leave in the '. . .' of Anna's speech)

ANNA: . . . oh, I believe you, I do believe you. Alexei, I've stopped now. The demon has gone.

VRONSKY: I don't enjoy that kind of life any more. I thought you understood that.

ANNA: I do, I do. I'm sorry.

She kisses him.

I propose that there's a MOMENT OF DECISION on Vronsky's part embedded in the '. . .' punctuation of Anna's speech, in which he chooses to make a move to leave or executes some other gesture of impatience. If he were to do this, he'd demonstrate that he's simply not going to pursue this conversation as long as Anna is in her particular frame of mind. If he *were* to make as if to leave, Anna would have to change both her tactics and her TEMPO-RHYTHM pretty radically and pretty quickly – which indeed she does in the text.

You could follow either of these sets of divisions for this extract of dialogue: neither is more or less right or wrong than the other. It would take the two actors playing Anna and Vronsky to sit down with the director and clarify where the divisions into BITS occur, and it may well be that five BITS in so sparse a piece of dialogue would be too much. Or it might be that the staccato rhythm of five short BITS reflects the inner emotional fragmentation of the scene more accurately than four. There's no gospel: each leads to a different, but equally valid, interpretation. What this does do, however, is provide an inroad into the way in which BITS and OBJECTIVES interconnect and cross-reference in terms of labelling, as we'll look at now.

The first list of BITS (taking the scene from Anna's PER-SPECTIVE) is:

- Tit-for-tat
- Anna cuts to the chase
- Anna's explosion
- Anna digs herself out of a hole

Here are some possible OBJECTIVES and COUNTER-OBJEC-TIVES for this list of BITS:

Bit 1: Tit-for-tat

ANNA: I want to enjoy Vronsky's discomfort.

VRONSKY: I want to chastise Anna for putting me in an uncomfortable position.

Anna's OBJECTIVE and Vronsky's COUNTER-OBJECTIVE reflect the sparring that's clearly going on in BIT 1: neither character is in a mood to be particularly open to the other, as each feels let down by the other.

Bit 2: Anna cuts to the chase

ANNA: I want to find out the truth from Vronsky about what he has been up to lately.

VRONSKY: I want to appease Anna for my absence.

Here in BIT 2 Vronsky readjusts his PERSPECTIVE to accommodate Anna's questioning, as he doesn't really want a row. After all, why bother meeting up with your mistress if you're only going to have a bad time?

Bit 3: Anna's explosion

ANNA: I want to convince Vronsky of the untenability of my situation.

VRONSKY: I want to straighten Anna's delusions concerning my behaviour.

In BIT 3, Anna can no longer pretend that the reality is anything other than what it actually is, and so she lets all her emotions out, while Vronsky remains anchored to his integrity.

Bit 4: Anna digs herself out of a hole

ANNA: I want to re-engage Vronsky's love for me.

VRONSKY: I want to distance myself from Anna's madness.

The final BIT 4 shows how Anna realises things aren't going the way she wants them to, so she has to change her tactics. Vronsky's COUNTER-OBJECTIVE reflects the fact that this isn't a scenario he particularly wants to pursue.

Thus we have four BITS and four possible OBJECTIVES and COUNTER-OBJECTIVES.

If we were to look at the scene from Vronsky's PERSPECTIVE and divide the scene into five BITS rather than four, this is how our OBJECTIVES and COUNTER-OBJECTIVES might shift. Our new, extended list of BITS is:

- Tit-for-tat
- Vronsky defends himself
- Vronsky corrects Anna
- Vronsky challenges Anna
- Vronsky straightens the situation

The OBJECTIVES and COUNTER-OBJECTIVES might be as follows (noting that for BIT 1 they remain the same as they did when we considered the encounter from Anna's PERSPECTIVE):

Bit 1: Tit-for-tat

ANNA: I want to enjoy Vronsky's discomfort.

VRONSKY: I want to chastise Anna for putting me in an uncomfortable position.

As we've already discussed, the sparring inherent in this OBJECTIVE and COUNTER-OBJECTIVE reflects the fact that neither character is in a mood to be particularly open to the other, as each feels let down by the other.

Bit 2: Vronsky defends himself

VRONSKY: I want to retain a certain sense of my professional status, even within the context of our domestic encounter.

ANNA: I want to put him on the spot and let him know that I have 'inside information'.

The OBJECTIVE and COUNTER-OBJECTIVE proposed here for BIT 2 reflect the tension between the public and the private, between the professional and the romantic, between He who can be seen publicly and She who has to remain behind closed doors. It reveals a profound and underlying inequality of circumstances.

Bit 3: Vronsky corrects Anna

VRONSKY: I want to correct Anna's misinterpretation of my work.

ANNA: I want to convince Vronsky that he can't fob me off.

In BIT 3, Vronsky will not let Anna contort the reality into anything other than what it actually is, while Anna tries to retain control of the conversation.

Bit 4: Vronsky challenges Anna

VRONSKY: I want to challenge Anna into being straight with me.

ANNA: I want to work this situation out to our mutual benefit.

Vronsky is not prepared in BIT 4 to be railroaded by Anna. Anna's COUNTER-OBJECTIVE reflects the fact she needs to be more compliant if she's going to hang on to some kind of loving *status quo*.

Bit 5: Vronsky straightens the situation

ANNA: I want to re-engage Vronsky's love.

VRONSKY: I want to clarify for Anna that this madness is not acceptable behaviour.

In this final BIT 5, Vronsky doesn't want to let Anna contrive what, in his opinion, is a misguided PERSPECTIVE. Anna's COUNTER-OBJECTIVE is not so much 'counter' as 'pro': she obliges in the straightening of the situation.

Obviously with both of these lists – whether the scene is divided into four or five BITS – I've taken certain interpretational decisions with which you might completely disagree, but we can begin to see how the words chosen for a BIT then become fine-tuned into workable, action-driven OBJECTIVES for the characters. We also see how one character will have an inciting OBJECTIVE (i.e. he or she is driving the BIT) and the other character will have a resisting COUNTER-OBJECTIVE (i.e. he or she is impeding or creating an obstacle which stops the achievement of the first character's OBJECTIVE). It's the conflict between Character A's inciting OBJECTIVE and Character B's resisting COUNTER-OBJECTIVE, which creates the inherent dramatic tension of the scene. Do we come away from this piece of dialogue between Anna and Vronsky believing that any rift or jealousy has been healed or diffused? Or is this one helluva doomed love affair? The answer may lie in the final stage direction of the dialogue: note that '*She kisses him*', rather than '*They kiss*' . . .

I'd suggest that ultimately OBJECTIVES can be distilled down to one critical thing. If you want something so badly – if your survival (be it financial, physical, emotional, professional, romantic, erotic, political) depends upon your attainment of it – what will you *lose* if you don't get it? Just how high are the stakes? And there's no question: the higher the stakes of the OBJECTIVE, the more exciting it'll be for you to play. There has to be a dimension which takes it beyond the mundane.

After all . . .

'I want to make a cup of tea' won't inspire you for very long.

'I want to make my long-lost aunt feel welcome, so I'll make her a cup of tea' might endure longer.

'I want to ensure my long-lost aunt keeps me in her inheritance so I'll make her feel welcome by making her a cup of tea', will add coal to the furnace.

Furthermore . . .

The higher the stakes, the more satisfaction you'll get from achieving your OBJECTIVE. Conversely, if you fail to achieve it – through the power of the other characters pursuing their own COUNTER-OBJECTIVES with more success than you, i.e. the obstacle with which they present you is too great for you to surmount – the greater will be your sense of defeat, dissatisfaction, or maybe even fear.

Fear is a many-splendour'd thing, which in terms of acting processes themselves can be eliminated with a well-defined OBJECTIVE. I've often found that if there's a scene coming up in the performance of a play which I'm dreading, the chances are I'm dreading it because I haven't actually found the right OBJECTIVE. The stakes *need* to be high. You *need* to want to go out onto that stage or in front of that camera and achieve it. If at any point you're thinking as an actor, 'Oh, I hate that scene in Act 3 where I have to lure the priest into the cave', it's probably because you haven't identified a sufficiently inspiring OBJECTIVE. Change the OBJECTIVE – sharpen your verb, raise the stakes, CONCENTRATE YOUR ATTENTION on what the scene's really about – until the point where you think, 'Wow, yes! I can't wait to get out on that stage or in front of that camera, and show that priest what I'm worth!' There need never be a moment of performance in which you – as an actor – experience dread or fear. Simply re-examine your OBJECTIVE – and make it burn.

That said, you don't have to bust a gut over it. In all fairness, it's rare to find a potent OBJECTIVE immediately or through pure intellect. If you go about your MENTAL RECONNAISSANCE creatively, you'll usually find that the right OBJECTIVE gradually formulates itself into a valuable, forward-moving desire. And it's worth spending time doing this, as – according to Stanislavsky – the right OBJECTIVE can prepare the most propitious ground for INSPIRATION:

> When an actor is completely absorbed by some
> profoundly moving objective, so that he throws his
> whole being passionately into its execution, he reaches
> a state that we call *inspiration*.[73]

It's in these moments of complete commitment to attaining your OBJECTIVE that you'll find yourself coming up with all sorts of moments in rehearsal or performance which were completely unplanned and yet utterly in keeping with the character and the action. That's when you know you're acting from a state of INSPIRATION.

So, one of the most exciting things about an OBJECTIVE is that it ensures you're motivated and focused in rehearsal or performance. And perhaps one of the sexiest ways of using this tool is to keep much of your character's OBJECTIVE hidden from the other characters. That way, there's a resonant gap between what you *actually* say or do, and the intention *behind* what you say or do. And this is what Stanislavsky called SUBTEXT.

Subtext

As we go through our daily lives pursuing our various OBJEC-
TIVES in the workplace, around the social sphere and at home,
we don't necessarily communicate all our desires through the
words we choose to speak. Stanislavsky maintained that only
about 10% of what's actually going on in our heads is expressed through words; the remaining 90% remains unspoken
and, in drama, that 90% lies bedded beneath the script. He
came to this conclusion while directing and acting in the plays
of Anton Chekhov. In fact the term SUBTEXT was first coined
by Nemirovich-Danchenko and Stanislavsky in 1898 when
they were working on *The Seagull*, and they used it to describe
the undercurrents of thoughts which flowed beneath the text.
Never – before Chekhov – had a writer left more *unsaid* by the
characters than was actually *said*, and the combined artistic
forces of Stanislavsky and Nemirovich-Danchenko realised
that a whole new approach to text analysis was now required.

What exactly is SUBTEXT?
As Stanislavsky says, it is that which:

> flows uninterruptedly beneath the words of the text,
> giving them life and a basis for existing . . . It is the
> subtext that makes us say the words we do in a play.[74]

Let's translate that into practicalities.
There's a cyclical and ongoing sequence inherent in all
human behaviour, which flows as Action – Reaction – Decision.
And it goes like this:

CYCLE I

- A executes an Action on B (e.g. A hits B);
- B has a gut Reaction to A's Action (e.g. 'I'm going to hit you back, you bastard!');

- B then makes a Decision about that Reaction (e.g. 'Okay, so you're having a heavy time at work and you're not behaving in your usual measured and compassionate way. Well, on this occasion, I'm not going to retaliate by giving like-for-like').

CYCLE II

- B instigates a new Action towards A (e.g. B embraces A).
- In turn, A has a gut Reaction to B's Action (e.g. 'Weird! You're embracing me and I thought you'd hit me back . . . ');
- A makes a Decision about his response to B's Action (e.g. 'Wow, that's incredible! And I'm going to let you know how grateful I am for your generosity and understanding!').

CYCLE III

- A executes a new, corresponding Action (e.g. A kisses B).

And on it goes: Action – Reaction – Decision —— Action – Reaction – Decision.

This process unfurls naturally and continually through all human intercourse. And often the Reaction moments and/or the Decision moments lie beneath our spoken words.

However . . .

Although they may be unvoiced, they're not absent. Far from it. Those Reaction or Decision moments are the instigating impulses behind our physical ACTIONS and our spoken words. They *are* our SUBTEXT.

To discover the layers of SUBTEXT in a script – the moments of Reaction and/or Decision – you've got to head for your character's OBJECTIVE: what your character *really* wants will determine how much and what they choose to say.

Let's take a piece of dialogue from Brutus and Portia in *Julius Caesar*, Act 2, Scene ii, shortly after the conspirators have gathered to plot the murder of Caesar. Note in this dialogue that one character (Portia) has a good deal of TEXT but very little SUBTEXT, while the other (Brutus) says very little and yet

his SUBTEXT and his psychological journey *through* that SUBTEXT
are as clear as daylight:

PORTIA: Brutus, my lord!

BRUTUS: Portia, what mean you? Wherefore rise you now?
   It is not for your health thus to commit
   Your weak condition to the raw cold morning.

PORTIA: Nor for yours neither. You've ungently, Brutus,
   Stole from my bed: and yesternight, at supper,
   You suddenly arose, and walk'd about,
   Musing and sighing, with your arms across,
   And when I ask'd you what the matter was,
   You stared upon me with ungentle looks;
   I urg'd you further; then you scratch'd your head,
   And too impatiently stamp'd with your foot;
   Yet I insisted, yet you answer'd not,
   But, with an angry wafture of your hand,
   Gave sign for me to leave you: so I did;
   Fearing to strengthen that impatience
   Which seem'd too much enkindled, and withal
   Hoping it was but an effect of humour,
   Which sometime hath his hour with every man.
   It will not let you eat, nor talk, nor sleep,
   And could it work so much upon your shape
   As it hath much prevail'd on your condition,
   I should not know you, Brutus. Dear my lord,
   Make me acquainted with your cause of grief.

BRUTUS: I am not well in health, and that is all.

PORTIA: Brutus is wise, and, were he not in health,
   He would embrace the means to come by it.

BRUTUS: Why, so I do. Good Portia, go to bed.

PORTIA: Is Brutus sick? And is it physical
   To walk unbraced, and suck up the humours
   Of the dank morning? What, is Brutus sick,
   And will he steal out of his wholesome bed,
   To dare the vile contagion of the night,

And tempt the rheumy and unpurged air,
To add unto his sickness? No, my Brutus;
You have some sick offence within your mind,
Which, by the right and virtue of my place,
I ought to know of: and, upon my knees,
I charm you, by my once-commended beauty,
By all your vows of love, and that great vow
Which did incorporate and make us one,
That you unfold to me, yourself, your half,
Why are you heavy, and what men tonight
Have had resort to you: for here have been
Some six or seven, who did hide their faces
Even from darkness.

BRUTUS: Kneel not, gentle Portia.

PORTIA: I should not need, if you were gentle Brutus.
Within the bond of marriage, tell me, Brutus,
Is it excepted I should know no secrets
That appertain to you? Am I yourself
But, as it were, in sort or limitation,
To keep with you at meals, comfort your bed,
And talk to you sometimes? Dwell I but in the suburbs
Of your good pleasure? If it be no more,
Portia is Brutus' harlot, not his wife.

BRUTUS: You are my true and honourable wife,
As dear to me as are the ruddy drops
That visit my sad heart.

PORTIA: If this were true, then should I know this secret.
I grant I am a woman; but withal
A woman that Lord Brutus took to wife:
I grant I am a woman; but withal
A woman well-reputed, Cato's daughter.
Think you I am no stronger than my sex,
Being so father'd and so husbanded?
Tell me your counsels, I will not disclose 'em:
I have made strong proof of my constancy,
Giving myself a voluntary wound
Here, in the thigh: can I bear that with patience,
And not my husband's secrets?

BRUTUS: O ye gods,
Render me worthy of this noble wife! (*Knocking within.*)
Hark, hark! One knocks: Portia, go in awhile;
And by and by thy bosom shall partake
The secrets of my heart.

Notice how Portia states very directly what she's thinking and she's feeling, she doesn't mince her words. Her lack of SUBTEXT forces Brutus's lies and deflections to simmer like boiling blood beneath the surface. He begins by fobbing her off with, 'Don't worry, darling, I'm fine – just a bit of a headache, that's all', the SUBTEXT of which the audience knows must be something like, 'Actually, sweetheart, I'm bloody awful – I just can't tell you about it now'. Portia's utter directness – her lack of game-playing or contrivance – forces Brutus to a point where he agrees to tell her exactly what the secrets of his heart are. Thus his OBJECTIVE changes from being something like 'I want to protect Portia' to 'I want to share my heart with her'. However, he's saved at the moment of confessing his PRESSING ISSUE by the rather timely knocking at the door. As an audience, we're completely in-the-know about his SUBTEXT, because we've just seen the previous scene with the conspirators; therefore, we absolutely understand how his PRESSING ISSUE fuels his SUBTEXT. Portia knows him well enough to sense he's pre-occupied and has a powerful SUBTEXT going on, but as yet she has no idea what exactly that PRESSING ISSUE might be. She presents very clearly in her opening speech how it has manifested itself in highly physical ways over the last few days: from everything she says, we get a tangible sense that Brutus's 90% unspoken life has found other, very noticeable means of expression: musing, sighing, ungentle looks, head scratching, foot stamping, etc.

So SUBTEXT can be conveyed either non-verbally (be it through body or through silence) or through the *disparity* between what a person actually says and what he or she means. SUBTEXT is a great tool for actors. It's the means by which you can personally engage with a role, because you can join the dots between what the writer has written and how you bring it to life in a way that's utterly unique to you. If you can find the counterpoint between the spoken word and the unspoken SUBTEXT – the disparity between what's said and what's meant – you'll begin, according to Stanislavsky, to manifest the 'melody of the living soul'[75] of the character. And this is what good theatre or cinema acting is all about – sounding out the living soul of a character as conjured up by its SUBTEXT. If a performance *wasn't* about sounding out the SUBTEXT, then as far as Stanislavsky was concerned the audience might as well stay at home and read the script.

There's one final component we should consider here, because without it we can't possibly convey our own SUBTEXT or read another person's. And that's the PAUSE. This is only a brief reference as there's further detail on this tool in the section on ACTIVE ANALYSIS. For the moment, we just need to bear in mind that if a writer marks PAUSES (or 'beats') in a script, it's often an indication that there's an active SUBTEXT at work – whether we're talking Anton Chekhov, Harold Pinter, David Mamet, Mark Ravenhill or any one of a number of powerful contemporary writers of stage and screen. As we'll see, the PAUSE is your means of breathing life into the Action – Reaction – Decision sequence. And if good psycho-physical acting is about good listening, then the PAUSE is the perfect tool for listening to your own inner thoughts and feelings, as well as to the words of the other characters. As Stanislavsky puts it:

> You convey, you pause, your partner absorbs what you conveyed, you continue, you pause again and so on.
> Of course, as you do this you must have in mind the whole of what you are to convey. To you as author of the subtext this is automatically clear, but to your partner it is all new, it must be decoded and absorbed.[76]

In brief:

- SUBTEXT is the key to unlocking OBJECTIVES.

- SUBTEXT is the 'melody of the living soul'.

- SUBTEXT is the reason why audiences want to see a performance and not just read a script.

- SUBTEXT is your means of personalising a role.

- SUBTEXT is the kernel of the Action – Reaction – Decision sequence.

- SUBTEXT works in conjunction with OBJECTIVES to propel everything we do and say as the character.

- SUBTEXT is revealed through PAUSES or 'beats' which a writer may mark in a script or which an actor might insert into dialogue.

You can begin to see how significant a tool SUBTEXT is in the toolkit. Stanislavsky felt very strongly that your ability to affect the audience through SUBTEXT was vital and should be shared:

> Do not conceal from us the hints you yourselves get from beneath the words, between the lines . . . just as you yourselves see, hear, and sense the life of a human spirit in the play. *Be creators, not mere narrators.*[77]

'Be creators, and not mere narrators' is a powerful incitement: of course, it's the writer's story that you're telling, but it's *you* who's creating it for this spectator or this camera, 'HERE, TODAY, NOW', as if for the first time. You can enhance your skill to 'create' and not just 'narrate' by understanding how to use every clue embedded in the text. That means developing your ability to understand the words and the PAUSES, as well as to decode the all-important PUNCTUATION.

Punctuation

As we 'mine a text', we shouldn't underestimate the number of clues given to us by the black-and-white dots on the writer's scripted page. Actually, the key to a script's SUBTEXT often lies in its PUNCTUATION. If the writer hasn't written 'pause' or 'beat' (which many contemporary writers now do), there may be suspension marks (. . .) indicating a silent thought-process or a moment where the character cannot complete a sentence for fear of giving too much away. If there are lots of suspension marks in a speech, you can probably deduce that the character's thought-processes are either changing rapidly, or that those thoughts are deep and complex, and therefore the character is struggling to find the appropriate means to articulate them. Take a look at Masha's speech in *Three Sisters* after Vershinin has left town towards the end of the play:

> By a curving shore stands a green oak tree, hung with a golden chain . . . A green cat . . . A green oak . . . I'm getting all mixed up . . . (*drinks some water.*) My life's ruined . . . I don't want anything . . . I'll be all right in a minute . . . It doesn't matter . . . What does that mean, a curving shore? Why do those words keep going through my mind? My thoughts are all mixed up.[78]

Clearly there has to be some thinking time in those suspension marks. It doesn't necessarily mean that the actress playing Masha has to mentally fill in the dots night after night. But it would probably be helpful if, at some point in her preparation of the role, she works through for herself the inner MOMENTS OF DECISION – uncovering the thoughts that Masha chooses to voice and those she chooses not to voice. What may only look like dots on a page are profound and important sources of information.

Obviously suspension marks aren't the only indicators of SUBTEXT: all PUNCTUATION provides clues as to the TEMPO-

RHYTHM, intention and inner content of a script. Stanislavsky had a very keen eye for this: he saw PUNCTUATION marks as being distinct directives as to how you manipulate your listener. So:

- you can use an exclamation mark (!) to provoke sympathy, approval or protest in your listener;

- you can use a question mark (?) to invite your listener to answer, even if you're asking a rhetorical question and therefore inviting a silent, rhetorical answer;

- you can use a colon (:) to invite your listener to wait for further information.

And as for the comma:

'Love the comma!' Stanislavsky constantly said, 'because it is in it that you can make people listen to you.' He compared the comma with a hand raised in warning, which makes the audience wait patiently for the continuation of an incomplete phrase.[79]

There's actually some really intricate detective work to be done on PUNCTUATION as far as Stanislavsky was concerned:

> You need to work out why the author put a full-stop here and not a semi-colon or suspension marks . . . Perhaps he wants to emphasise this thought particularly. Perhaps he wants to pick out the following thought and therefore prepares [the listener] for the expression of a whole thought. Only when you have thought through and thoroughly analysed a whole chunk in toto, and when a distant musical enticing perspective has opened up before you, will your speech become (as it were) long-sighted and not short-sighted as it is now. Then you will be able to speak not separate phrases or words, but whole thoughts.[80]

It's fair to say that not all writers are as attentive to PUNC-TUATION as Stanislavsky suggests. C. P. Taylor, for example, wrote huge numbers of suspension marks sometimes between *every* line of dialogue, and so we get:

HELEN: Don't just say things to pacify me, John . . . will you not, love? . . . I couldn't stand that . . .

MOTHER: John . . . John . . .

HALDER: Oh, Jesus . . . I cannot cope with that bloody woman just now . . .

MOTHER: John . . .

HALDER: I'm coming . . .

MOTHER: I thought you were in the toilet.[81]

And Shakespeare scholars are at pains to point out the disparity between folios and quarto texts with regard to PUNCTUATION. So we may not need to be as reverential to the dots and commas as Stanislavsky implies. That said, there's no harm in taking hints from his suggestions, and there are plenty of excellent thoughts and exercises in the books of contemporary voice teachers, including Patsy Rodenburg, Cicely Berry and Barbara Houseman to which you might refer. What's of particular interest here is that even from the first rehearsals of a script, when the actors and directors were simply sitting round a table 'mining the text', Stanislavsky's eye for the details of the printed page and all the psycho-physical information embedded in the sentences was incredibly sharp.

It's almost time to stop 'mining the text' imaginatively and cerebrally, and to start physicalising our discoveries about character and action. Before we do, there's one final tool to consider, as Stanislavsky said that without this tool you shouldn't go on stage: namely the SIX FUNDAMENTAL QUESTIONS.

The Six Fundamental Questions

The SIX FUNDAMENTAL QUESTIONS are referred to in Chapter 4 of *An Actor Prepares* ('Imagination') and they're very closely allied to the basic GIVEN CIRCUMSTANCES of a script. The first three of the six questions are directly related to the facts provided by the writer, though the second three are more up for grabs. The SIX FUNDAMENTAL QUESTIONS are:

- 'Who?'

- 'When?'

- 'Where?'

- 'Why?'

- 'For what reason?'

- 'How?'

During my actor-training in Moscow in the 1990s, I discovered just how vital these six questions are, yet their significance is curiously underplayed in the English translation of *An Actor Prepares*. So here and now, we're going to put them slap-bang in the middle of the table as we complete our first stage of 'mining the text'.

Who? is fairly straightforward, as in '*Who* is my character?' You can find the answer to this question in the 'social plane of the text' (see GIVEN CIRCUMSTANCES), and it'll probably stem from an accumulation of the rock-solid facts in the script. So, if I'm Masha in *Three Sisters*: 'I'm Russian. I'm the daughter of a general who died a year ago, and I've been married to a schoolteacher since I was eighteen. My mother is also dead. I'm the middle of three sisters, and I was brought up in Moscow. I'm a woman. I'm a wife. I'm a sister. At the start of the play, I'm twenty-two. I tend to dress in black. I play the piano. I read. I'm adored by my husband, despite the fact that I'm so rude to him and he knows by the end of the play I'm having an affair; yet despite all this he even describes me as "kind" and "good". I'm bored with life. I have no job. I'm emotional: I laugh, I cry, I sob, I whistle, I hum. I can be outspoken to people sometimes. As the play unfurls, I fall in love . . . '

Where? is equally straightforward, and operates on a number of CIRCLES OF ATTENTION – from the immediate surroundings to the larger geographical placement. So with Masha at the beginning of *Three Sisters*: 'I'm at my younger sister's name-day party in the house she shares with my older sister, along with my brother and the old nanny, Anfisa. I'm in the living/dining room. The house is quite big (as indicated by the hoards of officers we regularly entertain and the number of people who take shelter here in Act 3 when the fire breaks out). I'm in a provincial town in Russia maybe a hundred miles from Moscow, possibly Perm. The town is small – both in size and outlook – and I despise the civilians, seeing myself as one of the few intelligent and sophisticated inhabitants.' For *Three Sisters*, place is immensely important, as the omnipresent desire to be somewhere other than here is a vital cog in the inner workings of the play's action and the characters' psyches (reflected in the repeated chorus, 'To Moscow, to Moscow'). There's also a huge sense of *movement* in the play: the three sisters are gradually moved out of the house by their sister-in-law Natasha through the course of the action; the inhabitants of the town are severely disrupted by the fire in Act 3 so that they have to decamp and find shelter in other houses including the Prozorov house; Baron Tusenbach leaves this life to die in Act 4; and the soldiers leave the girls to go off to their next posting. Place. Displacement. Belonging. Ownership. Loss. All these issues fuel the plot and the characters on every level. There's also a psychological dimension to *Where?*: 'Am I on the periphery of the play's action or at the centre? Am I one of the key players in the drama or am I a supporting participant?' If I was Masha, I could go on to ask myself: 'Am I at the centre of Vershinin's life, or on the periphery? Is my husband Kulygin at the centre of my life, or on the outskirts?' It's probably fair to say that in most scripts, the arc of a character's journey – be it a geographical movement from one place to another or a psychological one – is the main thrust of the overall dramatic ACTION.

When? is also drawn from the particular facts in the text. In Act 1 of *Three Sisters*: 'It's the late nineteenth century. It's May. It's mid-morning. It's not only my sister's name-day, but also the first anniversary of my father's death.' As with the 'Where?' question, there are various CIRCLES OF ATTENTION: with Act 1 of *Three Sisters*, the big circle is the nineteenth century, the next circle down is May, the smallest circle is mid-morning, and resonating in the background is the contradictory combination of the sister's name-day (present tense) and the father's death (past tense). Act 2 projects us into February 21 months later: it's shrove-tide, it's snowing outside, and the atmosphere is quite different from the early summer optimism of Act 1 – both inside the house and out. This means a whole 21 months have passed since Vershinin and Masha clapped eyes on each other and before they actually act upon their feelings. Act 3 takes place 2 ¾ years after Act 2, therefore 4 ½ years since the start of the play, yet it's only now that Masha chooses the time is right to declare her love affair to her sisters. This means that she and Vershinin have been keeping their romance subterranean for a very long time in a very closed community – that's quite something. By Act 4, it's autumn: death is in the air, along with departures and farewells, the end of a year, the turning of the leaves and the halting of hopes. In terms of the time-scale surrounding the duel between Tusenbach and Solony, it's significant that they've been at loggerheads over Irina for nearly five years: their fight stems from no hot-headed irrationality, it's a chronic ongoing dispute. Throughout the whole of this play, time affects atmosphere and psychology and motive. The inertia is tangible. In fact, it's not until you pick between the lines of *Three Sisters* that you realise just how much time passes in the course of the play. It's so important for the actors to get a feeling of that slowness, in order for the audience to truly appreciate the lack of action within the lives and hearts of these girls: their house and their town and their jobs and their marriages really are prisons for them.

Why? is the first of the SIX FUNDAMENTAL QUESTIONS which begins the creative voyage into the actor's IMAGIN-ATION: we're no longer dealing with pure textual facts, we're now starting to interpret and personalise whatever information the writer has given us. To some extent, the answers to 'Why?' come directly from the dramatic structure of the play or the scene: Why is this scene present? Why did the writer write it? In what way is it driving the action forward? What do we learn about a particular character from this scene? What's her OBJECTIVE? If this scene weren't in the play, would the narra-tive continue seamlessly? The chances are – with a good script – you couldn't take away any scene or any character, without the narrative falling apart or shifting so radically that it would become a completely different script. Once you've identified the dramatic function of a particular scene or a particular character, then it's highly likely that the answer to the question *Why?* will become crystal clear. Why is Masha in *Three Sisters?* On the one hand, there's a very revealing fact to consider: Chekhov wrote the part for his wife, Olga Knipper, so he obvi-ously knew her temperament, her repertoire, what kind of role would suit her, what kind of part he wanted to see her in and what kind of part she wanted to play. On the other hand, there are the ensemble dynamics to consider: it's very significant that the most emotional of the sisters is the least physically active, in the sense of being the one without a job (see EMPLOI). Irina and Olga are always working and talking about working, as if they're trying to distract themselves from their dissatisfaction with life through physical and intellectual occupations. In fact, everyone else in the play has a job except Masha (if you con-sider that Natasha's job is to be a mother), and because Masha has time on her hands, she's able to go deep into the core of her emotional appetites – and we know from his own descriptions of his plays, as well as his numerous encounters with women, that Chekhov loved love!

Obviously, there's a certain amount of room for interpre-tation with the FUNDAMENTAL QUESTION *Why?*, in the sense that every character's OBJECTIVE will be up for debate, and the choice you personally make for your OBJECTIVE is a huge part of the answer to your interpretation of 'Why am I here?' One actor might consider Vershinin's OBJECTIVE is, 'I want to seduce Masha because I love her' – and that's why he's here rather than hanging out with his mess-mates. Another actor might feel the Lieutenant-Colonel's behaviour is far more manipulative and his OBJECTIVE is, 'I want to seduce Masha because I need some personal gratification' – and that's why he's here rather than staying with his suicidal wife. The answers to the FUNDAMENTAL QUESTION *Why?* combine the facts of the writer's text with your own interpretation of those facts, which in turn leads to you creating your own particular SUBTEXT.

The fifth FUNDAMENTAL QUESTION, *For what reason?* is a curious one. In the English language, *Why?* and *For what reason?* could seem remarkably similar. In Russian, however, the two words are quite different: *pochemu* is 'Why?' and *zachem* is 'For what reason?' And it's with this FUNDAMENTAL QUESTION that the appeal to your IMAGINATION grows even stronger. As Stanislavsky suggests, the question, 'For what reason?'

> obliges you to clarify the object of your meditations, it suggests the future, and it impels you to action.[82]

Each of these three phrases is very significant: you have to clarify what you're CONCENTRATING YOUR ATTENTION on, i.e. *whom* or *what*; create a possible future for your character, i.e. *what* could arise if you CONCENTRATED YOUR ATTENTION fully on the object of your meditations; and propel yourself into the appropriate ACTIONS to secure that future.

The significance of the question *For what reason?* was made crystal clear to me in 2003, when I was playing the small, but perfectly formed part of Pimple the maid in Max Stafford-Clark's production of Goldsmith's *She Stoops to Conquer*. It was my National Theatre début, so I invited my Russian Scenic Movement teacher, Vladimir Ananyev, over from Moscow to share the excitement. After the performance, Ananyev hung his head in his hands and asked, 'Why are you such a hooliganka? Don't you see? Your performance is all happening on the stage.' This confused me, as I thought that was the whole point, wasn't it? Everything *should* be 'happening on the stage' – a phrase which I interpreted as 'Everything should be born "in the moment" of performance'. However, that wasn't at all what Ananyev meant. As far as he was concerned there was no 'reverberation' to what I was doing; my performance stopped at the wings, as he could sense there was no *For what reason?*

Little by little, as I questioned him about what he meant, I began to unravel the significance of the question, *For what reason?* Pimple, for example, works hard in Mr Hardcastle's house, and from the way in which Stafford-Clark had staged the production – with Pimple bringing on various props and furniture and generally being on hand – it was clear to see that she was good at her job. Efficient. Effective. And personable.

'*Why* does Pimple bring in the tray of lemons and cinnamon?' asked Ananyev.

'Because I want to help Mr Hardcastle prepare his hot punch for his guests,' I replied.

'*For what reason* do you want to help him?' asked Ananyev.

'Because I want to do my job well,' I replied.

'*For what reason* do you want to do your job so well?' pressed Ananyev.

'Because I want to earn more money,' was my reply, interpreting Pimple's OBJECTIVE as being a basic matter of survival: money buys food and clothes, food and clothes keep you alive.

'And *for what reason* do you want to earn more money?' pursued Ananyev.

By now, my mind was blank. Beyond feeding and clothing herself, I couldn't really find a 'reverberant' answer for Pimple. After all, she didn't really need anything else in terms of the GIVEN CIRCUMSTANCES of the play. So Ananyev offered up some suggestions:

'Maybe she wants to improve her lot romantically as well as financially. If she earns more money, she can buy the beautiful shawl she saw last week at the market. Once she's wearing that, then she might attract the attention of the young squire who lives on the neighbouring estate. He might then fall in love with her and take her from Hardcastle Hall and raise her up from her humble position and change her life forever.'

Suddenly – by virtue of some proposed answers to the FUNDAMENTAL QUESTION *For what reason?* – Ananyev had plunged me deep into the realm of IMAGINATION and invention.

First of all, the answers to the question *For what reason?* 'clarified the object of my meditations' – i.e. the OBJECTIVE which drove my character through the play. And so my OBJECTIVE shifted from 'I want to help Mr Hardcastle' to 'I want to earn more money'.

Secondly, the answer 'suggested a future': If I earn more money, where might my future lie? In much better circumstances with much happier prospects.

And thirdly, the answer 'impelled me to action': I wanted to fulfil the simple physical tasks before me (bringing Hardcastle the ingredients of lemons and cinnamon to make his special hot punch for his guests, along with cleaning the tables and moving the furniture). By achieving these simple tasks, I could strive towards a more complex psychological OBJECTIVE – 'I want to improve my lot romantically and financially' – which in turn had the potential to transform my life.

Now my character had a whole set of imaginative dimensions beyond the simple physical tasks before me. Of course, the audience was completely oblivious to the specifics of my imagined scenario, and yet I found that the imaginative background immediately gave my playing of the character a certain volume, or 'reverberation' beyond the GIVEN CIRCUMSTANCES of the script, and that 'reverberation' rapidly enhanced my sense of play *as an actor* and my sense of impulse *as a character*.

Going back to *Three Sisters*, what might be the answers to Masha's 'Why?' and 'For what reason?' Let's take Act 1: 'Why does she stay for lunch when Vershinin arrives?' Because she wants to spend time with an interesting man. She's bored: she doesn't love her husband, she has no children – there's a certain emptiness to her existence. Spending time with an interesting man would give some content to her life. After all, she has no job and therefore she has nothing to occupy her *body* . . .

. . . and she's bored by her husband and therefore she has nothing to occupy her *mind* . . .

. . . and so the one aspect of herself through which she might find fulfilment is through her *heart*.

Thus her body, mind and heart might all be drafted into unified occupation.

Let's take it further: 'For what reason does Masha want to spend time with an interesting man?'

Because she wants to fall in love.

'*For what reason* does she want to fall in love?'

Because . . . she wants to live at the extremes of her nerve endings.

Because . . . she wants to fulfil her romantic potential.

Because . . . she doesn't want to wither away emotionally as spinster-sister Olga seems to have done. And she doesn't want to throw her life away domestically with a man she doesn't love as she sees Irina about to do and as she perceives that she herself is doing in her own marriage.

Because . . . she wants to sense the utter completion that you feel when you're heart-and-soul-and-body in love.

And '*For what reason* does she choose Vershinin?'

This is where the investigation could become rather fun and complex. If we adopt a somewhat Freudian perspective on the GIVEN CIRCUMSTANCES as indeed I hinted at earlier in this chapter with reference to the 'psychological plane', it's clear to see that Masha doted on her father: isn't that why, after all, at the start of the play she's still in black one year after his death, while Olga and Irina have abandoned their mourning weeds for blue and white respectively? The similarities between Vershinin and her father are manifold: the military connection; the intellectual capability; the fact that the wind howled in the chimney the night father died just as it's howling in the chimney at the moment Vershinin declares his love in Act 2; then there's the age gap between Masha and Vershinin of about twenty years. Maybe she seeks through Vershinin a connection she thought she might have had with her husband Kulygin – whom she also thought was clever and intelligent and a little daunting when she first married him – a connection which will link her to a man (her father) who was no doubt an impressive and romantic figure in her life. And if her father hadn't died a year ago (from when the play begins), the whole family might well have gone back to Moscow, and thus her escape might have been managed. Falling in love with Vershinin fills a space in her heart and a place in her family home.

Who knows? This might be reading far too much into the text – but you can see how the imaginative impulse supplied by the FUNDAMENTAL QUESTION *For what reason?* can suddenly give all manner of textures and reverberations to an interpretation of a part beyond the written word.

The sixth FUNDAMENTAL QUESTION, *How?* was clarified for me by another of my Russian mentors, acting master Albert Filozov. Filozov trained at the Moscow Art Theatre Studio, as a result of which his own acting practices are steeped in all the playful aspects of Stanislavsky's later work, including ACTIVE ANALYSIS. He believes that if you're truly alive to the myriad nuances of your fellow actors' behaviour, then your *How?* will never be fixed: it will inevitably and necessarily change each night or during each take on a minuscule level (see ADAPTATION) as you respond to *their* ever-changing performances. Filozov suggests that as long as you've put all the other pieces in place in your preparation of a part and you've done all the necessary detective work on the character and the dramatic ACTION, you don't actually have to know the answers to *How?* You can simply get out there – in front of that camera or onto that stage – and see what happens: just dive into Mamet's 'terrifying unforeseen'. Filozov argues that it's your prerogative as an actor to change the ongoing moment-by-moment answers to the FUNDAMENTAL QUESTION *How?* every night, as you respond truthfully and spontaneously to your acting partners. These are not disruptive changes that you're making: often they're almost imperceptible to the outside eye, but they're highly 'reverberant' to the INNER CREATIVE STATE. So, the real FUNDAMENTAL QUESTION that you're asking yourself is '*How* will I behave tonight in response to this actor in front of this audience given these actions?'

In terms of film, of course, a certain amount of fixedness is necessary to ensure the continuity of each take, but that doesn't mean you can't remain alive *within* the technical and rigid structure. The inner *How?* – the very light in your eye – can be bright and nuanced and constantly alert and attentive to the tiny changes in your partner on every single take. It's crucially important to remember that just because the physical and technical elements need to be rigid, your inner life *can't* be rigid or your performance will be dead. You can *never* stop listening – and if you truly listen, it's impossible to fix your inner life. Fixedness and spontaneity are as incompatible as trying to open and close a door in the same moment.

Before you get to the actual performance, however, it's possible to set some potential *How?*s in place during rehearsal. The director Max Stafford-Clark calls this process 'actioning a text', a technique for which he has become internationally famed. The process involves finding a transitive verb which motors every line in a text, be it 'I excite', 'I threaten', 'I educate', 'I charm', etc. These are the ACTIONS that you seek to play upon your fellow characters – i.e. they are the means by which you strive in each moment of a scene to achieve your larger OBJECTIVE. As Stafford-Clark details in his wonderful book, *Letters to George*,[83] this is a Stanislavsky-based practice that he has refined over the years at Joint Stock, the Royal Court, and Out of Joint.[84]

A very useful development of this technique was introduced to me by acclaimed British actor, Miles Anderson, who had worked for several years under the directorship of Richard Cottrell at the Bristol Old Vic Theatre, UK. During a discussion out in Australia in the spring of 2005, Cottrell suggested to Anderson, who was at the time working with me in Stafford-Clark's re-staging of *The Permanent Way* at the Sydney Theatre, that an actor might colour each line-by-line transitive verb with an adverb. So, for example 'I seduce cautiously', 'I threaten playfully', and 'I tease assertively'. Alternatively, 'I seduce playfully', 'I threaten assertively' and 'I tease cautiously'. Then again, perhaps 'I caution seductively', 'I play threateningly' and 'I assert teasingly'. Instantly you can sense the subtleties involved in the combination of verb and adverb. The transitive verb pinpoints *what* you're trying to do, the adverb adds a nuance to *how* you're going to do it.

You can make all these preliminary decisions about the answers to your *How?* questions while sitting round the table, as long as you have the caveat that once you put the scene on its feet, you're free to make any necessary and natural adaptations and refinements, which will inevitably occur once you're eye-balling your fellow actors. This is certainly what Stafford-Clark advocates with his *actioning* technique: for him, his idiosyncratic rehearsal process simply forms a platform from which the rocket of the play can launch, it's not the rocket itself.

In brief:

- You can find the answers to the first three of the SIX FUNDAMENTAL QUESTIONS (*Who?*, *Where?* and *When?*) *in the script* and from your factual research *around the script*.

- The fourth FUNDAMENTAL QUESTION (*Why?*) takes you into the structure of the play and what might be the

character's psychological OBJECTIVE underpinning the
ACTION.

- The fifth FUNDAMENTAL QUESTION (*For what reason?*)
leads you even further into the realm of your personal
IMAGINATION and JUSTIFICATION.

- All five of these FUNDAMENTAL QUESTIONS can be
explored through 'mining the text'.

- The sixth FUNDAMENTAL QUESTION (*How?*) really
becomes clear once you get onto the rehearsal-room
floor, where you physicalise the role and interact with
your fellow performers, responding to their ever-
changing subtleties.

- You can fine-tune your *How?*s by selecting a transitive
verb to be the ACTION you play on your partner. You
can then colour that verb with an adverb which
determines how you intend to play the ACTION.

*

Overview

So what has 'mining the text' entailed?

First of all, we've used four general tools for basic textual
analysis, addressing all the information embedded in the script.
This has involved:

- a conscientious FIRST READING;

- an appreciation of the raw material – i.e. the TEXT;

- an assessment of the TEXT through our MENTAL
RECONNAISSANCE (including looking at the seven
'planes');

- a reaping of the facts and figures in the text which
comprise the GIVEN CIRCUMSTANCES.

We've then looked at five tools for understanding how the actual structure of a scene can take us further into our process of characterising a role. We've:

- broken a text down into BITS of action;

- come up with some psychological OBJECTIVES and COUNTER-OBJECTIVES (or 'obstacles');

- fuelled those OBJECTIVES and COUNTER-OBJECTIVES with some SUBTEXT;

- examined the way in which the PUNCTUATION itself can deepen our understanding of the script's inner mechanism;

- merged the writer's information with our own interpretation by asking the SIX FUNDAMENTAL QUESTIONS, and thus we've begun a true personalisation of the part.

All this 'mining of the text' – which might occur collectively with the director and the rest of the company round a table, or individually as part of your own exploration of a role – has been a vital stage in our detective work. But it's time to transmute that brain-work into physical work, as we begin the complex process of 'Embodying the Role'.

Section 2
Embodying the Role

Getting your body into the space is an exciting and daunting part of rehearsals, as suddenly your sense of responsibility as an actor comes to the fore. Every physical movement you make delivers a mass of encoded messages to the receiving audience, so you need to be sure those messages are relevant. In an age of psychological realism, the message you usually have to communicate is one steeped in TRUTH.

TRAY 6

THE TOOL WHICH UNDERPINS
OUR CREATIVE WORK ON A ROLE

Truth

TRUTH is a tricky word and an even trickier concept. In the twenty-first century, there's no such thing as 'objective truth' any more: *your* perspective is as legitimate as *my* perspective which is as legitimate as *anyone else's* perspective. Each person's vision of the world is as justified as anyone else's. Which is fine, because when it comes to TRUTH, what we're really looking for is a context for what we're seeing, some rules which determine our expectations, some kind of LOGIC AND SEQUENCE.

LOGIC AND SEQUENCE are a tantalising duo, which crop up with curious regularity in Stanislavsky's writings, including being displayed on placards in an acting class described at the end of Chapter 11 of *An Actor Prepares*.[85] LOGIC doesn't have to mean mathematical logic: our emotions can have their own logic, which at first may seem utterly chaotic, but with time reveals itself to have an absolute coherence. However, it doesn't really matter whether we're talking rational logic or emotional logic: the audience aren't going to buy into what we're doing unless we've created some sort of truthful context for the action – be it *Star Wars* or *West Wing* or *Woyzeck*.

The key to this sense of TRUTH is the ongoing sequence of Action – Reaction – Decision, described earlier in reference to MOMENTS OF DECISION. In this sequence:

- A does something to B (Action);
- B has a gut response to A (Reaction);
- B makes a choice about what A has done (Decision);
- and B does something back to A (next Action).

The audience stops believing what they're watching when one of those steps (usually Reaction or Decision) is omitted. Instead, they start questioning the sense of TRUTH in what they see: 'I don't understand why Character X did that' or 'I don't believe Character Y would respond like that'. But I repeat, the TRUTH doesn't have to be a realistic TRUTH. It can be absurd, abstract, science-fiction, horror. As long as there's a LOGIC AND SEQUENCE to the rules and the context of the piece, I can 'believe' in an episode of *Star Trek* or Ionesco's *The Bald Prima Donna*, just as I can believe in an episode of *E.R.* or Ibsen's *A Doll's House*.

Stanislavsky was hot on TRUTH. He believed that a sense of TRUTH marked the difference between a craftsman and an artist. And he pinpointed three different kinds of TRUTH which he saw arising in acting practice:

1. 'make-believe truth'[86] (which draws on clichés and short-cuts);

2. 'actual fact'[87] (which is life as we know it);

3. 'scenic truth'[88] (which is 'actual fact' distilled into a creative form).

'Make-believe truth' isn't great, but neither is it utterly useless, as half the time with a 'make-believe truth' you can con your audience into accepting what they see. (If that's what you want to do . . .) You've usually based your choices on certain stereotypes: 'Oh, this is what a colonel in the army would be like: stick on a moustache, slick down my hair and bark a few orders as I strut about in khaki.' These stereotypes of 'make-believe truth' are quite different from what we might term 'fantasy'. Of course, if you're playing a hobbit in *Lord of the Rings* or a talking lion in *Narnia* or a superhero in *X Men*, there's going to be an element of fantasy involved in the choices you make. But fantasy is quite different from 'make-believe truth'. 'Make-believe truth' stems from *generalities* as opposed to realms of reality: it doesn't matter what genre, medium or character type you're exploring or how far-fetched the realms of the script's 'reality' might be, your choices as an actor can have the same degree of specificity that you'd apply to psychological realism, if you simply engage your creative IMAGINATION. There is no need for you as an actor to ever fall into the abyss of 'make-believe truth'.

That said, you have to be on your guard: even if you don't intend it to happen, clichés can creep into your performance surreptitiously and (in Stanislavsky's words) 'clip your wings'.[89] So to prevent the conventions and lies kicking in, Stanislavsky proposed that you should consciously develop an inner sense of TRUTH to use as a metaphoric internal sounding-board during your creative process, since a sense of TRUTH

> supervises all [an actor's] inner and physical activity, both when he is creating in rehearsal and when he is performing his part. It is only when his sense of truth is thoroughly developed that he will reach the point, where *every pose, every gesture, will have an inner justification.*[90]

If you really listen to yourself as you train your psycho-physical co-ordination, you'll know when an action rings true or not – you'll hear the inner sounding-board of your sense of TRUTH chiming in or out of key.

The second kind of TRUTH – 'actual fact' – is what you see around you. But however valuable OBSERVATION may be as a tool, it's not always appropriate to transport 'actual fact' into performance. Here's a simple example. Suppose the colonel you're playing has a Glaswegian accent: if your accent is too accurate, too 'truthful', the audience will have no idea what you're actually talking about. So as you 'embody the role', you have to introduce a degree of moderation, of artistic 'untruth'.

And indeed, the third kind of TRUTH – 'scenic truth' – involves that kind of moderation. In the process of embodying a role, you draw upon your OBSERVATION of the real world.

('Oh, that's what a colonel looks like, so let's consider how this individual deals with the conflict of duty and desire, given his military status. And how does he communicate that conflict in his broad Glaswegian accent?') Then you artistically and intuitively filter that factual information into a format you can use in performance. So, the 'true'-sounding Glaswegian accent is filtered through your IMAGINATION to make it a credible *impression* of the required accent, while still remaining truthful to the writer's intentions and understood by the audience; at the same time, your OBSERVATIONS and psychological assimilations of the real-life colonel filter out your 'make-believe' generalisations.

I discovered how this filtering process worked when I was playing an Investment Banker in Hare's *The Permanent Way*. I could have begun my journey into the character by going for the 'make-believe truth' and considered what the broad brushstrokes of an Investment Banker meant to me. I'd watched enough Wall Street movies, I'd seen enough documentaries and news programmes to come up with a formula. But because *The Permanent Way* was based on real people, I decided to visit the actual man in his high-powered merchant bank in the City of London. The guy was in his fifties, coming up to retirement, extremely successful, absolutely loaded – and generally very at-one with the world. Back in the rehearsal room, I tried to take on the 'actual facts' that I'd observed in the real banker and portray them in my own way through my body and voice. I adopted his laidback posture, I spoke in his gently timbred tone, and I beamed his beatific smile. After a while, the director asked me what on earth I was doing. The problem was that, as a five-foot-one female in her mid-thirties, I couldn't convey with much sense of TRUTH the cool aplomb of the fifty-five-year-old male. In the process of embodying the role, I needed to convert the 'actual facts' of life into an appropriate 'scenic truth'.

To do this, I started with something as simple as shifting my *physical* weight from my heels (which felt cool and laid-

back) forward to the balls of my feet (which felt more plugged
in and switched on). Suddenly my *psychological* focus felt more
switched on too. My mind was keener and my diction was
sharper. It was more scenically affective and dramatically
connected.

'Scenic truth' relates to the emotions as well. We tend to
think that Stanislavsky's 'system' is about beating your breast
and tearing your hair out. In fact, he called upon his actors to
be 'cool and impartial',[91] as a sense of TRUTH isn't about being
so wound up in an emotion that it floods your entire performance like an emotional tsunami. Inherent in your sense of
TRUTH you have to have a sense of artistic detachment. This is
important, because if you take some of Stanislavsky's words on
emotional TRUTH out of context, they can sound as if he
wanted actors to use *real* emotions – real joy and real distress,
for instance:

> Each and every moment must be saturated with a
> belief in the truthfulness of the emotion felt, and in
> the action carried out, by the actor.[92]

But there's a significant difference between *feeling the real
emotion* and *believing in the truthfulness of the emotion*. It's
subtle but significant, a little like the difference between
believing in what's going on in the enacted drama and
believing in its *possibility*. To help actors develop their inner
TRUTH sounding-board or monitor, Stanislavsky came up with
'three steps'.[93] These three steps built on the idea that we need
to adjust the facts of life ('actual fact') to the fictions of
performance ('scenic truth').

1. First of all, you need to *reconstruct all the experiences*
    that the character has in the script, colouring in even
    the smallest details with your own IMAGINATION. [Look
    at everything the writer gives you and ask the SIX
    FUNDAMENTAL QUESTIONS, so that you can supply
    information from your own IMAGINATION to fill in the
    blanks left by the writer.]

2. There then has to be a certain *identification* with the character and its surroundings. [Go back to your initial trigger into the character, the original 'lure' between you and the role, so you can pinpoint your connection with the part and your empathy with its circumstances.]

3. Having reminded yourself of the 'lure' – the point of 'identification' – you need to *clarify your character's specific 'objectives'*. [If you sharpen your OBJECTIVES, every moment will make sense for you; it'll have some kind of LOGIC AND SEQUENCE, however tangential or whacky or idiosyncratic that LOGIC AND SEQUENCE may be.]

Once you've taken these three steps, Stanislavsky believed the ground should be ready for your sense of TRUTH towards the character to flourish within you.

Your next task is to put that sense of TRUTH to the test by finding a series of simple physical ACTIONS, which you can execute from your character's PERSPECTIVE. And it really is through the *simplest* of physical ACTIONS that you can hear your inner sounding-board. In some ways, the smaller those ACTIONS are, the easier it is for you to believe in them. And you have to believe in what you're doing, because if you can't believe in your smallest *physical* ACTION, how can you possibly execute complex *psychological* tasks with any degree of conviction?

Let's take a simple example. Suppose my OBJECTIVE in leading a workshop is 'I want to create a good learning environment in which I can inspire the actors with the value of Stanislavsky's "system"'. In itself, this is a pretty complex psychological task. Yet I can make life easier for myself. To achieve my complex OBJECTIVE, I can execute a series of ACTIONS so simple that there's no way my sense of TRUTH in them can be questioned. So I enter the studio, switch on the light, turn on the heaters, sweep the floor, set out the chairs in a welcoming circle, lay out my handouts in an accessible way, do my warm-up, grab a bottle of water and await the arrival of the participants. Through this series of very simple ACTIONS – which will either ring true or they won't, in that I either switch on the light or I don't – I can begin to create within myself the feeling of an informative, capable, well-organised acting tutor. If I can prepare the ground in this way, my complex psychological OBJECTIVE should be much easier to achieve. (We'll come back to this in greater detail later in this chapter with 'Approaches to Rehearsal', re: the METHOD OF PHYSICAL ACTIONS and ACTIVE ANALYSIS.)

Stanislavsky was adamant that if you can *feel* the TRUTH of what you're doing, you'll stir your passions. It's as simple as that. There's an age-old jibe aimed at a mythical Method actor, whose director asks him to execute some simple physical task – something like bringing in a drinks tray. The actor asks, 'But what's my motivation?' To a director who just wants to get the play on its feet and create beautiful stage pictures, it doesn't really matter what the motivation behind the action is: 'Just bring in the drinks, for Chrissakes!' Yet if there's no sense of TRUTH for the actor, the moves will be empty, formal and, worse still, there'll be no creative passion to be stirred within him. He might as well quit and let the director hire a robot to do the job instead. It's not naïve or difficult or earnest of an actor to want to fathom out the motivation behind a move: it's simply his IMAGINATION desiring some creative food with which to fuel the ACTION. And we shouldn't forget that through tiny physical movements, we can unlock big complex EMOTIONS. As Stanislavsky insists:

> You will come to know that in real life . . . many of the great moments of emotion are signalised [sic] by some ordinary, small, natural movement . . .

> We artists must realise the truth that even small, physical movements, when injected into given circumstances, acquire great significance through their influence on emotion.[94]

The long and short of all this is that TRUTH – a big and mighty word – actually lies in the smallest of physical ACTIONS. (As

I've said, we'll keep revisiting the importance of ACTION throughout *The Toolkit*.) So from the first moments of physic- ally 'embodying a role', we should be absolutely attentive to our inner sense of TRUTH. If we metaphorically knock the marble off its course by one millimetre, we might find our interpretation of a role ends up being formal and uninspiring. Yet if we CONCENTRATE OUR ATTENTION on the tiniest physi- cal ACTIONS, we prepare the best imaginable ground in which to stir our passions and arouse our IMAGINATIONS in the most unexpected and exciting of ways.

In brief:

- TRUTH isn't dependent on naturalistic detail; as long as the context of the script has its own LOGIC AND SEQUENCE, then any genre, style or medium can build its own sense of TRUTH.

- TRUTH in acting has three manifestations:

  – 'make-believe truth' (which tends to consist of broad brushstrokes and clichés);

  – 'actual fact' (which stems from your direct experience of life);

  – 'scenic truth' (which involves filtering your real experiences into something aesthetically usable in performance).

- Your sense of TRUTH can be used as an inner monitor or sounding-board in rehearsal or performance to ascertain what feels physically and psychologically appropriate.

- You have to be 'cool and impartial' when it comes to creating something with an emotional 'scenic truth'.

- You can create a sense of TRUTH if you:
- flesh out the details of the text;
- find a point of identification with a character;
- clarify the specific OBJECTIVES of your character.

- You can test the TRUTH of a dramatic situation by constructing a series of simple physical ACTIONS, which feel appropriate and right when you execute them.

- TRUTH is a physical sensation, as much as an inner feeling.

Having determined at this point in *The Toolkit* that we're working towards a sense of TRUTH, there are three key tools which can help in the first steps of embodying a role. They are

- imagination
- the Magic 'If'
- observation

TRAY 7

THREE BASIC TOOLS FOR
BUILDING A SENSE OF TRUTH

Imagination

IMAGINATION is perhaps one of the most vital tools in any artistic endeavour, and, as we've seen with the toolkit so far, you won't get very far without it. In fact, you might think it's superfluous to talk about the role of IMAGINATION either regarding acting in general or Stanislavsky's toolkit in particular. And yet it would seem odd if we omitted it, especially as Stanislavsky devotes a whole chapter to it in *An Actor Prepares*.

As a tool, IMAGINATION is closely connected with 'scenic truth', and Stanislavsky's words on the subject dispel any myth that he was wrapped up in some kind of fourth-wall mysticism:

> There is no such thing as actuality on the stage. Art is a product of the imagination, as the work of the dramatist should be. The aim of the actor should be to use his technique to turn the play into a theatrical reality. In this process imagination plays by far the greatest part.[95]

When you start to build a role, the first thing you do – whether you realise it or not – is appeal to your IMAGINATION. However, Stanislavsky's own relationship to the actor's active IMAGINATION is curious. As I've mentioned already, he spent his early years as a director completely ignoring his actors' IMAGINATIONS: instead, he gave them very physical directions and told them exactly where to stand and sit and how long they should pause or kiss. (All of this is revealed in vivid detail in his 1898 production plan for *The Seagull*.)[96] With time and experience, he came to realise that it's actually the *actors'* imaginative pictures which 'serve as lures to our feelings when we are dealing with words and speech'.[97] As we've seen, this realisation radically altered his approach as a director.

In fact, your relationship with a director reveals exactly how you're using your IMAGINATION tool. If your IMAGINATION is fully functional, you can take on board any direction proposed to you, and all those 'What's my motivation?' questions can be answered effortlessly without rubbing the director up the wrong way. In fact, if you *don't* exercise your IMAGINATION, you can run the risk of becoming little more than a pawn in the director's hands. Stanislavsky himself warned:

> The kind [of imagination] that does not respond to suggestions presents a more difficult problem. Here the actor takes in suggestions in a merely external,

formal way. With such an equipment, development is fraught with difficulty, and there is very little hope of success unless the actor makes a great effort.[98]

A well-developed IMAGINATION is your key to artistic freedom: it enables you to make physical adaptations to whatever GIVEN CIRCUMSTANCES arise, it helps you to find psychological JUSTIFICATIONS for any directions you're given, and it's a muscle that can be exercised. Indeed, it *should* be exercised.

So how do you exercise your IMAGINATION?

First of all, your IMAGINATION is stimulated by your powers of OBSERVATION. In Stanislavsky's words:

> The more an actor has observed and known, the greater his experience, his accumulation of live impressions and memories, the more subtly will he think and feel, and the broader, more varied, and substantial will be the life of his imagination, the deeper his comprehension of facts and events, the clearer his perception of inner and outer circumstances of the life in the play and in his part.[99]

The second way of exercising your IMAGINATION is to combine OBSERVATION with the stimulation of *the five senses* (taste, touch, sound, sight and smell). When our senses are stimulated, we usually find that powerful EMOTION MEMORIES are aroused. These three areas – OBSERVATION, sensory stimulation and EMOTION MEMORY (also known as 'affective memory') – work together in conjunction with our IMAGINATION. As Stanislavsky puts it, IMAGINATION

> stirs up our affective memory, calling up from its secret depths, beyond the reach of consciousness, elements of already experienced emotions, and re-grouping them to correspond with the images which arise in us . . . That is why a creative imagination is a fundamental, absolutely necessary gift for an actor.[100]

There's an important note here: when you're working with creative IMAGINATION, you start by taking something you've already experienced. You then 'regroup' the thoughts, images and memories which come to you, so that they correspond with the ideas in the script. It's a bit like restacking your inner building blocks to make a turret out of a cottage, or a wall out of a chicken shed. This means that as you embody a role, you're not using your own materials in their *raw* state: it's the *imaginative* use of your emotions, memories, experiences, etc., which enables you to transform your personal 'actual facts' into usable 'scenic truths'. Which is why you need to keep your IMAGINATION exercised and fully operational, so you can remember a time in your life when you drowned a spider in the bath or dissected a frog in the backyard, and you restack those memories to get inside the psyche of Lady Macbeth or Sweeney Todd.

The third aspect of IMAGINATION is that it's *physical*. You don't just sit poring over the text and understanding what the SIX FUNDAMENTAL QUESTIONS might mean to you intellectually. All the information you've gleaned from 'mining the text' around the table becomes transformed by your IMAGINATION into physical challenges: how your body moves, what actions your body takes, how your body interacts with the other characters, with the set, with the props, with the costumes, etc. IMAGINATION both fuels your desire to get up and do something active and physical, and then it fills those physical impulses with inner content. Again, Stanislavsky is quite clear about this:

> [The actor] *must feel the challenge physically as well as intellectually*, because the imagination . . . can re-flexively affect our physical nature and make it act . . . Not a step should be taken on the stage without the cooperation of your imagination.[101]

In other words, don't cross the stage, stand up, sit down, let alone carry the drinks tray, unless your IMAGINATION is engaged in the whole process.

As far as Stanislavsky was concerned, the quickest and most powerful way of feeling the pulsating connection between your IMAGINATION and your body is to improvise:

> Student actors who have been trained in improvisations later find it easy to use their imaginative fancy on a play where this is needed.[102]

This maxim was to influence Stanislavsky right up until his death, with the rehearsal processes of the METHOD OF PHYSICAL ACTIONS and ACTIVE ANALYSIS focusing heavily on improvisation.

In brief:

- IMAGINATION is closely allied to 'scenic truth'.

- IMAGINATION can provide the bridge between you as an actor and your director.

- IMAGINATION is the key to artistic freedom.

- IMAGINATION is developed through OBSERVATION, and works intricately with your five senses and EMOTION MEMORY.

- IMAGINATION becomes physical when you take all your MENTAL RECONNAISSANCE and feed it into your body.

- IMAGINATION is developed most directly through improvisation.

From early on in his discussions of acting, Stanislavsky proposed that one of the most direct ways to convert your imaginative processes into physical responses is by means of the tool he named THE MAGIC 'IF'.

The Magic 'If'

What would I do *if* . . . there were a mad axe-murderer behind the door? (Stanislavsky's Gothic example in *An Actor Prepares*.) What would I do *if* I knocked someone over in my car? . . . *if* I were nominated for an Oscar? . . . *if* I were to discover I was pregnant with triplets? THE MAGIC 'IF' is the springboard from your IMAGINATION into the GIVEN CIRCUM-STANCES of the script, and in effect it works by appealing to your sense of ACTION: 'What would I *do* if . . . ?'

In many ways, THE MAGIC 'IF' combines the outer sphere of ACTION with the inner sphere of psychology, as it provides one short hop from the world of the text to your own world as an actor, and its successful use lies in the fact that:

> The circumstances which are predicted on 'if' are
> taken from sources near to your own feelings, and they
> have a powerful influence on [your] inner life . . . Once
> you have established this contact between your life and
> your part, you will find that inner push or stimulus.[103]

Of course, this doesn't mean that you've got to have killed someone in order to play Macbeth. As I've already suggested, you can use your IMAGINATION in a number of ways: you've seen films in which characters are killed, or news items portraying dead bodies, or you yourself have killed a wasp or an ant or a spider or a mouse, or maybe you've even dreamt about killing a person. You've seen through film or novels or documentaries what happens *if* people find themselves in situations where killing is the only option. So with THE MAGIC 'IF', you're not looking for the re-enactment of actual experiences, but you *are* seeking the stimulants to your IMAGINATION which will fill in the gaps between you and the ACTIONS of the script. You're restacking your inner building blocks, creating a prison cell not a conservatory, or a chapel not a schoolroom.

One of the most complicated challenges for me as an actor arose with the Second Bereaved Mother in Hare's *The Permanent Way*. The real mother's eldest son had been killed in the 1999 Paddington train crash, the blaze of which was so intense there was literally nothing left of the young man's body. At first, I had no idea how to connect with the overwhelming pain and anger that the real mother must have suffered. Not only did I have no children, but mercifully I'd never experienced a loss so shocking and unexpected in my own life. I had huge gaps in the connection between myself and the role, and I had to find a means of understanding what I would do *if*... How would I feel *if*...?

To find some imaginative fuel to give integrity and taste to my embodiment of the role, I decided to go and visit the memorial site near what's known as the Paddington 'throat' in Ladbroke Grove where a number of main train-lines converge into a smaller number of tracks on the busy approach into central London. I knew that the real-life mother went there every year on the anniversary of the crash: as this was the last place her son had been seen alive, she felt perhaps his spirit was still there somewhere. I needed to stand where she stood each year and ask myself, 'What would I do *if* someone close to me had been killed?'

I found myself walking in the bright October sunshine and reading the simple commemorative plaque on the nearby wall of the Sainsbury's car park right by the crash-site. I watched the trains hurtling by – looking (in this context) more like animated coffins than means of transport. I noticed the heavy wooden sleepers linking the tracks and understood in this moment that the 'eternal sleepers' of the crash were indeed somewhere in this landscape. And soon I found myself effortlessly answering the questions, '*What if* someone I loved dearly had been destroyed in this place? How would I feel? What would I do? What actions would the sensations propel me towards? How would I channel my anger?'

Very quickly, my original 'What if ...?' question had spawned a whole heap of follow-up questions, connected powerfully with animated ACTIONS and impassioned EMOTIONS. From those questions came new ACTIONS: I'd want to know what had happened that day to cause the crash; I'd want to know who to blame; I'd want to make someone answerable. So I'd attend inquests, I'd rally other 'victims', challenge judgements, overturn politicians' arguments. I'd do politically active things when previously I'd simply been a mother of four, happily bringing up my family. I'd do everything I could to ensure my remaining children's lives were a little better, safer, richer.

THE MAGIC 'IF' is a surprisingly non-coercive tool, in the sense that the question 'What if . . . ?' doesn't ask you to believe blindly in the circumstances of the text. It simply asks you to consider the possibilities of what you might do *if* . . . 'If' implies supposition, it suggests that what you're proposing is not for real – it's asking you what you would do *supposing* these GIVEN CIRCUMSTANCES were real. Because it's non-coercive, it's incredibly liberating. And through its liberating quality (replacing the command 'Thou shalt believe in this fiction' with the provocation 'What would you do *if* this fiction were true?'), it accesses all manner of imaginative ideas and creative possibilities.

It's also incredibly simple – almost childishly simple. Using this tool, you can cross the threshold from being an objective observer of a script's ACTION to becoming a subjective participator in the embodiment of that ACTION. From: 'Mother. Bereaved. From Cambridgeshire.' To: '*What if* I were a bereaved mother whose idyllic life was smashed to smithereens?' And from there, into the heart of the writer's world.

In brief:

- THE MAGIC 'IF' propels you from your own self into the script's dramatic narrative.

- THE MAGIC 'IF' urges you towards ACTION.

- THE MAGIC 'IF' opens your IMAGINATION to the possibilities of the GIVEN CIRCUMSTANCES without coercing you emotionally.

Time and again, we see with *The Toolkit* that the individual tools interconnect and inter-depend. The greater your IMAGI-NATION, the more intricate, unexpected, truthful and idiosyncratic may be the answers to your 'What if . . . ?' questions. The IMAGINATION is widened through your life experience, and as we saw with the IMAGINATION tool, the first way you can widen your experiences of life is through OBSERVATION.

Observation

Supplying THE MAGIC 'IF' with resources on which you can draw depends to a great extent on your individual powers of OBSERVATION. You could say that IMAGINATION comprises two aspects of your inner realm: what you've *experienced* of life and what you've *observed* of life. The difference between the two is similar to the difference between finding yourself actually caught in a war zone, and watching media reports on the television and films of soldiers in battle. Essentially, OBSERVATION supplements the parts of your experience which might not be direct. So it's back to THE MAGIC 'IF' scenario: even though I'm not a murderess, I can play Lady Macbeth extremely convincingly because I've read accounts of murders, I've seen film footage of murderers, maybe I've even spoken to one. Through my OBSERVATIONS, I've woven into the fabric of my experience an understanding of what it might mean to me to be a murderer, of what it might entail in terms of the weapon to use or possible methods, of the kind of psychology that might generate a murderer, and what circumstances in my own life might theoretically provoke in me the impulse to kill. The filtering of those OBSERVATIONS through my personality can feed my IMAGINATION with sufficient psycho-physical information for me to embody the role.

OBSERVATION is not just an inner, mental process: like IMAGINATION, it has a very *physical* aspect to it. Whatever ACTION or EMOTION I'm playing, I have the outside world from which to draw, but more than that: I have the OBSERVATION of my own body, how my muscles respond to certain GIVEN CIRCUMSTANCES, and how my BREATHING changes according to the emotional content of an experience. I've experienced laughter, I've experienced tears: when I have to portray those emotions on stage or screen, I can apply a sense of 'self-OBSERVATION' to monitor whether my portrayal is authentic or compelling. Is there a sense of TRUTH in what I'm doing? Am I faking it or feeling it? Does my body feel right in this manifestation of this emotion? Stanislavsky suggests that you can use this quality of 'inner observation' in a very practical way. Following a rehearsal or performance, you can inwardly observe which aspects rang true or false for you. If your part goes wrong one night,

listen in silence to the voice of your subconscious.[104]

It's like striking a tuning-fork and listening for the resonance. The 'voice of your subconscious' is your 'inner observation' – that inner monitor or sounding-board which we've already mentioned – letting you know whether or not you found the sense of TRUTH tonight. We'll come back to this idea of *self-observation* in Chapter 3 when we consider DUAL CONSCIOUSNESS. The main notion to hold onto here is that OBSERVATION has a surprising number of dimensions and some very practical uses.

In brief:

- OBSERVATION is a means of developing IMAGINATION.

- You can strengthen your inner muscles as an actor, by homing in on physical OBJECTS or people and, through observing them, allowing your IMAGINATION to springboard into fantasy, and from fantasy into ACTION.

- OBSERVATION of your own body and inner self will alert you to whether what you're doing in rehearsal or performance feels appropriate and 'truthful' within the context of the script.

Each of the tools so far in this section of 'Embodying the Role' – TRUTH, IMAGINATION, THE MAGIC 'IF', and OBSERVATION – is used for inherently 'inner' or imaginative processes: the path we've followed shows that having established the need for a sense of TRUTH, the three accompanying tools provide ways of developing it.

The next four tools in the kit are geared towards further evolving your sense of psycho-physical co-ordination as you embody your role. They are:

- action
- tempo-rhythm
- emotion memory
- emotion

TRAY 8

FOUR TOOLS FOR
BUILDING PSYCHO-PHYSICAL
CO-ORDINATION WITH A CHARACTER

Action

Throughout *The Toolkit* so far, ACTION is a term I've used quite liberally: it's now time to look at some specifics and discover why it's arguably the most vital tool available to us.

Everything you do on the stage – even if you're simply sitting in silence – has to be *for a purpose*: this was the fictional director Tortsov's instruction to his student-actors in *An Actor Prepares*. And it's important to remember this. For all the emphasis on the emotional and psychological processes which characterise spin-off interpretations of Stanislavsky's 'system', his overwhelming concern – even from his early production plans for *The Seagull* – was with ACTION. He believed that as soon as you take your focus off meaningful, purposeful ACTION, then what he termed 'stock trade work' (in which you simply go through the motions of the onstage 'blocking') almost inevitably obliterates your art. And for Stanislavsky:

> *Action* is the chief element of our art – genuine, organic, productive, expedient action.[105]

Implicit within this list of adjectives is the idea that every ACTION you perform must have some kind of LOGIC AND SEQUENCE, otherwise you distort your sense of TRUTH. I once saw an essentially realistic production of *The Seagull*, in which the actor playing the estate manager Shamrayev came storming onto the stage in Act 2 to tell Arkadina that she couldn't have any horses to go into town. Within seconds, the actor had thrust his hands into his pockets. Instantly, my belief in the TRUTH of the situation was fractured: after all, this was a working farm man, who vividly describes how all the men are carting the rye today, so presumably he has just come into the scene hot and sweaty and dirty. To thrust his hands into his pockets seemed to me to be totally incongruous. The ACTION was arguably more like that of an actor who didn't know what to do with his hands than the logical and sequential ACTION of a farmer. Unless of course, Shamrayev had suddenly grown aware of how dirty his hands were in the company of the fragrant ladies, in which case he might have taken a moment to notice that detail, before thrusting them into his pockets to hide his filthy fingernails. As it was, there seemed to be no integrated LOGIC AND SEQUENCE in what the actor did and I had the vague sense of being served up Stanislavsky's notion of 'stock trade work', rather than art.

I've talked about ACTION several times already in relation to the three-step sequence of Action – Reaction – Decision. I've also discussed how a performance can cease to affect the audience if a link in that chain is omitted. If there's no LOGIC

OR SEQUENCE in what they're seeing, they simply stop believing in the possibility of those events – like Shamrayev and the trouser pockets. Time and again, we return to the notion that ACTION has both a physical dimension and a psychological one. We'll look specifically at physical ACTIONS shortly: before we do, I'm going to bring in two of the SIX FUNDAMENTAL QUESTIONS: 'Why?' and 'How?' to illustrate how in many respects they're the tools for moving your ACTIONS from the inner (psychological) realm to the outer (physical) realm:

Why you do something comes from your OBJECTIVE: it's your inner, psychological drive.

How you do something is the way in which you behave in order to try and achieve your OBJECTIVE: it's a physical sequence of ACTIONS.

So let's say you're banging your hand on the table. The *way* in which you bang your hand (the physical ACTION: the *how*) will depend on the *reason* behind your physical ACTION (the psychological ACTION: the *why*). Do you want to test the firmness of the table before you climb onto it and change a light-bulb? Do you want to wake your friend who's dozing on the table? Do you want to quieten a rowdy meeting which is getting out of hand? Do you want to emphasise a point in an argument? Even the simplest deed (i.e. a physical ACTION) is motivated by a reaction or a decision (i.e. a psychological ACTION) which in turn is spurred by your OBJECTIVE.

You see how your OBJECTIVE is fundamental to any ACTIONS you might make. It's your desire. It burns. It compels. And for you to really achieve what you want in a situation, you need to inject an equally burning, vital, compelling energy into your physical and psychological ACTIONS: in other words, those ACTIONS can't just be empty shells. For Stanislavsky, this is the root of a truly artistic performance:

> Out of desires, inclinations, impulses to act I am naturally moved to that important thing: inner action . . .

External action on the stage when it is not inspired,
not justified, not called forth by inner activity, is
entertaining only for the eyes and ears; it does not
penetrate the heart, it has no significance in the life
of a human spirit in the role . . .

Real life, like life on the stage, is made up of
continuously arising desires, aspirations, inner
challenges to action and their consummation in
internal and external actions.[106]

There's a huge amount of energy to be invested into each
ACTION. Your 'external actions' can't just be activities, they are
the *physical* manifestation of your desires and aspirations. Likewise, your 'inner actions' are in no way diluted just because
they're inner: they are the *psychological* manifestations of your
desires and aspirations, as you 'warn, threaten, educate, assure,
impress, undermine, delight, intimidate, or enchant' (in the
way that we saw with Stafford-Clark's practical use of psychological 'actioning'). If your OBJECTIVES are strong enough, you
should reach the point where you can't help but be propelled
into ACTION, be it physical or psychological. Your ACTIONS
become the only way for your internal desires to find sufficient
outlet, like a boiling kettle or a stopcock under pressure.

And this is why Stanislavsky places so much emphasis on
ACTION, because it's through ACTION that you can contact your
EMOTIONS more directly. There's often a danger, when you're
confronted with a juicy, emotional part, that you feel the need
to dredge up your emotions and connect yourself straightaway
with the psychological core of the script. The result, as
Stanislavsky warns, is that you end up taking short cuts or
generalising the emotion:

If you tell an actor that his role is full of psychological
action, tragic depths, he will immediately begin to
contort himself, exaggerate his passion, 'tear it to
tatters', dig around in his soul and do violence to his
feelings. But if you give him *some simple physical problem*

to solve and wrap it up in *interesting, affecting conditions*,
he will set about carrying it out without alarming
himself or thinking too deeply whether what he is
doing will result in psychology, tragedy or drama.[107]

So that's your task as an actor: to combine a 'simple physical
problem' with some 'interesting, affecting conditions'. I'd suggest that those 'interesting, affecting conditions' are a combination of your OBJECTIVE, your psychological ACTIONS and
your GIVEN CIRCUMSTANCES.

Here's what I mean.

Suppose my OBJECTIVE is 'I want to seduce you': that
OBJECTIVE in itself is one of my 'interesting, affecting
conditions', as it involves my inner desires and it's bound to
provoke some psychological ACTIONS (such as 'I entice you', 'I
delight you', 'I amuse you', 'I enthuse you'). But I'm not going
to worry too much about those psychological ACTIONS.
Instead, I'm going to give myself 'a simple physical problem':
I'm going to put my hand on your knee. Achieving that 'simple
physical problem' may be easy enough: who knows? It'll
depend on your COUNTER-OBJECTIVE: you might quite enjoy
the hand-on-knee encounter (and so you facilitate my
OBJECTIVE) or you might find it deeply intrusive of your
personal space (and so you counter my OBJECTIVE). But let's
not worry about that too much, either. Instead, let's wrap the
scenario up in a few more 'interesting, affecting conditions' by
throwing in some GIVEN CIRCUMSTANCES to spice up my
OBJECTIVE and my psychological ACTIONS.

Let's suppose we're in a crowded restaurant: this GIVEN
CIRCUMSTANCE in itself will add some danger to my 'simple,
physical problem'. But the stakes can be even higher if we add
a heap more GIVEN CIRCUMSTANCES: maybe you're a millionaire
and I'm a struggling actress; maybe you're married and so am
I; maybe you're a famous football coach and I'm an undercover
journalist. Each little detail will crank up the creative energy
and the performative fun, all the while marrying my
OBJECTIVE ('I want to seduce you') with my psychological

ACTIONS ('I entice you, I delight you, I amuse you, I enthuse you') and my 'simple, physical problem' ('I'm going to put my hand on your knee'). I can guarantee that some kind of EMOTIONS will arise from this scenario, without us really having to worry about them.

So ACTION combines the physical and the psychological in a highly performative and very enjoyable way. In fact, Stanislavsky saw appropriately chosen ACTIONS as a true acting palliative:

> Just as a breath of fresh air will clear the atmosphere in a stuffy room these real actions can put life into stereotyped acting. It can remind an actor of the true pitch which he has lost. It has the power to produce an inner impetus and it can turn a whole scene down a more creative path.[108]

In brief:

- ACTION exists even in stillness and silence.

- ACTIONS should always be purposeful, and have some kind of LOGIC AND SEQUENCE.

- ACTION is both internal / psychological (i.e. a decision or a reaction) and external / physical (i.e. a deed or an activity).

- ACTION is a crucial part of the Action – Reaction – Decision sequence which underpins all human intercourse.

- ACTION can be a direct way of accessing EMOTIONS.

- Physical ACTION is particularly powerful when you endow it with 'interesting, affecting conditions' (which can include OBJECTIVES, psychological ACTIONS and GIVEN CIRCUMSTANCES).

- An appropriately chosen sequence of physical ACTIONS
  will provoke interesting psychological ACTIONS, and
  together they can create the role that you're embodying.

For a sequence of *physical* ACTIONS to be truly effective and
affecting, it needs to resonate with the appropriate TEMPO-
RHYTHM, a tool which can also be applied both to *psychological*
ACTIONS and emotional states.

Tempo-rhythm

TEMPO-RHYTHM is an unavoidable part of natural life.
According to Stanislavsky:

> Wherever there is life there is action; wherever action,
> movement; where movement, tempo; and where there is
> tempo there is rhythm . . .[109]

The whole universe is subject to the laws of rhythm, whether
it be the night following the day, the spring following the
winter, the beating of a heart, the ebbing and flowing of the
tides, or the waxing and waning of the moon. At the centre of
the rhythmic law for all living creatures is the continual
inhalation and exhalation of breath, and as we've already seen,
through BREATHING we access EMOTION. There's no doubt
that TEMPO-RHYTHM is at the very heart of acting.

Stanislavsky himself understood from early in his professional development that TEMPO-RHYTHM should form the
foundation of all creative work. As a young performer in 1884,
he explored the effect of TEMPO-RHYTHM on the body, when
he and his fellow acolyte actors walked and stood and sat while
a pianist hammered out different TEMPO-RHYTHMS. Then in
1908, he wrote to his friend Vera Kotlyarevskaya, drawing
together what he then considered the three most significant
strands of his burgeoning 'system':

> What fascinates me most is the *rhythm of feelings*, the
> development of the *emotion memory* and the *psycho-
> physiology* of the creative process.[110]

By the time of the 1919/20 season at the Moscow Art Theatre, he had established a system of classes addressing

> the feeling of rhythm not only in movement, but in the inner sensations and in sight, and so on. The process of sight is the raying out of spiritual juices that come from us and enter into us. These rayings out have movement, and once there is movement, there is also its tempo and its rhythm.[111]

(I look at these 'rayings out' in GRASP and COMMUNION below.)

Then again, Norris Houghton, in his famous descriptions of Stanislavsky's work with the Moscow Art Theatre, tells how ten specific TEMPO-RHYTHMS were used in rehearsal, from (1) which was that of a man almost dead, to (2) that of a man weak with illness, through to (9) which was that of a person seeing his house burning, and (10) that of a person jumping out of a window.[112]

Given its evident importance in the development of Stanislavsky's practices, what exactly is TEMPO-RHYTHM?

At its most simple, 'tempo' is the *speed* at which you carry out an action, and 'rhythm' is the *intensity* with which you carry it out.

For Stanislavsky, TEMPO-RHYTHM was the key to putting yourself into a state of genuine, creative excitement and, through that genuine excitement, arousing within yourself the relevant emotional state. It wasn't just a question of speeding up or slowing down your breathing patterns or physical movements and then you'd suddenly feel emotional: TEMPO-RHYTHM also had the power to conjure up exciting images and memories. Finding those images and locating a character's TEMPO-RHYTHM happens to a great extent when you start to physically embody the role and carry out the script's ACTIONS on the rehearsal room floor. Though not exclusively . . .

You can actually fathom quite a lot about the necessary TEMPO-RHYTHM directly from what you see in the printed script. Just by looking at a page, you get a sense of how the basic rhythm of the dramatic ACTION unfolds. Take the abrupt lines of a Caryl Churchill script with lots of '/'s indicating where characters' short speeches overlap, compared to a Shakespeare scene involving long monologues in iambic pentameters. All this visual information is incredibly useful, and it becomes fully embellished and embodied once you put the scene on its feet. Not forgetting, of course, that TEMPO-RHYTHM exists as vibrantly in PAUSES as it does in moments of ACTION. The Russian actor Vasily Toporkov, who worked with Stanislavsky in his later years, illuminates this point very lucidly in his description of a rehearsal:

> [*Stanislavsky*:] 'You are not standing in the correct rhythm!'
>
> [*Toporkov*:] 'To stand in rhythm! How – to stand in a rhythm! To walk, to dance, to sing in a rhythm – this I could understand, but to *stand*!' [. . .]
>
> [*Stanislavsky*:] . . . 'To stand and watch for a mouse – that is one rhythm; to watch a tiger that is creeping up on you is quite another.'[113]

However . . .

Your inner (psychological) TEMPO-RHYTHM and your outer (physical) TEMPO-RHYTHM may not necessarily be the same. The waiter in a busy restaurant may be physically darting from table to table but, inside, his TEMPO-RHYTHM may be perfectly calm and measured. Meanwhile, the person sitting quietly at the bus-stop may have just received the most terrible news and her heart is in deep turmoil. I vividly remember the acute contradictions in my own inner–outer TEMPO-RHYTHMS after I'd just received the tragic news of the untimely death of a very close friend. As I stood on the crowded commuter train journeying home, I could barely contain the cauldron of sensations which bubbled inside me, yet my physical body was, to all appearances, as still as the jolting train would allow. Often in everyday life we hide immensely turbulent emotions behind a façade of coping strategies, yet these inner–outer counter-points of TEMPO-RHYTHMS can be rich spoils for a psycho-physical actor.

That said, there are times when a fracture between your inner TEMPO-RHYTHM and your outer TEMPO-RHYTHM is very unhelpful and deeply disconcerting. This can happen, for example, when whatever you're undergoing rhythmically *as the actor* contradicts the appropriate TEMPO-RHYTHM *for your character*. I experienced this uncomfortable reality when I played the Investment Banker in Hare's *The Permanent Way*. The character was essentially cool and unflusterable, yet as I stood on the stage at the opening preview, I became horribly aware that my first-night excitement had raised my own inner TEMPO-RHYTHM to a pitch far more intense than that of the Investment Banker. Suddenly I felt a bizarre schizophrenia, as if the character was in front of me or to the side of me, but I certainly wasn't 'in the centre' of it. Over the course of the first few shows, I was able to calm my own inner TEMPO-RHYTHM down to a pitch more suited to the character. Which was a huge relief – as my own performance experience then became far more pleasurable and my portrayal of the character decidedly more centred.

My experience isn't uncommon: Stanislavsky analyses this first-night phenomenon by describing the actor as being at a personal tempo of Number 200, when the character is at a tempo of Number 20. If you can somehow bring yourself to a tempo of Number 100, you can at least begin to reintegrate yourself with the character.[114]

During his lifetime, Stanislavsky became ever more con-vinced that TEMPO-RHYTHM was an extremely powerful tool due to its influence over an actor's emotions and inner sensations. By the time he had established the METHOD OF PHYSICAL ACTIONS in his mature years, he stated categorically:

> You cannot master the method of physical actions if
> you do not master rhythm.[115]

In brief:

- 'Tempo' is the speed at which you execute an ACTION, and 'rhythm' is the intensity with which you execute it.

- TEMPO-RHYTHM is directly connected with your BREATHING and your arousal of EMOTION.

- You can often see the embryonic TEMPO-RHYTHM of a scene just by looking at the lay-out of a script on a page.

- TEMPO-RHYTHM exists even in stillness: standing watching a mouse is quite different from standing watching a tiger.

- Your inner TEMPO-RHYTHM might be very different from your physical TEMPO-RHYTHM.

- TEMPO-RHYTHM lies at the heart of the METHOD OF PHYSICAL ACTIONS.

Having talked so much about the TEMPO-RHYTHM of feelings and the power of ACTION to arouse EMOTION, it's time to turn our attention to an extremely provocative tool in Stanislavsky's toolkit, yet one without which – as human beings, let alone actors – we wouldn't fully function. It's EMOTION MEMORY.

Emotion memory

EMOTION MEMORY is also known as 'affective memory', 'emotion recall', and 'sense memory'. It's one of the most controversial of Stanislavsky's tools partly because it became the kernel of the 'Method' in America from the 1930s onwards under the directorship of Lee Strasberg in the Group Theatre and later at the Actors Studio, New York. Although plenty of stars of genius and acclaim have emerged from the Method school, EMOTION MEMORY has gained something of a bad reputation for seemingly spawning a whole host of actors with psychoses and neuroses. But there are plenty of healthy and effortless ways of applying EMOTION MEMORY, which illustrate how it's a natural and vital part of any imaginative and creative process.

Stanislavsky originally came across the term 'affective memory' in two works by the French psychologist Théodule Ribot, which were entitled *Les Maladies de la Mémoire* and *Les Maladies de la Volonté*, and which were published in Russian in 1900. Basically, Ribot discovered that those patients who thought about positive experiences during their illness recovered more quickly than those who allowed their illness to take its course. Ribot also discovered that memories of past experiences might not be instantly accessible to the conscious mind, but if you stimulated one of the senses – be it taste, smell, touch, sound or sight – you could provoke your memory in unexpected ways.

Stanislavsky was struck by the power that past-tense memory has on present-tense experience, as well as by the power of the senses over the memory itself. And this is very important to remember: EMOTION MEMORY doesn't mean you have to dredge up the dark times in your life when you experienced grief or disappointment or jealousy or hatred. Or even the good times when you experienced excitement, love or pride. Powerful emotions can be stimulated as much by the smell of your boyfriend's aftershave, the feel of a velvet glove, the taste of a pickled gherkin, a photograph of a concentration camp victim, or the vibrational rumblings of a didgeridoo. Your senses are a direct avenue to your IMAGINATION and your EMOTION MEMORY, and they're generally pretty reliable.

Another thing we should be clear about is that EMOTION MEMORY is natural and unavoidable. We draw upon it all the time in our everyday transactions. The decisions I make in each moment of my life are based on my *memories* of what has gone before and my *imaginings* of what may happen in the future. So, I don't walk down that particular alleyway, because I remember once a big black mastiff leapt out and scared the living daylights out of me, and I imagine it might happen again. Yet I do sit down for ten hours at a time at my laptop and write this book, because I remember the response to my first book, and I imagine the future joy of clarifying ideas through these pages and sharing thoughts with other practitioners.

These memories and imaginings affect my present-tense decisions. I've had the experience of *fear* in my life, which – courtesy of my *memory* – alerts me to the fact that I don't enjoy the pounding heart and sweaty palms provoked by the barking mastiff. Ergo: I find a different way home. I've also had the experience of *success* in my life, which – courtesy of my *imagination* – I can inflate into the idea of future acclaim and reward. Ergo: I carry on writing this book! And thus, my EMOTION MEMORY and IMAGINATION work together continuously to shape my present-tense decisions, by bridging and merging with my past and my future. This is how we operate as human beings. And we simply can't escape the power that EMOTION MEMORY – or 'affective memory' or 'sense memory' or whatever else we choose to call it – has over us at every moment of our lives.

And it should be celebrated, not feared. For Stanislavsky, a colourful EMOTION MEMORY is your 'store-room' as an actor. It's piled high with riches from all sorts of places. Not only from your own experiences, but also from your communication with other people, seeing how they live in Madrid or Minnesota, Kabul or Kyoto, Outer Hebrides, Inner Mongolia, the Australian outback or the African inland. It's supplemented by visiting the Hermitage Museum and the British Library and the Uffizi Gallery, by watching Warner Brothers movies and Sky TV. It's a rich resource that, on the one hand, can enable you to find more out about your own inclinations and emotional predilections and, on the other hand, can help you access the initial trigger or 'lure' into a character which we've already discussed.

But why might EMOTION MEMORY be useful when you're embodying a role?

First of all, EMOTION MEMORY can put you right at the centre of a dramatic situation. Just like THE MAGIC 'IF', it can turn you from being an objective 'listener' into the subjective 'doer'. As Stanislavsky describes it:

> The emotions of a reader or a hearer differ in quality from those of an onlooker or principal in [a tragic] event.
>
> An actor has to deal with all these types of emotional material. He works it over and adjusts it into the needs of the person whom he portrays . . .
>
> [Thus sympathy] might be transformed into direct reaction . . . From the very moment when the actor feels that change take place in him he becomes an active principal in the play of life – real human feelings are born in him – *often this transformation from human sympathy into real feelings of the person in the part occurs spontaneously.*[116]

When it doesn't occur spontaneously, you have to work a little harder. This usually means tapping into your EMOTION MEMORY 'store-room' to find a situation from your own life which is analogous to that of the character.

And this is where the terrain becomes a little controversial. So, let's go back to Macbeth. The idea is not that in playing Macbeth you recall a time in your life when you killed a king, as the chances are not many of us have had that particular experience. Rather, you find the broader brushstrokes of connection with the character, which then take you into the depths of the character's 'realm'. Stanislavsky provides a clear example of what he means, as quoted by Gorchakov in *Stanislavsky Directs*: he's giving notes to a young actress, Titova, who is exploring the role of a prostitute during a rehearsal at the Moscow Art Theatre:

'Everything is very sincere, touching, and good, in touch with what you are doing, Titova. You don't have to reveal any of your actress' secrets . . . [but tell] me just one thing: what were you thinking about when Jacques left you alone on the square?'

'I was thinking, Konstantin Sergeyevich, that for the last year whatever I do in the theatre doesn't come off and if I don't do better this time you will throw me out of the Moscow Art Theatre.'

Stanislavsky turned to everyone: 'Please listen to this attentively. This is a very important statement. It was intuition that put Titova on the right road to work. She didn't imagine herself as a prostitute, but she imagined very vividly what would happen to her as an actress if I threw her out of the theatre. As a result, she gave us an impression of a woman in a most desperate situation. The right intuition gave birth to all her actions. What were you thinking about in the following moments?'

'I didn't care what happened to me afterward.'

'That's exactly what I felt when I watched your acting. And I want you all to remember how the right movement and right external actions follow from the correct organic state. Now, Titova, please don't think that when you're rehearsing next time you must remember and repeat mechanically what you did today. If you do that, you will have only the external form. Each time you have to repeat this scene, think only of the personal equivalent that can generate this emotion in you . . .

'We will not throw you out, Titova, but you must always believe in this now, and you must imagine each time in a different way what would happen to you if this really took place.'[117]

There's a whole heap of things to be unpacked from this quotation.

First of all, we see how Titova uses a range of tools. She begins with her 'lure' – called here her 'intuition' ('It was intuition which put Titova on the right road to work'): her intuitive 'lure' helps her to empathise with the character's sorry state. She then shifts to EMOTION MEMORY as she reflects on the past ('I was thinking . . . that for the last year whatever I do in the theatre doesn't come off'). She then combines her EMOTION MEMORY with IMAGINATION as she contemplates what she considers to be an almost inevitable future ('if I don't do better this time, you will throw me out of the Moscow Art Theatre'). She then adds a further imaginative impulse with THE MAGIC 'IF' ('she imagined very vividly what would happen to her as an actress *if* I threw her out of the theatre'). These imaginative tools then propelled her into ACTION. Those ACTIONS then generated genuine feelings, thus completing the cycle from the past-tense EMOTION MEMORY to the future-tense IMAGINATION to the present-tense experience of an EMOTION.

It's important to note that Stanislavsky and Titova are *in rehearsal*, and indeed this current chapter of *The Toolkit* is about 'Rehearsal Processes'. In a good rehearsal process, *any* tools should be used to find your inroad into the character, according to the genre and style of the script. Today it might be EMOTION MEMORY, tomorrow it might be IMAGINATION, on Wednesday it might be physical ACTIONS. The rehearsal room is your laboratory: you should dare to try anything, whether it works or not. Stanislavsky reckoned that only 10% of what you do in the rehearsal room remains in your final performance. So let's use that laboratory – and experiment! I stress this because it's important that we don't extract particular sections from any of Stanislavsky's writings and say, 'Aha, see! – This is how it should be done!' Stanislavsky's account of Titova's process is just one example: a different actress might have found it quite easy to imagine exactly what she would do 'if' she *were* a prostitute, and her IMAGINATION might have been avid enough to conjure up warm and creative sensations without using the tool of EMOTION MEMORY.

A final point to draw from this quotation is the fact that the same memory won't necessarily work every time:

> Do not count on always recovering the same impression. Tomorrow something quite different may appear in its place. Be thankful for that and do not expect the other. If you learn how to be receptive to these recurring memories, then the new ones as they form will be more capable of stirring your feelings repeatedly. Your *soul* in turn will be more responsive and will react with new warmth to parts of your role whose appeal had worn thin from constant repetition.
>
> . . . On the other hand, don't spend your time chasing after an inspiration that once chanced your way. It is as unrecoverable as yesterday . . . Bend your efforts to creating a new and fresh inspiration for today.[118]

If you're working psycho-physically, this isn't a problem: you can hop from one stimulus to another to another with equal affectivity. It may well be that a certain EMOTION MEMORY works perfectly well for six rehearsals in a row; then suddenly something completely unexpected will supersede it, and you'll find yourself open to a whole new range of images and impressions and memories. Keep yourself alert, keep yourself fresh, keep yourself responsive – and then you stand a chance of an unexpected emotional INSPIRATION ambushing you.

As we work through *The Toolkit*, you should feel quite free with the tools. They can be used in the way in which you need them, and at times you don't need to use them at all. Sometimes in rehearsal, we find we just get on a creative roll, and if that's the case, don't mess! As one of Stanislavsky's actresses, Solovyova, advised:

We use 'emotional recall' or 'affective memory' when
our inspiration [fails], or in Stanislavsky's expression,
when 'Apollo does not answer readily'. But if your intuition gives you what you need, you don't have to use
affective memory. Stanislavsky used to say, 'If the part
comes to you spontaneously, you don't have to go
through affective memory. Just thank Apollo and act!' . . .
I never knew what key would open the door to the heart
of a part for me. Would it be through affective memory
or would I feel the part from the first reading of the
play? Seeing myself in the same situation would I have
the same feelings, the same understanding and response
to the character I was to portray – finding the same
feeling in my heart? Or would I visualise it so clearly
that it would awaken in me the necessary feelings?[119]

Solovyova is maverick, as indeed we should all be. As I said in
the Introduction, if it ain't broke, don't fix it.

However . . .

We shouldn't take short-cuts, either. One of the key criti-
cisms of EMOTION MEMORY is that, if you're always trawling
your own memory store-room for material, you'll reduce all
your characters to variations of your own personality. Stanislavsky had a very clear response to this argument:

The musical scale has only seven notes, the sun's
spectrum only seven primary colours, yet the combinations of those notes in music and those colours in
paintings are not to be numbered. The same must be
said of our fundamental emotions, which are preserved
in our affective (emotion) memory, just as things seen
by us in the external world are preserved in our
intellectual memory: the number of these fundamental
emotions in our own inner experience is limited, but
the shadings and combinations are as numerous as the
combinations created out of our external experience
by the activity of our imagination.[120]

Your individual EMOTION MEMORY supplies you with the 'primary colours', but your IMAGINATION then mixes those primary colours into an endless palette. This means you have the potential to play a mighty myriad of roles. Which gives us another equation: *Emotion Memory* + *Imagination* = *the breadth of the dramatic canon at your fingertips.*

So how do you activate your EMOTION MEMORY? Stanislavsky offers five clear steps, which I've adapted here.[121]

1. You have to put yourself in a sufficiently relaxed and playful psychological 'place' (your INNER CREATIVE STATE) to access your emotions. He suggests that this means knowing your character's biography in as much detail as you know your own. So keep adding new details to that biography – even after the play is up and running, or the movie's started filming, so that it becomes as deep and textured and varied as your IMAGINATION will allow.

2. Then you have to define the exact EMOTION for each bit, not being afraid to stumble on an ugly one. So it might be love, jealousy, anger, resentment, delight – whatever. Enjoy playing the ugly EMOTIONS as much as relishing the refined ones.

3. You then go beneath the TEXT to see what the particular EMOTION is really about. The example that Stanislavsky gives is that 'egotism is first of all pity for oneself'.

4. Having defined the nature of the EMOTION, you then search for the ACTIONS which will arouse that EMOTION. 'This is the bait which the feeling will rise to.' And this is what the process of rehearsing is all about: finding the physical ACTIONS to 'bait' your EMOTIONS. (Yet again, we're back to ACTION.)

5. Finally, once you've found the way to arouse the EMOTION, you then have to know how to control it. As a creative artist, you have to be the master of your materials, and not their slave.

While I don't for one minute suggest that following these five steps will lead to you having your EMOTION MEMORY at your utter beck and call, there's certainly a lot to be said for points 1, 4 and 5. (1) The correct 'psychological place' or INNER CREATIVE STATE is incredibly useful. (4) Accessing EMOTIONS through ACTIONS is sound advice. And (5) being able to control your EMOTIONS is absolutely crucial. After all, we're professional actors, not patients in a therapy clinic, so once you've found the 'right bait' to arouse your EMOTIONS, you've got to be able to work with them creatively and appropriately. Stanislavsky was very clear about this:

> [The actor] must have the willpower to control these feelings, to stop their action when it is necessary, or to change them.[122]

If you're a psychologically healthy artist, I don't really see that there's a problem. Especially if you adopt Michael Chekhov's image of holding your EMOTIONS metaphorically in the palm of your hand. There, they're connected to you via the umbilical cord of your arm, but it's up to you whether you offer them up or hold them back, whether you metaphorically open your palm or close your fingers over them. You're in control of them, they're not in control of you.

This degree of control is even more vital in the strict conditions of performance. Although this chapter is called 'Rehearsal Processes', let's look briefly at how EMOTION MEMORY might be used and controlled *in performance*. By way of illustration, I'll draw upon two working examples, one from my own experience and one from that of actor, Miles Anderson.

Anderson has played numerous emotionally charged roles on stage, film and television. Among them, two of the most notable are the volatile, coke-snorting, political publicist Roger O'Neill in the BBC drama *House of Cards* and Elizabeth Sawyer's familiar, Dog, in the Royal Shakespeare Company's *The Witch of Edmonton*. I was therefore intrigued to discover that, over the years, he's found the use of any personal EMOTION

MEMORY when he's performing a role can actually *distance* him from the character's inner life, rather than drawing him into it. For Anderson, the best use of EMOTION MEMORY *in performance* is to tap into all the relevant work he has already done *in rehearsal*, rather than to dredge up any personal cargo.

To this end, he uses rehearsal time to get right inside the body and psyche of a role, to such an extent that he knows exactly what makes the character tick, laugh, cry, emote. In other words, he builds up an emotional store-room *for the character*, which he can then access more or less at will:

> I have to have a 'thin skin' in rehearsal, as if there's a bubble of emotion inside my chest, which responds to whatever the character's going through. It's also like having antennae everywhere, going from your knees, toes, fingers.[123]

Once he's actually playing the role – on screen or stage – Anderson's goal is to make an imaginative connection with the character's GIVEN CIRCUMSTANCES and engage in the drama's ACTION with a full-blooded commitment, putting any personal cargo temporarily on the backburner. He keeps the 'thin skin', while the emotional bubble remains inflated and the antennae are tingling, but it's all in response to whatever's going on in performance.

Given the ease with which Anderson can tap into his emotional reservoir both in front of a camera and a live audience, his inner palette is clearly very rich. Yet it's curious to discover just how little of that emotional activity stems from the recall of autobiographical experiences, and just how much of it arises from his imaginative exploration of the role.

My own use of EMOTION MEMORY was significantly challenged when I played the Second Bereaved Mother in *The Permanent Way*. To some extent, I embarked on a similar journey in rehearsal to the one described by Anderson: I took time to investigate the mother's own psychology so that, when I was in performance, I could imaginatively enter her inner 'realm'.

However, my major challenge was how to access those powerful feelings every night for a total of 10½ months.

I discovered that my attitude to EMOTION MEMORY altered dramatically during that time. Over the course of those 10½ months, I used all manner of stimuli to provoke the relevant EMOTIONS, depending on how I felt each night. I usually spent some time before going on stage, preparing an appropriate INNER CREATIVE STATE; however, whatever I CONCENTRATED MY ATTENTION on during that prep-time varied from night to night. Sometimes I connected imaginatively with what the real-life mother had been through. Sometimes I recalled my visit to the memorial site at Ladbroke Grove. Sometimes I imagined how I'd feel if I suddenly lost someone whom I loved dearly without having had the chance to say goodbye to them or even to see the body once they'd died. Sometimes I lingered on something I'd seen on the news. Sometimes I used Ananyev's 'In-in-in-out' BREATHING pattern for a minute or so (see BREATHING above). Sometimes I simply contemplated the darkness of the backstage area. One night I noticed the emergency sign with the outline of a person running away with a flame at their heels, and in my IMAGINATION I saw the victims of the train crash trying in vain to escape from the blazing inferno. Sometimes I thought about a myriad of sad things that had happened to me in my own chequered life. Basically, I opened myself to whatever stimuli wanted to flood my mind each night. I didn't censor myself – and it didn't really bother me whether the thoughts were personal EMOTION MEMORIES, imaginative provocations, physical sensations, or action-based EMOTIONS stemming from the events portrayed on stage. I simply developed a kind of inner monitor over those 10½ months – an inner sounding-board for my sense of TRUTH – which knew when an appropriate INNER CREATIVE STATE had percolated my body and I could then enter the stage in that INNER CREATIVE STATE, ready to tell my character's story.

There were even times when I relied on nothing but pure technique, when my own emotional reservoirs felt arid and dry.

On those occasions, I simply re-enacted – as accurately and with as much commitment as I could – the tiny physical ACTIONS of the mother whom I'd witnessed break down in front of me: how her voice faltered, how long she paused before talking again, how her vocal pitch cracked, how she boldly endeavoured to regain her composure as quickly as possible by brushing away her tears, straightening her back and munching on a chocolate digestive. If I succeeded in getting the tiny physical details accurate, then more often than not, the emotion-wells sprang forth again.

I began to understand over those 10½ months, that PSYCHO-PHYSICALITY really can work from the *inside out* or the *outside in*: I could appeal to my EMOTION MEMORIES and my IMAGI-NATION in order to create the desired INNER CREATIVE STATE, or I could externally mimic the physical ACTIONS of a person in deep distress, which in turn would invoke the EMOTIONS I was seeking. Both usually worked as far as the audience were concerned and, therefore, both seemed to be perfectly legiti-mate strategies. After all, it's the audience who have to feel the real emotions, not necessarily the actors: you can be weeping and wailing as hard as you like, but if your audience is left feeling 'cool and impartial', then you've hardly fulfilled your OBJECTIVE.

What emerges with *The Toolkit* is that not only will different actors use different tools, but different actors will use the same tool in different ways. And that's exactly how it should be. A toolkit is there to be used as best suits you.

In brief:

- EMOTION MEMORY is also known as 'affective memory', 'emotion recall' and 'sense memory'.

- EMOTION MEMORY works inextricably with IMAGINATION, influencing all your daily decisions by bridging your past-tense memories and your future-tense fantasies.

- EMOTION MEMORY is your store-room as an actor, coming from your own experiences and supplemented by your 'second-hand' experiences as gained from museums, books, galleries, films, television, etc.

- EMOTION MEMORY can shift you from the position of an objective 'listener' to that of a subjective 'doer': all you have to do is find something analogous from your own life which links you to the GIVEN CIRCUMSTANCES of the character.

- EMOTION MEMORY works with IMAGINATION to mix the 'primary colours' of your life experience into a whole palette of possibilities, from which you can construct a character and break the limits of your own autobiography.

- You'll find that the same EMOTION MEMORY won't work for you every time, so you need to be open and playful to all manner of stimuli.

- Your memory of what you discovered about the character in rehearsal can be just as useful a springboard in performance as any autobiographical stimuli; in other words, the EMOTION MEMORY of your rehearsal discoveries can be just as stimulating as any EMOTION MEMORY from your own life.

- EMOTION MEMORY is inevitably used in correlation with other tools including IMAGINATION and THE MAGIC 'IF', to assist you when you need it, and not to be used when you don't need it.

Having examined the power of EMOTION MEMORY and its close dialogue with IMAGINATION, it's worth addressing Stanislavsky's attitude to EMOTION *per se*.

Emotion

EMOTION is not so much a tool as an intrinsic part of the 'system'. Just as you can't perform without a body, you can't act in a truly vibrant manner without your EMOTIONS being drafted into your psycho-physical work at some level or another.

So what is an emotion? Many fine and accessible books exist on the subject, some of which argue that EMOTIONS are *physiological responses to situations*, including sweaty palms, increased heart rate and muscular tension. Others argue that EMOTIONS are *cognitive interpretations of situations*: Am I in danger or am I safe? But here and now, we need to be clear about the parameters of what it is that we're considering. Often the word 'emotional' can be alienating, as images of weeping at weddings and sobbing at sad movies spring to mind; however, this is not the way in which, as actors, we can most usefully approach the notion of 'being emotional'. We're talking about something much more nuanced, something which appears in upbeat manifestations as well as melancholy ones, and the phrase 'being emotional' can apply equally to a composer or a jazz singer, a playwright or even a lighting designer, as it can to an actor. 'Being emotional' is really about being creatively responsive and openly playful.

Whether an EMOTION is considered physiological or cognitive, the most important question for us as actors is arguably: what causes it?

The simplest answer is: an EMOTION arises when something or someone stops us from getting what we want. *Or* when something or someone makes it easier for us to get what we want.

If I do get what I want, I experience positive emotions. If I don't get what I want, I experience negative emotions. Here's a simple scenario: I'm walking to the sorting office to pick up an important package, and there's half an hour to go before the sorting office shuts. My mobile rings: it's my boyfriend, saying he's locked himself out, can I go back home and let him in? Damn . . .

Alternatively: a car horn toots and it's my boyfriend: he's spotted me walking along the street and he's offering to give me a lift to the sorting office. Hoorah!

In the first instance, my boyfriend's behaviour (his COUNTER-OBJECTIVE) blocks the achievement of my OBJECTIVE: it serves as an obstacle. In the second instance, his behaviour (still, in principle, a COUNTER-OBJECTIVE) accelerates the achievement of my OBJECTIVE: it serves as a facilitator. Each situation produces a different emotional response in me, ranging from the negative to the positive.

The magnitude of my emotional response will depend on how important it is for me to achieve my OBJECTIVE. The higher the stakes, the greater will be the impact on me when my circumstances are changed.

So: if my OBJECTIVE is 'I want to pick up my passport from the post office, because I'm off to Japan in the morning', the consequences of achieving it or otherwise will have a greater significance for me than if my OBJECTIVE is 'I want to pick up a book that I ordered off the Amazon website'.

The emotional weight of my experience will also be altered if my boyfriend's COUNTER-OBJECTIVE has higher stakes.

So: if my mobile rings and my boyfriend has not only locked himself out but he's also left a chip pan on the stove which might catch fire, the stakes are suddenly raised: if I go back home to let him in, I risk losing the opportunity to collect my passport and jeopardise the whole trip to Japan. If I'm just collecting the book that I ordered from Amazon, my emotional response to the change in my path won't be so great: 'Hey, big deal, I can pick up the book another time.'

Maybe it's not a chip pan on the stove. Maybe our baby is locked in the house on her own – up go the emotional stakes still further.

There's one more thing to consider, and that's my boyfriend's PERSPECTIVE towards my OBJECTIVE. If his PERSPECTIVE towards my trip to Japan is *laissez-faire*, he won't think twice about asking me to go back home and let him in. If he thinks the trip is as important as I do, he won't think twice about trying to find another way of getting back into the house. It's a question of whether my OBJECTIVE is more important than his COUNTER-OBJECTIVE – both in my eyes and in his. Of course, if we add in the home-alone baby, I guess the passport's a goner!

Let's recap:

- EMOTIONS arise when something or someone either stops you from achieving or enables you to achieve your OBJECTIVE.

- The more you need to achieve your OBJECTIVE, the greater will be your emotional response either when you're blocked in your pursuit or when that pursuit is made easier.

- The PERSPECTIVE of the other person towards your OBJECTIVE versus their need to pursue their own COUNTER-OBJECTIVE will also affect the nature of your emotional response.

So where does Stanislavsky fit in to all this EMOTION talk?

EMOTION was a doubled-edged sword for Stanislavsky. He wanted actors to realise that they couldn't rely on a beautiful voice and a versatile body to do their job for them: they also needed an accessible emotional reservoir. Yet he was fully aware of the risks and pitfalls involved in using EMOTIONS:

> The more [an emotion] is violated, the more it resists and throws out its invisible buffers before it, and these, like hands, do not allow emotion to approach that part of the rôle which is too difficult for it . . . And the more the buffers are developed, the harder it is for emotion to appear when needed and the more necessity there is for old stencils and stagy craftsman-ship. The more stamps and staginess, the farther the emotion runs from them.[124]

I've often heard actors bemoan the fact they can't cry in performance. Somehow they've allowed their emotional buffers to develop and they find themselves chasing their own EMOTIONS like frightened sheep. But why do we put so much attention on crying? Maybe it's because tears seem to be physiological 'proof' that the actor has achieved the desired EMOTION (though most actors will reach for the tear stick on the twentieth shoot of the day . . .) And there are certainly other EMOTIONS with equally challenging physiological manifestations, such as blushing with embarrassment or blanching with fury. But because (partly due to skin pigmentation of course) not everybody does blush or blanch – though arguably everyone has the capacity to cry – a good deal of emphasis is laid upon the actor's ability to weep.

In fact, all EMOTIONS are complex – laughing, crying, blushing, blanching: they aren't just simple primary colours. Stanislavsky himself was acutely aware of their complexity:

> Every passion is a complex of things experienced
> emotionally, it is the sum total of a variety of different
> feelings, experiences, states. All these component
> parts are not only numerous and varied but they are
> also often contradictory.[125]

And we shouldn't be afraid of those contradictions: contradictions are good. If your character appears to behave in one way during Scene 3 and another way during Scene 5, then celebrate it and develop it and allow those contradictions to flourish. After all, we know that the LOGIC AND SEQUENCE of the EMOTIONS aren't like the mathematical logic of reason.

And this is where rehearsal time is crucial when you're embodying your role. It's important to use rehearsal time to explore your emotional palette and see how you can mix the myriad 'colours' to create your characters. It's the only way to find out what you're made of. After all, Stanislavsky believed that:

> There lies in the nature of every gifted actor the seed
> of every human feeling and sensation. One only needs
> to find the right bait to arouse him.[126]

The rehearsal period is the very time for finding that bait –
through your ACTIONS and interactions with other characters.
So be daring in your explorations, not dormant. Be brave in
your rehearsals, not boring. In fact, you might even say the
fundamental reason for working with EMOTION MEMORY and
EMOTION is to get to know your inner palette, so you're free to
be the master of your own emotional repertoire. As Stanislavsky put it:

> When you know the inclinations of your own nature,
> it is not difficult to adapt them to imaginary
> circumstances.[127]

Once you start to look at EMOTIONS and EMOTION MEMORY in
this light, they're both good fun. Using them is your chance to
get those creative juices flowing, rather than feeling you have to
dredge up lots of dark, mysterious sensations. Because when
you've found your 'lure' into the character, your main EMO-
TION – both in rehearsal and performance – becomes the actual
joy of *creative play*. As we saw with PSYCHO-PHYSICALITY,
simply being on the stage or in front of the camera – embodying this role and dialoguing with these actors, and moving this
audience to laughter or tears – is a hugely emotional experience
in its own right. So EMOTION doesn't have to be dark and
psychotic. We can take immense pleasure in laughing and
crying, expressing anger, jealousy, love and hate, not to
mention incandescent joy. All this energy can imbue our
embodiment of the character with great artistic dimension.

*

Here are the tools we've covered so far in 'Embodying the Role':

- truth (which we strive for in any performance)

Followed by:

- imagination
- the Magic 'If'
- observation

These three help us in our pursuit of a sense of TRUTH.

Then:

- action
- tempo-rhythm
- emotion memory
- emotion

These four develop our PSYCHO-PHYSICALITY by co-ordinating and harmonising our inner sensations and outer expressions.

All of these tools offer us some psycho-physical means of accessing our own resources and making a personal connection with a TEXT.

It's time now to turn more directly to some concrete issues of character and characterisation, as we continue the complex and fascinating task of 'embodying the role'. There are four more tools which help us add textures to our characters. They are:

- inner psychological drives
- heroic tension
- *emploi*
- objects

TRAY 9

FOUR TOOLS FOR TEXTURING A CHARACTER

Inner psychological drives (see Preface)

Stanislavsky devotes a whole chapter of *An Actor Prepares* to the INNER PSYCHOLOGICAL DRIVES: although the chapter is one of the shortest in the book, the INNER PSYCHOLOGICAL DRIVES are actually some of the most useful tools in the whole toolkit. He describes them as:

> *three impelling movers in our psychic life, three masters who play on the instrument of our souls.*[128]

And those 'three masters' are our 'thought-centre', our 'emotion-centre' and our 'action-centre', and they intricately interconnect throughout the course of our daily lives, as well as in the construction of a character.

First of all, our 'thought-centre' creates mental pictures about the character.

Through their potential to 'lure' us towards the character, those images stir our 'emotion-centre'.

As our 'emotion-centre' is stirred, we find ourselves driven towards doing certain things to make manifest that character, as our 'action-centre' kicks into work.

We've touched upon some of these ideas already through the tools of IMAGINATION (linked to our 'thought-centre'), OBJECTIVES (linked to our 'emotion-centre') and ACTIONS (clearly linked to our 'action-centre'). Each of these three 'drives' is very complex and very exciting.

Let's take the 'thought-centre' first. Imagine that physically it's associated with your head: we usually associate our thoughts with our head, so this makes sense. The 'thought-centre' operates on a whole array of paradoxes, as your thoughts can comprise both wild fantasies and mathematical logic, all-consuming daydreams and philosophical reason. In other words, a thought-centred person could be as imaginative as Walter Mitty or as scientifically-gifted as Einstein, an inspired artist or a leading statistician.

Imagine that the 'emotion-centre' is physically associated with your solar plexus, which is the nucleus of nerve endings located anatomically between your stomach and your spine. You can actually *feel* that this area is your 'emotion-centre': we talk about butterflies in the stomach, or being sick with rage, or losing your appetite when you're passionately in love. In fact, it's been scientifically proven that there are more nerve endings in your stomach than in your brain: in other words, more processing of information takes place in the stomach area than in the head. Yet the intelligence of this area of the body is completely underestimated by most people who are inclined to think our rational brains do most of the decision-making in our lives. As with the 'thought-centre', the 'emotion-centre' is also an extremely complex centre because it houses the whole range of emotional responses which comprise your inner landscape from jealousy to delight to rage to excitement to anguish.

Imagine that the 'action-centre' is associated physically with your pelvic area: in many respects, this centre is the equivalent of the base chakra in eastern meditational practices. That said, the potential of the 'action-centre' courses throughout your whole body: after all, it's through the actions of your body that your thoughts and feelings can be manifested in the world, as I touched upon in the discussion of PSYCHO-PHYSICALITY. If we didn't have a body, we would have no means of making tangible the most ingenious of thoughts or the most textured of emotional responses. Like the 'thought-centre' and the 'emotion-centre', the 'action-centre' is also a very complex centre in that it houses both unbridled sexual energy and restrained formal etiquette. This is a curious combination. It's fairly evident this centre would have some sort of sexual energy given its predominant location in the groin. The idea of formal etiquette is a little harder to make sense of, but if you think about it, any ritual – from shaking hands to brushing teeth to starting the ignition of your car – has a kind of active component to it which doesn't necessarily involve very much thought or emotion: you just do it. These kinds of rituals are pure ACTION, with their impulse stemming directly from the 'action-centre'. Here's a quick example to illustrate the 'action-centre' impulse behind most etiquette:

Imagine we're at a drinks party and I meet you for the first time, so I shake hands with you, perhaps saying, 'Hi, my name's Bella. Pleased to meet you, John.' As we shake hands, we don't need to invest a huge amount of emotion or thought in our gesture: it's just an action, a ritual, a formality. I'm giving you my name, you're giving me yours: it's a simple exchange of information to facilitate any further interaction.

Imagine we're at the party again, but this time suppose you're my all-time favourite actor. My physical action is the same as in the first instance, in that I simply shake your hand, but now my energy impulse stems from my 'emotion-centre': 'Oh, my God! You're Johnny Depp, aren't you? How fantastic to meet you!' This is no longer pure etiquette (i.e. pure ACTION): there's now an emotional investment.

Now let's suppose we had a big row last night about whether Stanislavsky is better than Mamet and we're meeting again this morning; we tentatively shake hands, sheepishly trying to fathom each other's light-of-day responses. 'Hi, Johnny . . . how are you doing? Okay . . . ? Yeah, me too, I'm fine, I'm okay . . .' Again all we do is shake hands as we did in both the first and the second instances, but this time my energy is coming from my 'thought-centre' as I ask myself the inner questions, 'Can I shake hands? Is he still angry? Will he reject me? Will he accept me?'

Thus you can see that simple ritual (i.e. the first of these three scenarios) is essentially an 'action-centre' impulse. And I'm sure we all know that wild sexual chemistry is an 'action-centre' impulse too.

It's incredibly useful when you're embodying a role to figure out whether a character is predominantly led by their brains ('thought-centre'), feelings ('emotion-centre') or involuntary impulses ('action-centre'). All three INNER PSYCHOLOGICAL DRIVES interconnect on a very rapid-response level, but each of us can probably answer the question, 'Are we fundamentally thoughtful? Emotional? Or action-driven?' I often find I flit between the three: after days of working on a book ('thought-centre'), I want to do nothing but paint walls or plant broccoli ('action-centre'). After working on a role for a long time ('emotion-centre'), I'm very happy reading a good book ('thought-centre') or going to the gym ('action-centre'). If one centre dominates our lives for too long, we soon feel the internal fragmentation, whether we consciously process it or not.

Let's take Chekhov's three girls in Act 1 of *Three Sisters*: Olga keeps herself continually busy, marking books and preparing Irina's name-day party, so she doesn't have to think or feel: her 'action-centre' dominates her behaviour. Masha does very little other than malinger in the dark mood which she brings into the scene until suddenly her 'emotion-centre' is stimulated by the arrival of Vershinin. Irina is head-based, always fantasising about a future that might come into being, with images of working hard, living in Moscow, being in love with the right man: her 'thought-centre' dominates her behaviour.

Obviously, the division isn't entirely that cut-and-dried, as each INNER PSYCHOLOGICAL DRIVES stimulates elements of the other two, but you can test your intuitive responses to a role by asking the questions: 'What would this character *do* in this circumstance? What would this character *feel* about this? What would this character *think* about this? How much of a delay would there be between the *emotional* reaction and the *physical* response? Would they *think* long and hard before they did anything? Would they *do* something first and *consider* the consequences later? Would their *emotions* obscure their *thoughts* and colour their *actions*?'

To some extent we can take it back to the Action – Reaction – Decision sequence. Is there a long or short time-lapse between the character's Reaction-and-Decision and ensuing Action? In other words, does my Action fly like a dart either into your *head* (provoking lots of thoughts and questions) or into your *gut* (provoking a rapid emotional response)? How quickly do you respond physically to my Action: i.e. how rapidly does your *body* kick in? Alternatively do you process your gut Reaction through your 'thought-centre' so you can make a very considered and deliberate Decision about your ensuing Action? There's a myriad of combinations of responses and sequences, all of which can help you colour and texture a character.

And these kinds of questions need not apply only to dialogue. The INNER PSYCHOLOGICAL DRIVES can be particularly useful when you're working on a soliloquy, as you're never just talking to yourself or just talking to the audience: there's always some kind of inner dialogue going on between your *thoughts*, your *feelings* and your *actions*. Let's take Hamlet's 'To be or not to be' speech from Act III, Scene i. He begins in his 'thought-centre' as he contemplates, 'To be or not to be – that is the question': in other words, he's asking himself: 'Shall I live or shall I kill myself? That's my dilemma.' Killing oneself is a *physical* action. So Hamlet's *thoughts* are battling with his *body*: should he use his own body to snuff out his own life force? And before long, his *emotions* start pouring forth as he thinks about all the dreams and fantasies (which are thought-based activities) that might haunt him. ('For in that sleep of death what dreams may come/When we have shuffled off this mortal coil/Must give us pause.') The soliloquy is an immense and complex conversation between all his INNER PSYCHOLOGICAL DRIVES, ending with the realisation that his dreams and fears may actually curb his actions:

> And thus the native hue of resolution
> Is sicklied o'er with the pale cast of *thought*,
> And enterprises of great pitch and moment

With this regard their currents turn awry
And lose the name of *action*. [My emphasis]

Furthermore, it's curious to note that this intellectual, bookish man is seen to feign madness – or genuinely become mad – the implication being that his 'thought-centre' goes from the rational to right-off-the-scale.

Once you've located the predominant INNER PSYCHOLOGICAL DRIVE of your character, it's then very useful to consider the opposites:

I've said that the 'thought-centre' houses both mathematical logic and wild fantasy, so if your character is very *rational*, where in the script might they be seen to be very *imaginative*?

I've said that the 'emotion-centre' houses all sorts of complex responses, so if your character is emotionally very *volatile*, where might they be seen to be emotionally *restrained*?

I've said that the 'action-centre' is both etiquette and sexuality or impulsiveness, so if your character seems to be very *formal* or *detached*, where might they be seen to be very *spontaneous* or *sexual*?

The energy behind the opposites of each INNER PSYCHOLOGICAL DRIVE is incredibly useful, and the dynamic between such opposites was called by Stanislavsky HEROIC TENSION.

Heroic tension

There's a wonderful term in psychology called 'enantiodromia' – the Law of the Pendulum. Just as a fully working pendulum will swing the same number of degrees each way – i.e. 45° to the left and 45° to the right, not 27° to the left and 92° to the right – so too will our psychologies. If I have the capacity to like you a little bit, I also have the capacity to dislike you a little bit. If I have the capacity to love you passionately, I also have the capacity to hate you inexorably. This is a great idea to bear in mind when you're embodying a role in order to stop you from opting for the obvious choices. It's what Stanislavsky meant by HEROIC TENSION,[129] which is a little tool that you find in the part of your toolkit with those odd screws and miscellaneous bolts, but it's invaluable – as those odd screws always are.

Finding the tension of contrasts in your role can be very creatively energising. It allows for contradictions to co-exist, which is vital, since – as we've considered before – we mustn't feel that LOGIC AND SEQUENCE iron out all the complexities of a character and its innate human nature. For Stanislavsky:

> Extremes extend the gamut of human passions and enlarge the palette of the actor. Therefore when he is playing a good man, he should seek out what there is of evil in him; if he is playing an intelligent character, find his mentally weak spot; if he is playing a jolly person, find his serious side.[130]

After all, 'black only becomes black when white is introduced'[131] and the 'logical behaviour of a drunken man is not that he staggers but that he tries *not* to stagger'.[132] So as we embody a role, we're looking both for the psychological juxtapositions and the physical counterpoints: all too often, we can fall into the trap of going for the broad brushstrokes, the 'make-believe truth' which relies on generalisations and quick-fix choices. Finding the HEROIC TENSIONS between opposites – in the character's psychology and physicality – can be both fun and authentic.

That said, there are certain broad brushstrokes which can give us some valuable starting points in our embodiment of a role. One of these brushstrokes is considering what the character does for a living: in other words, what is their EMPLOI?

Emploi

EMPLOI has two connotations.

First of all, EMPLOI *as type*. Stanislavsky's general concern with EMOTION in the early formation of his 'system' stemmed from his desire to retaliate against those actors who, following the traditions of the nineteenth and early twentieth centuries, stuck to their own particular 'types' or EMPLOIS. That 'type' might be Juve Lead, Soubrette, Old Character part, or Comic Servant, for example. To some extent, it wasn't the actors' fault as these types were often written into texts and an individual would be hired by a company specifically to play that EMPLOI. This fact in itself locked actors into certain shortcuts, 'make-believe truths' and sterile stereotypes.

Secondly, EMPLOI *as occupation*. And this is where the tool becomes incredibly useful, as it's another angle on ACTION and 'doing'. What a character does for a living and what they choose to do with their time have a huge influence on their OBJECTIVES and ACTIONS throughout a script. When you're building a character and embodying a role, it's intriguing to ask, 'What does my character *do*? What's my character's *profession*?' These are questions we usually ask of someone when we meet them in real life, so why not ask them of our characters? Most of us spend more time at work than anywhere else, so the choices we make about our professions and the demands that our jobs make on us provide a snapshot context of the kind of life we lead. So we see in *Three Sisters* how Olga is a schoolteacher who becomes a headmistress; Irina becomes a postmistress and then trains to be a teacher; Tusenbach surrenders his commission to work in a brick factory.

Of course, it's just as interesting to note when a character doesn't have an EMPLOI. With Masha in *Three Sisters*, it could well be that part of her *ennui* stems from the fact she has so much time on her hands. Furthermore, it's curious that she marries a schoolteacher and falls in love with a Lieutenant-Colonel: the EMPLOIS of her men-folk reflect something of her own psychology and the kinds of people who interest her. A character's EMPLOI indicates how they might spend their days and occupy their nights: it influences their wishes, their dreams and their fears. Even if they've no paid employment, they still – like Masha – make choices about how they spend their time, and all this information can be extremely lucrative as we 'embody a role'.

Indeed, EMPLOI also affects a character's *physicality*, as it determines to some extent how they inhabit their body. Do they work on the land? Do they sit at a desk? Are they posted in Iraq? Do they teach Tai Kwan Do? Their body will reflect their daily pursuits, and their EMPLOI will even dictate the way they stand. And this is a very handy hint: one of the first things to consider once you start physically embodying a role is how your character stands and walks, as their EMPLOI will affect their contact with the ground. In turn, that contact with the ground will influence the alignment of their spine. And that alignment of the spine will in turn inform the character's *emotional* experiences and *thought* processes. Joan of Arc is a soldier, she wears boots and armour: put her in the Dauphin's perfumed court and see how she stands. Lear is a king, he wears fine footwear: let him hobble barefoot on a blasted heath, and watch how he deports himself. Marlene in Caryl Churchill's *Top Girls* is a business woman, power-dressed in fitted suits and heels: how does she behave when off-duty in her sister's threadbare home?

EMPLOI also affects a character's *psychology*. Let's consider this in relation to the three INNER PSYCHOLOGICAL DRIVES of thinking, feeling, doing. Is the character's job *action*-based, like a plumber or a personal trainer? Is their job *emotion*-based, like a poet or a therapist? Is their job *thought*-based, like a computer analyst or a politician? And how do these 'centre'-led jobs interact with each other? I once facilitated an international conference for senior managers in a major internet company. Over the course of the two days, I noticed how the 'ideas people' (the designers) were in effect the company's *head*, while the marketing people (the enthusers) were the company's *feelings*, and those who made everything that the designers designed and the marketing people enthused about (i.e. the engineers) were the company's *body*. Together they constituted this high-powered, international company: each needed the others.

There are other psychological aspects implicit in the *physical surroundings* of our EMPLOI. Why does someone choose to be a florist, not a haberdasher? A cobbler, not an electrician? How does a man feel who spends his days standing among people's worn-out shoes, putting his hands inside their boots? How does a woman feel standing amidst daffodils and dahlias, making up wreaths as well as bouquets? And what if the cobbler is a woman and the florist is a man? The surroundings which form part of our daily occupation influence who we are psychologically and what we do physically. And that includes the space in which we work. The taxi driver in his cramped cab. The priest in his chilly church. The football manager on his newly mown pitch. Suddenly we see how a simple GIVEN CIRCUMSTANCE – a person's job – yields a huge harvest in terms of psycho-physical information.

And it's not just the surroundings in which a person works – it's the OBJECTS that they use.

Objects

For Stanislavsky, everything on stage could be a partner: a lighting state, a sound effect, a costume, a piece of the set, and even an inanimate OBJECT.

Beginning with your powers of OBSERVATION, you can start to develop a fascinating 'dialogue' with an OBJECT. In Stanislavsky's words:

> Intensive observation of an object naturally arouses
> a desire to do something with it. To do something
> with it in turn intensifies your observation of it. This
> mutual inter-reaction establishes a stronger contact
> with the object of your attention.[133]

As your OBSERVATION works upon your OBJECT, it quickly activates your IMAGINATION and before long you may find yourself projecting your OBJECT into an imaginary context. The imagined circumstances surrounding the OBJECT

> can transform the object itself and heighten the
> reaction of your emotions to it.[134]

So, swiftly we move from OBJECT to OBSERVATION to IMAGINATION to EMOTION, with a little bit of ACTION thrown in. Immediately we see how the resonances of an OBJECT can be startlingly profound. Look at Masha in *Three Sisters* clutching her pillow in Act 3 as she fantasises a life with Vershinin. See how Mary Warren in Arthur Miller's *The Crucible* presents a hand-made poppet to Elizabeth Proctor in Act 2 as she conjures up her possible powers of witchcraft. Where would Beckett's Krapp be if he didn't have his tape recorder, and what about Brecht's Mother Courage and her cart and war accoutrements? Your dialogue with an OBJECT can reveal a range of nuances about your character's inner state. So a cigarette can be an aid to an alluring seduction or a weapon of personal destruction. The lipstick on that coffee cup delights you if the drinker has just popped out to powder her nose, and taunts you if the drinker left without a farewell kiss. Does the unopened letter contain the news of a long-lost lover? Or the results of your recent blood test?

The power of props and their emotive potential is summed up brilliantly in Stanislavsky's example of how to play a murderer:

> The only thought, the first one, with which you
> should enter the circle is your knife. Concentrate on
> the physical action: examining the knife. Look at it
> closely, test its edge with your finger, find out whether
> its handle is firm or not. Transfer it mentally into the
> heart or the chest of your rival. If you play the villain
> try to estimate the force of the blow that would be
> needed to thrust the knife into your rival's back. Try
> to think whether you would be able to deal the blow,
> whether the blade should not have been a bit shorter
> or longer, whether it should not have been a little
> stronger, or whether it would stand the blow without
> bending? All your thoughts are concentrated on one
> object only: the knife, the weapon.[135]

The effortless way in which you can combine IMAGINATION, THE MAGIC 'IF', EMOTION and OBJECTIVE, as well as physical and psychological ACTION, is summed up and summoned up wonderfully in this simple relationship with a prop. You can begin to see just how powerful an OBJECT can be as a tool for propelling you from page to stage – from your MENTAL RECONNAISSANCE to your embodiment of the role – in an easy, imaginative leap.

*

We've looked at a range of tools so far in 'Embodying the Role', from the amorphous sense of TRUTH to the rock-solid physical OBJECT. Before we move onto the third section of this chapter – 'Approaches to Rehearsal' – let's consider the tool towards which all the other tools are ultimately geared: the arousal of the SUBCONSCIOUS.

TRAY 10

THE MEAT OF THE TOOLKIT
AND THE 'SYSTEM'

Subconscious

In many ways, the SUBCONSCIOUS is the twin sister of INSPIRA-TION. I specifically put INSPIRATION in Chapter 1 on Actor-Training to encourage a sense of bravery in the first stages of developing a psycho-physical technique. And I've included the SUBCONSCIOUS here to understand how its life is engendered when you've prepared a character thoroughly. Igniting INSPIRA-TION and accessing the creative genius of the SUBCONSCIOUS is what we're really seeking as actors as we 'embody a role'.

The final chapter of *An Actor Prepares* is called 'On the Threshold of the Subconscious', and Stanislavsky has a very clear vision of what you experience on *this* side of the threshold as opposed to *that* side of the threshold:

> We see, hear, understand and think differently *before*
> and *after* we cross the 'threshold of the subconscious'.
> *Beforehand*, we have 'true-seeming feelings', afterwards
> – 'sincerity of emotions'. On *this* side of it we have
> the simplicity of a limited fantasy; *beyond* – the
> simplicity of the larger imagination. Our freedom on
> *this* side of the threshold is limited by reason and
> conventions; *beyond* it, our freedom is bold, wilful,
> active and always moving forwards. *Over there* the
> creative process differs each time it is repeated.[136]

You know when you've stepped over the threshold into your
SUBCONSCIOUS, because your IMAGINATION and your body and
your sense of daring push you into places of which your conscious brain couldn't conceive. You suddenly find yourself doing things which fit absolutely with the decisions you've made
about the character, which adhere truthfully to the words of
the writer, and which don't disrupt the director's aesthetically
constructed MISE-EN-SCÈNE or the camera's carefully posi-
tioned shot. Creatively you're absolutely flying. The audience
feel it, the camera sees it, your fellow actors are with you, the
stage or the film-set becomes your 'home', you're utterly relaxed,
you feel totally in possession of the space and the text and the
moment and the 'spirit'. And – paradoxically – there's an
exciting sense of danger, because to some extent even *you* don't
know what you're going to do next, let alone the spectator!

Wow! What an adrenalin rush!

But it's not a fix that we can have whenever we fancy.

By its very nature, the SUBCONSCIOUS is elusive. We can't
consciously call upon it. That said, we *can* consciously do things
to prepare the ground for its arousal. We can know our
OBJECTIVES, we can understand the structure of the scene – its
BITS, the GIVEN CIRCUMSTANCES – we can open ourselves to the
INNER CREATIVE STATE, etc. As we saw with INSPIRATION, this
is what Stanislavsky's whole 'system' was designed for: to put
the *conscious* scaffolding into place so the SUBCONSCIOUS can
do its unexpected and inspired work.

But your careful preparation is only a springboard. You have to play dangerous in order to evoke the SUBCONSCIOUS. If night after night after night, or take after take after take, you merely go through the motions of every word and action as if you know them like the back of your hand, then forget the SUBCONSCIOUS. All that will happen is that artistic boredom and inertia will set in.

Playing dangerous isn't so easy, though, and there's a simple reason why we often play safe: we're afraid we're going to forget our lines. That's the base line. Even with film, when you have the option of another take, it's still a fear which haunts us all – from acolyte student to seasoned pro. Even Laurence Olivier and Derek Jacobi have suffered incapacitating stage fright: Antony Sher actually documents his battle with what he calls The Fear, in his book, *Primo Time*.[137]

The curious thing is that knowing our lines is the least the audience will expect of us, and it's the least we should expect of ourselves. And that's just it – it's The Least. If you stay in the safety zone, you make it incredibly hard for the SUBCONSCIOUS to work. So you have to develop a blind faith in yourself. As you step out onto that stage or in front of that camera, you have to trust that you do know the lines, that they are in your head – and even better, that they're in your body.

Paradoxically, it's often in those moments when we lose our lines that the SUBCONSCIOUS steps in and takes us somewhere truly exciting. The SUBCONSCIOUS is both a safety net and a wild horse. And that's the joy of the paradox: the SUB-CONSCIOUS springs into action either when we're incredibly prepared or in a moment of crisis. And we just have to ride the wild pony.

To be this brave, one of the most useful things we can do is to nurture a sense of TRUTH for ourselves in the realm of the piece – whatever its genre or style or medium. If we can believe in the possibility of our GIVEN CIRCUMSTANCES, then our SUB-CONSCIOUS has the chance to pick up the creative baton and run with it:

Have you noticed that each time this *truth* and *your belief in it* is born, involuntarily, the subconscious steps in and nature begins to function? So when your conscious psycho-technique is carried to its fullest extent, the ground is prepared for nature's subconscious process.[138]

It would be foolhardy and facetious to offer any specific exercises for arousing the SUBCONSCIOUS, as it's a product of your overall psycho-physical technique, combined with your physical relaxation, your mental and imaginative playfulness – enhanced by a good script and a collaborative ensemble. Plus a certain degree of raw talent, of course, which allows you to forego the safe and dive across the threshold into Mamet's 'terrifying unforeseen' – like a Marlon Brando! Do the prep, and trust the rest.

*

Overview

In the first two sections of this chapter, we've 'mined the text' for the various details provided by the writer to whet our creative appetites. Then we've looked at how to turn that textual analysis into something physical as we 'embody the role'.

This has included considering the nature of TRUTH, and how to build it through

- imagination
- observation
- the Magic 'If'

Having developed a sense of TRUTH in what we're doing, we've begun to build a psycho-physical connection with the character using

- action
- tempo-rhythm

- emotion memory
- emotion

We've then begun to texture that character using the tools of

- the inner psychological drives
- heroic tension
- emploi
- objects

Once we're familiar with the text and we're working with our bodies, the power of our SUBCONSCIOUS can then start to work its creative magic.

It's time now to look at what happens when we meet our fellow actors on the rehearsal-room floor. This is where the real work begins . . .

Section 3
Approaches to Rehearsal

The important element in this final section of Chapter 2 is *your partner* – whether it's on stage or in front of the camera. You can do as much textual analysis as you like and any amount of individual work, but only when you put yourself physically into relevant situations with other living, breathing human beings can you really start to penetrate the inner workings of the script.

'Approaches to Rehearsal' focuses on two particular rehearsal processes – the METHOD OF PHYSICAL ACTIONS and ACTIVE ANALYSIS. They're both hugely liberating for actors and they can lead to all sorts of creative discoveries. You'll see in Chapter 4 that there aren't many exercises offered to accompany this section, as essentially we're looking at holistic rehearsal processes: if we try and fragment them too much, they'll simply unravel. The best thing is to attend to each of the components and then give the approaches a go – under the watchful eye of an attentive and sensitive director.

In fact, THE ROLE OF THE DIRECTOR is vital with both processes, as the responsibility of orchestrating the vast range of creative discoveries and finding the appropriate MISE-EN-SCÈNES lies fundamentally with him or her.

TRAY 11

GENERAL PRINCIPLES OF DIRECTING AND STAGING

The role of the director

How a director conducts a rehearsal greatly affects the tools you choose as an actor to manifest a role. He or she also influences how you then use the tools you've chosen. So before probing the rehearsal processes themselves, it's worth investigating Stanislavsky's own attitude to THE ROLE OF THE DIRECTOR.

We've seen how Stanislavsky's approach to directing changed radically over the course of his life. This was partly due to the problems that he himself encountered as an actor and partly in response to the discoveries he made as a trainer of other actors. We know that in the early days of the Moscow Art Theatre, he started out as a 'director dictator', with his score for his 1898 production of Chekhov's *The Seagull* indicating to the very second the precise length of every pause and even the length of each kiss. But in his defence, what choice did he have? The aspiring new Moscow Art Theatre of 1897 had some big ambitions to fulfil:

> We . . . wanted to give luxurious performances, to
> uncover great thoughts and emotions, and because we
> did not have ready actors, we were to put the whole

power into the hands of the stage director. He had to
create by himself, with the aid of the production,
scenery, properties, interesting mise en scène [sic] . . .

I demanded that the actors obey me, and I forced
them to do so. True, many of them performed what I
directed them to do only outwardly, for they were not
yet ready to understand those directions through the
medium of emotion. But what was I to do? I could see
no other means, for we were faced by the necessity of
creating a complete troupe and a new theatre with
new tendencies in the space of a few months.[139]

Under these restrictions, it could only be a matter of time
before some of his highly talented young actors, including
Vsevelod Meyerhold and Olga Knipper, rebelled. He was
forced to admit that this style of directing utterly blocked the
actors' own creativity, rendering them mere puppets in the
director's hands. In response, he began to include his actors
much more directly in the rehearsal process, by introducing
lengthy periods during which the company would sit round the
table engaging in the kind of MENTAL RECONNAISSANCE that
we've already talked about.

There's no doubt that the 'round-the-table analysis' was
incredibly useful, but it had a major flip-side. The process was
so extensive and intensive that, by the time the actors actually
stood up and started to rehearse the play physically, their heads
were stuffed liked baked potatoes with too much diverse
information. Once again, their creative guts were constipated.

These two periods of experimentation (the 'director dictator' and 'round-the-table analysis') brought Stanislavsky to the
final stages of his creative life as a theatre maker. He realised
that, although some detective work on the script was absolutely
vital, the sooner the actors could start embodying the play
physically, the richer the rewards.

And it didn't really matter how much or how little cerebral
knowledge they might have of the text at first. Once they were

up on the rehearsal-room floor, the actors could integrate their bodies, imaginations, emotions and psychological energies all at the same time. In this way, their understanding of the script arose out of a genuine combination of their own creative resources: it came from the soul, not the cerebrum.

Out of this creative conflagration evolved the METHOD OF PHYSICAL ACTIONS and ACTIVE ANALYSIS. The director was still a vital cog in the rehearsal machine, but his responsibility shifted from being that of a puppet master: instead, he was something like a photographic technician, who slowly allows the negative film to emerge as a positive image by adding the right chemical solutions at just the right time. In this way, the film image develops into the most appropriate, brightly coloured, and sharply focused composition imaginable.

So what constituted a good director as far as Stanislavsky was concerned?

As a starting point, a director should have as profound an understanding of acting techniques as an actor. And it's no surprise to hear that in Russia today directing courses at drama schools can last for five years: a large part of the programme includes exactly the same actor-training as those students engaged in the full-time, vocational acting courses.

Stanislavsky then suggested that there are three key principles which a director has to tackle. They're all quite straightforward, but warrant inclusion here. A director should know:

- how to work with the author;
- how to work with the actors;
- how to work with everyone else involved in the production.

Let's look at the implications of each of these:

1. The author

The director should know *how to work with the author*, unless (of course) the author is dead. This may sound like an obvious piece of advice, but consider the complexities of Stanislavsky's relationship with, for example, Chekhov. If the contact between writer and director is problematic, your confidence as an actor can be seriously fractured, making it very difficult to generate a CREATIVE ATMOSPHERE. If, however, the director knows how to get inside the writer's mind, the animation in the rehearsal room can be deliciously compelling with everyone firing on all cylinders. I know this from working with Max Stafford-Clark. He's particularly good at the contact with a playwright, having spent a lifetime working both with new writers and new writing, teasing out THROUGH-LINES and untangling ACTIONS.

2. The actors

The director must know *how to work with the actors*. For Stanislavsky, one of the first steps in negotiating the production of a script is to provoke actors into asking all the right questions: many of these questions will come from the MENTAL RECONNAISSANCE and discussion of the script, which will then spur the actors to come up with appropriate OBJECTIVES for the characters. From their answers to those questions, they can fill in the necessary details to breathe life into the roles. This often means the director simply watches the living actors with all their quirks and idiosyncrasies negotiating their roles, and then he sensitively compares those living, breathing people with the qualities of the fictional characters. From there, he can gently guide them away from any unhelpful personal habits towards elements which may be useful for their parts. As Stanislavsky puts it:

> The most important function of the director, as I understand the definition, is to open up all the potentialities of the actor and to arouse his individual initiative.[140]

If a director can have as much understanding of the tools in *The Toolkit* as the actors, then he can watch the performers at work and he, in turn, can then ask himself the appropriate questions to help the actors manifest the roles: 'What would help this particular person at this particular point? Sharpening the OBJECTIVE? Clarifying the GIVEN CIRCUMSTANCES? Accessing a particular EMOTION MEMORY?' And the more the director can talk the same language as the actors, the more options they'll all have at their disposal, with the result that the final production may be potentially more detailed and captivating.

3. Everyone else in the production

The director should also know *how to work collaboratively with everyone else involved in the production* – screen or stage. This includes the composer, the designer, the wardrobe team, the sound designers, the production crew and stage management team or – in film – the multitude of vital technicians, including the cameraman or woman, the sound engineer, lighting designer, editor, etc. The director is as much an organiser of the final production's manifestation as a conduit between the writer and the actors. He needs to be a 'person-manager', as well as an artist.

There's also the question of *genre* and *style*. It's important to keep reminding ourselves that *The Toolkit* isn't restricted to realism or naturalism. Stanislavsky loved all forms of performance: from opera and operetta, to farce and melodrama. It's the director's challenge to encourage the actors to liberate a genre from its traditional trappings – in just the same way that it's important to free an individual actor from his or her own personal clichés.

With all these considerations in mind, Stanislavsky approached THE ROLE OF THE DIRECTOR from the literary, aesthetic, organisational and interpretational perspectives, as well as developing an intimate contact with his actors.

As we'll see with ACTIVE ANALYSIS, THE ROLE OF THE DIRECTOR for Stanislavsky became increasingly important and extremely textured, right up until the day he died. After all, the subtleties involved in a rehearsal process which places *improvisation* at its very core demand of the director a highly developed intuition towards each actor's process. It's his job to help every actor sound the true notes and ditch the false, and not just let them wallow about in a chaotic quagmire of artistic anarchy. Far from it. The director has to develop a sophisticated ability to take all the stage pictures that the actors spontaneously discover in their improvisations, and turn them into a coherent and aesthetic MISE-EN-SCÈNE.

Mise-en-scène

The term MISE-EN-SCÈNE – or 'putting on the stage' – may sound pretentious at first. But it's a vast improvement on the much used and utterly unhelpful alternative 'blocking'. So often we concern ourselves with 'blocking' a scene: 'Should I sit by the window on this pause? Should I walk over to the sideboard on that line? Where should I stand in relation to Hamlet during this opening speech?' The result can be startlingly phoney and two-dimensional. That's because 'blocking' does exactly what it says: it blocks you from any fluid, excitable, creative discoveries. And that's exactly what happened with Stanislavsky's company when he 'blocked' a play through a production plan. He knew in his heart of hearts that a theatrical production plan which remains a theatrical production plan can never truly resonate: the actors have to 'fulfil' it. As Vasily Toporkov describes:

> Daring directorial conceptions which could not be justified by the actors were rejected by [Stanislavsky]. Better something simpler within the capability of the actor than a fruitless rush to unattainable heights by unjustified means.

A director's plan, which is not fulfilled by the actors, remains a plan, not a performance. We can appreciate the director's imagination, but such a production can never touch the heart of the audience.[141]

Yet sometimes there's no alternative: there has to be a rigid choreography. Most television directors – just like Stanislavsky in the first years of the Moscow Art Theatre – are up against the limitations of time. So they usually have to ask the actors to 'block this scene for the camera quickly' just before the filming of a shot. It's a five-minute process. The economic pressures demand quick-fix performing. And it takes an open and confident professional to endow the kind of rigid choreography that most television requires with an inner, creative suppleness.

The need for inner suppleness, along with the other dilemmas which face us as actors when a MISE-EN-SCÈNE is thrust upon us, was of huge concern to Stanislavsky. Yet he also believed that if you were psycho-physically playful, you could usually make sense of any prescribed 'blocking':

> All disputes with your [director] about the mise-en-scènes [sic] are almost always a waste of time . . . The creative force in you suffers no diminution whether you sit, stand or lie down. The only point that may be considered pertinent in this connection is the extent to which your creative powers can be said *to have been set free*, and whether in a certain mise-en-scène [sic] your body does or does not obey your will because, somewhere inside you, you have not achieved the *proper degree of freedom* and have, consequently, failed to achieve the necessary harmony.[142]

This is quite a gauntlet that Stanislavsky throws down here. Basically he's saying that the more skilled we are in our art, the more we'll be able to work with a sense of inner freedom and creative play under even the most mechanical of directorial schemes. And the opposite is true: the less skilled we are, the more wooden we'll appear.

For all the impact of this gauntlet – 'Go where you're told and make it mean something' – Stanislavsky still made a radical turn-around as a director in his later years. As he said to his opera students in 1935:

> Before, we tried to squeeze the actor into the *mise-en-scène*, while the *mise-en-scène* should be born as the result of his work and his adaptation to his partner and the [objective]. In the theatre of the future we shall work without any fixed *mise-en-scènes* so as to preserve the freshness of all the organic processes. If we deprive the actor of the *mise-en-scène*, he will have to think more of the circumstances of his part . . .

> [So] now we shall proceed differently. We shall create the line of his action, the life of his body, and then the life of his spirit will be created indirectly by itself.[143]

And this process became known as the METHOD OF PHYSICAL ACTIONS.

TRAY 12

REHEARSAL PROCESS 1:
THE METHOD OF PHYSICAL ACTIONS

The Method of Physical Actions

The basis of the METHOD OF PHYSICAL ACTIONS is the basis of PSYCHO-PHYSICALITY as we've looked at it throughout *The Toolkit*. Physical ACTIONS affect EMOTIONS, and EMOTIONS provoke physical ACTIONS. The inner and the outer are entirely co-ordinated.

Although the METHOD OF PHYSICAL ACTIONS was crystallised during the last five years of his life, you can see glimpses of it very early on in Stanislavsky's professional career. His own performance of Dr Stockmann in Ibsen's *An Enemy of the People* in 1900 was something of a *eureka* for him, as he experienced very vividly the fluid interaction between his inner images and their outer expression:

From the intuition of feelings I went to the outer
image, for it flowed naturally from the inner image,
and the soul and body of Stockmann-Stanislavsky
became one organically. I only had to think of the
thoughts and cares of Stockmann and the signs of
short sight would come of themselves, together with
the forward stoop of the body, the quick step, the eyes
that looked trustfully into the soul of the man or
object on the stage with me, the index and middle
fingers of the hand stretched forward of themselves
for the sake of greater persuasiveness, as if to push
my own thoughts, feelings and words into the soul of
my listener. All these habits came of themselves,
unconsciously, and quite apart from myself . . .

I only had to assume the manners and habits of
Stockmann, on the stage or off, and in my soul there
were born the feelings and perceptions that had given
them birth. In this manner, intuition not only created
the image, but its passions also. They became my own
organically, or, to be more true, my own passions
became Stockmann's.[144]

As his acting theories developed over the years, Stanislavsky's
increasing emphasis on *the body* became something of a
survival tactic, as well as an artistic belief. Under the Soviet
regime, anything psychological was considered to be
dangerously idealistic and decadent. So the Socialist Realist
artists sought to illustrate in their works that human beings
were proactive, 'doing' creatures, whose actions had the potential to change society, rather than reactive, emotive beings,
whose psychologies were flawed. If Stanislavsky was going to
survive Soviet censorship, he had to get away from the
emphasis on EMOTION MEMORY which had characterised his
earlier work and adapt himself to the need for ACTION. This
led to his declaration that actors require

only physical actions, physical truths, and physical
belief in them! Nothing more![145]

So successful was his shift in perspective that, to Stanislavsky's
chagrin, the METHOD OF PHYSICAL ACTIONS was even exalted
by the Soviets as the ultimate form of actor-training – which
for him was the artistic kiss of death.

But what exactly was the basic premise behind the METHOD
OF PHYSICAL ACTIONS?

It was quite simply that actors could generate many of the
creative discoveries in a rehearsal room through their *bodies*,
rather than their *brains*. By getting up on their feet and
inhabiting the rehearsal space, the actors' bodies could feed
their IMAGINATIONS and prompt them into all sorts of emotional discoveries, without them having to squeeze their EMO-
TION MEMORIES like a tube of toothpaste. If they could turn
their attention away from big emotional delvings, leaving the
SUBCONSCIOUS alone and focusing instead on small, manage-
able, everyday, physical tasks, then the SUBCONSCIOUS had the
chance to spring to life and fuel the actors' creative impulses.

To this end, the main task in rehearsals using the METHOD
OF PHYSICAL ACTIONS was to find a sequence of small, achiev-
able ACTIONS, which would stimulate complex psychological
experiences in the actors if they carried them out with
precision and commitment. (We've alluded to this in ACTIONS
above.) To be sure that the SUBCONSCIOUS had the best chance
to work creatively, there needed to be a good, powerful and
burning OBJECTIVE behind each physical ACTION. Every actor
needed an inner canvas of psychological 'I want to's accompanying his outer 'score of physical actions', so there was an
inner JUSTIFICATION; the actions couldn't just be empty and
formal.

If that's the basic premise, how did the METHOD OF
PHYSICAL ACTIONS actually operate?

Through a sequence of simple stages (which have been set
out very clearly by Sharon Carnicke, whose list I've adopted
and adapted here):[146]

1. Identify the purposeful OBJECTIVE of the BIT you're exploring (e.g. 'I want to create an atmosphere in which I can run an inspiring workshop').

2. Compile your 'score of physical actions' by listing all the little things you have to do to pursue your OBJECTIVE (e.g. 'I open the door, I turn on the light, I switch on the aircon, I set up a circle of chairs', etc.).

3. Test that 'score of physical actions' by means of a SILENT ÉTUDE, so that you play out that BIT of the scene without words (e.g. I carry through my simple ACTIONS without any text, to understand whether the order of the ACTIONS and the nature of the ACTIONS feel appropriate: maybe I want to switch on the aircon *after* I've laid out the circle of chairs? And I certainly have to switch on the lights *before* I do anything else). (See ACTIVE ANALYSIS and CONNECTION below for details on SILENT ÉTUDES.)

Part of the reason there's so much emphasis on physical ACTION in this sequence is that, in the early stages of rehearsal, Stanislavsky intended to divert the actors *away from the spoken word*. He didn't want them learning their lines by rote; instead – as I hinted in the Introduction – he wanted them to 'create the living word'.

> The 'living word' is one in which the roots run down into one's soul, they feed on one's feelings; but the stem reaches up into the consciousness where it puts forth luxuriant foliage of eloquent verbal forms, conveying all the deep emotions from which they draw their vitality.[147]

'Creating the living word' was hugely important for Stanislavsky. He believed that when you first pick up a text, the distance between the writer's words and your own resources is of immeasurable size. It's all too easy to become very formal with the words, burying your head in the script and not having a true sense of contact with your partners or the environment or even with what the words of the text are *really* saying. In these situations, the word is far from living: it's *sans* roots, *sans* stem, and consequently *sans* foliage. To combat this scenario, he invited his actors to come to the first rehearsals with very little knowledge of the script. He would simply give them a broad outline of a scene and they would then improvise the circumstances *in their own persons* and *using their own words*. He was so keen that his actors should begin with a very intuitive and spontaneous relationship to a script, that when he was working on *Othello* in 1935, he didn't even want his students to read the play beforehand. He was worried their intellectual grapplings with Shakespeare's verse would violate their creative instincts on the rehearsal-room floor. Ignorance was bliss, and bliss was INSPIRATION.

Having taken away the writer's text, Stanislavsky then focused the actors' early improvisations on some of the basic tools in the kit. He took THE MAGIC 'IF', GIVEN CIRCUMSTANCES and OBJECTIVES, and prompted the actors towards questions with which we're now very familiar: 'What would I do if *I* was in this situation? What do I *want* from the other person in this situation? And what would I say?' Carrying these questions in their hearts, the improvising students would *do* the things they would naturally do and *say* the words they would naturally say. And so they set about improvising their way towards their characters. Then:

> After you have learned to act from yourself, define the differences between your behaviour and that of the character. Find all the reasons and justifications for the character's actions, and then go on from there without thinking where your personal action ends and the character's begins. His actions and yours will fuse automatically if you have done all the preceding work [i.e. considered the GIVEN CIRCUMSTANCES and clarified the OBJECTIVES] as I have suggested.[148]

Some of these ideas are already familiar from CONCENTRATION AND ATTENTION and merging with the character. And, as you saw with physical ACTIONS, the important part of the process at this point is that ACTIONS have the capacity to appeal to your EMOTIONS, primarily because of your *muscular memory*. You have a whole palette of emotions embedded in your musculature: by inciting your body into action as early as possible, the more likely you are to awaken those powerful muscle memories. The physical, three-dimensional improvisations are a vital way of provoking these muscle memories, as well as accessing your thought-based memories, as you fuse with the GIVEN CIRCUMSTANCES of the character.

Gradually, through merging yourself with the character, and blending your improvised text with the written word, you'll uncover the appropriate 'score of physical actions'. Once you've found it, you then start to road-test it through further ÉTUDES, so that you can eventually fix it. That doesn't mean pinning it like a butterfly to a board, but rather shaping it into a coherent whole. The idea is that each time you repeat it, it actually inspires you – much in the same way a virtuoso violinist plays exactly the same notes every night, but with an energy and passion that allows the strict structure to resonate and soar. (See ACTIVE ANALYSIS below for more details.)

But how do you ensure the process is unfolding appropriately?

The answer is: through ongoing textual analysis, both before an improvisation and after an improvisation. The METHOD OF PHYSICAL ACTIONS isn't anarchical chaos. There has to be some textual analysis, otherwise how can your improvisations evolve in their precision? So after each ÉTUDE you compare where you were psychologically at each point in your improvisations with where you still need to go in order to render faithfully the writer's TEXT.

That textual analysis still involves breaking a scene down into BITS and working out your OBJECTIVES. There's still plenty of reference to biographical research and historical details. But the information is now fed into the rehearsal when you're 'organically' ready for it, so it's not just slapped on like an oversized overcoat. In this way, all your discoveries become much more experiential, visceral and hot-blooded, rather than coldly academic or calmly intellectual.

Okay – so far we're improvising using our own words based on a simple scenario given to us by the director, and we're allowing our physical body to do much of the early exploratory work for us. Each improvisation is backed up by some MENTAL RECONNAISSANCE and little by little, we're uncovering a 'score of physical actions' which propels the scene forward.

At some point, surely, the writer's words have to come into play?

Indeed, they do. And at this point in rehearsals, Stanislavsky became very attentive: he didn't want to disrupt the 'creation of the living word' – i.e. the subtle evolution from the actor's im-provised words to the writer's text – for fear of catapulting the actors straight back into rote-learning and clichéd stereotypes. So he carefully fed the actual lines of the script to the actors during their improvisations from the sidelines like a football coach – *but only as and when he felt they were ready for them.*

> Generally, the lines of the play become indispensable to the actor only in the last phase of his creative pre-parations, when all the inner material he has accumu-lated is crystallised into a series of definite moments, and the physical embodiment of his role is working out methods of expressing characteristic emotions.[149]

If the writer's text was introduced too early, it only became

> a deterrent. The actor is not yet capable of making a full or deep or exhaustive estimate of it . . . The pure text of the playwright seems too brief and actors fill it out with words of their own, interpolations of 'well' and 'now' and so forth.[150]

So, Stanislavsky held back on the writer's words until the actors were virtually gagging for them, when those words were the only 'weapons with which to go into action'.[151] At the point when the actors were truly gasping for them, the words ceased to be a memorised lexicon belonging to another person and they became those very 'living words', which he so desperately sought. Their roots did 'run down into the actors' souls', they did 'feed on their feelings', and the stem did 'put forth its luxuriant foliage of eloquent verbal forms': the living word was created.

Although the point of the rehearsal process is that we do end up speaking the writer's words, we need to be very clear about why we start by improvising the text with the METHOD OF PHYSICAL ACTIONS. In no way are the improvisations an abuse of the writer's text, a means of legitimising an easy paraphrasing. Not at all. The METHOD OF PHYSICAL ACTIONS is a process by which ACTION is *verbal* as much as *physical* as much as *inner* as much as *psychological*. The writer's words become 'grafted on' to your psyche

> without any forcing, and only because of that they [retain] their most important quality – liveliness.[152]

There's one very particular – and rather cunning – reason why I find the METHOD OF PHYSICAL ACTIONS so attractive. Often when we pick up a script, we take the writer's words as gospel: we tend to believe that whatever the characters say is true. After all, unless the character is some sort of convicted felon or a compulsive liar, why should we *not* believe that what we're being told is the truth? Yet, as Stanislavsky points out – and as we discovered with SUBTEXT – frequently in life we only say about 10% of what we actually feel or think or mean: our words are just the tip of an iceberg, the body of which lies submerged in our SUBTEXT and embedded in our physical expression. The same is absolutely true of a fictional character. With the METHOD OF PHYSICAL ACTIONS, you form the hidden part of the iceberg organically: by improvising and exploring the text physically as well as discursively, you're able to evolve simultaneously all that can be seen and all that lies hidden beneath the surface. And through this holistic process, you might come up with an 'iceberg' which is completely different from the 'iceberg' the writer had in mind when he conceived the character. Yet it fits with the script, it resonates for you as the actor playing the part, and it can have a powerful 'subterranean' effect on the audience. They sense something is lurking beneath the words of the script, even if it slightly eludes them, and their own creative juices are stirred into action as they try and see through the mild sense of mystery.

The tendency with a more 'Learn-the-Lines-and-Don't-Bump-into-the-Furniture' method of rehearsal is that the nuances of the text develop *after* the surface area has been covered. Here with the METHOD OF PHYSICAL ACTIONS it's all happening simultaneously. Stanislavsky provides an interesting overview:

> Let us compare our method with what is done in any theatre of the ordinary type. There they read the play, hand out the parts with the notice that by the third or tenth rehearsal everyone must know his role by heart. They begin the reading, then they all go up onto the stage and act, while holding the script. The director shows them the business to do and the actors remember it. At the predicted rehearsal the books are taken away and they speak their lines with a prompter present until they are letter-perfect in their parts.[153]

Sound familiar?

One final thing about the METHOD OF PHYSICAL ACTIONS is that at its heart lies TEMPO-RHYTHM. It's not just the LOGIC AND SEQUENCE of your ACTIONS which arouse your EMOTIONS, but also the speed and intensity at which your 'score of physical actions' is executed:

> You cannot master the method of physical actions if you do not master rhythm. Each physical action is inseparably linked with the rhythm which categorises it. If you always act in one and the same rhythm, then how will you be able to embody a variety of characters convincingly?[154]

Mastering TEMPO-RHYTHM is not just about expanding the range of the characters you can play: TEMPO-RHYTHM is also your means of igniting the inner life of your 'score of physical actions' in the first place. The actor

> moves and, so to speak, takes a run-up, thanks to physical actions and gains momentum. At that moment with the aid of the given circumstances and the Magic Ifs he spreads the invisible wings of belief which carry him upwards to the realm of the imagination in which he sincerely believes.[155]

In brief:

• The METHOD OF PHYSICAL ACTIONS comes from the idea that you can work from *simple physical actions to complex emotional and psychological experiences*, as long as you fuel those simple physical ACTIONS with an OBJECTIVE. Your desire to fulfil that OBJECTIVE motors you through the physical ACTIONS, as long as there's a LOGIC AND SEQUENCE and you inject everything with a sense of TRUTH.

• You can test out your 'score of physical actions' through SILENT ÉTUDES.

• Once you've discovered the 'score of physical actions', you repeat it to strengthen your connection with the inner life of those ACTIONS. Each time you enact the 'score of physical actions', it grows and blossoms, rather than becoming stale and repetitive.

• You keep returning to a process of MENTAL RECON-NAISSANCE to draw out more facts and details from the script to enhance your merger with the character and draw your improvisations closer to the writer's text.

- From the SILENT ÉTUDE, you then add words – first of
  all from your own improvised ideas, and then gradually
  from the writer's text once all your inner preparation
  has been done and you're hungry for the actual script.

- The METHOD OF PHYSICAL ACTIONS is a powerful
  means of creating 'the living word', because you move
  from silent action to improvised speech to the director's
  sideline promptings of the author's actual text. You
  learn the words effortlessly, almost without knowing
  that's what you're doing.

Stanislavsky talks so passionately – even romantically – about
the potential of the METHOD OF PHYSICAL ACTIONS and its
awesome creative possibilities that you wonder why the script-
in-hand, 'Don't-Bump-into-the-Furniture' type of rehearsal
(described in *Creating a Role* and quoted above) still dominates
the Western world. Furthermore, you might think from the
passion with which Stanislavsky writes about the METHOD OF
PHYSICAL ACTIONS, that it was the pinnacle of his professional
experiments: after all, where else was there to go once you'd
'spread your invisible wings of belief'? Yet, for Stanislavsky,
there were still continents to discover.

   Let's turn to the equally psycho-physical, but arguably
rather more playful and anarchic approach to textual analysis
and embodiment of character known as ACTIVE ANALYSIS and
its various components which include:

- étude rehearsals

- events

- grasp

- connection

- 'here, today, now'

- justification

- adaptation

- super-objectives

- through-line of action

- verbal action

- pauses

- the second level

- inner monologue

- envisaging

- moment of orientation

TRAY 13

REHEARSAL PROCESS 2:
ACTIVE ANALYSIS AND ITS COMPONENTS

Active Analysis

There's some disagreement among scholars and practitioners as to whether there actually is a difference between ACTIVE ANALYSIS and the METHOD OF PHYSICAL ACTIONS. I propose that there most definitely is. The emphasis with ACTIVE ANALYSIS is still on finding the right 'score of physical actions' to spark powerful emotional responses within you as an actor. But I think there's a certain anarchy involved, which renders it far more applicable to the host of performance styles present in the twenty-first century than the more action-driven and scientifically logical METHOD OF PHYSICAL ACTIONS. From my own training in ACTIVE ANALYSIS in 1990s' Russia, along with what I've garnered from Maria Knebel's *On the Active Analysis of Plays and Roles*, I'd promote it as one of the most exciting and provocative means of embodying a role and engaging with other actors that I've yet to experience. I've put it to the test in three full-scale productions and I've used its basic principles in numerous workshops, and I know that I'm not alone in my endorsement of it.

The actual process of ACTIVE ANALYSIS is remarkably straightforward, and not dissimilar to the METHOD OF PHYSICAL ACTIONS. The sequence is:

1. you read a scene;

2. you discuss the scene;

3. you improvise the scene without further reference to the script;

4. you discuss the improvisation, before returning to the script;

5. you compare whatever happened in your improvisation with the words and incidents of the actual text.

You then repeat this 5-step sequence until the entire play is staged and the lines are learnt. It's as simple as that.

One of the problems that emerged for Stanislavsky from too much sitting round the table and discussing a text was that the actors' thought processes became disengaged from their physical and emotional resources. They could talk about the characters till the cows came home, but they hadn't a clue about how their roles might manifest themselves emotionally or psycho-physically.

Suddenly with ACTIVE ANALYSIS, all the available avenues of investigation – mental, physical, emotional, and experiential – were harnessed together holistically. All three INNER PSYCHOLOGICAL DRIVES – the 'thought-centre', the 'emotion-centre', and the 'action-centre' – were drafted into the process simultaneously, and each one had equal significance in uncovering the layers of the play. By using all their resources in this way, the actors could get right inside both the *inner action* and the *verbal action* from the very beginning of rehearsals. They could immediately flesh out the script's skeleton with blood and guts and sinews.

The reason why ACTIVE ANALYSIS is different from the METHOD OF PHYSICAL ACTIONS is that it didn't put all its eggs in one ACTION basket: as well as their bodies, the actors could follow their EMOTIONS or their fantasies. I'd say ACTIVE ANALYSIS generally had an exciting edge of play and anarchy and a 'Give-it-a-Go' bravura. Basically, it was less aesthetically 'anal' than the METHOD OF PHYSICAL ACTIONS.

So, what rehearsal conditions are required to put ACTIVE ANALYSIS into practice?

As with the METHOD OF PHYSICAL ACTIONS, the point of improvising a scene – rather than wandering around the stage with a script in your hand in an effort to find a decent 'blocking' – is that the organic link between your *scenic movement* and *the cause or reason that gave birth to that movement* can be forged with very little effort.

To make this linkage even easier, it's important for the rehearsal room to be decked out as closely as possible to the final stage-set. This is because every prop, every piece of furniture, every wall, door, lighting and sound effect, provides you with new pieces of psycho-physical information, all of which help you enormously in your journey towards the character. If you rehearse for three weeks with a broom-handle sword, and then at the technical rehearsal you're given a bloody great sabre, your whole psycho-physical perspective is altered. Obviously it's not always possible to have every prop available in its final form throughout rehearsal, but it's an ideal worth striving for.

Perhaps the most important condition of ACTIVE ANALYSIS is that it requires an incredibly astute director at the helm. Through your improvisations as an actor, you're searching out the LOGIC AND SEQUENCE of a physical and psychological blueprint for your character. Sometimes the *character's* LOGIC AND SEQUENCE may well be completely different from *your own*, and what might be nonsense to you makes complete sense in terms of the character. At this point, the director becomes supremely important. In the course of your improvisations, you may enact something which in terms of the bigger picture of the script makes perfect sense, but for you it feels unnatural and illogical. When this happens, the chances are that you're exploring a new flavour of LOGIC AND SEQUENCE, which fits perfectly with the character as written but feels utterly strange to you, as you push the boundaries of your own psychological comfort zone. A good director will develop an acute sensitivity to the rehearsal process so that he can single out those moments which are genuinely illogical, and those moments where the character's logic may *seem* strange to you as the actor but is in fact perfectly credible within the GIVEN CIRCUMSTANCES of the character and play as a whole.

This degree of sensitivity is crucial. ACTIVE ANALYSIS encourages actors to start *from themselves*: 'What would *I* do in this situation?' Yet you use the rehearsals – through the process of improvisations – to allow the character to 'find' its own voice and physicality. It's back to the idea of the positive photograph emerging from the negative film. Your physical analysis of the character becomes an artistic synthesis in a complex way, and you can best be assured of the success of this complex synthesis if your director is absolutely attentive to each and every actor's creative process. As Knebel writes:

> Responsibility and initiative in the creative organisation
> of rehearsals by means of ACTIVE ANALYSIS lie, of
> course, at the door of the director.[156]

Having directed three productions using pure ACTIVE ANALYSIS, I know how vital the 'creative organisation of rehearsals' can be. The improvisational basis of the rehearsals tends to be – and, in many respects, *has* to be – quite chaotic. As an actor, you have to follow whatever impulse may be guiding you at each moment, so you can genuinely 'actively analyse' your relationships with the other characters. At the same time, there

must be a sense of organisational overview in those improvisations, as each actor is not an island, but part of a collaborative
whole. Little by little, the director has to guide the whole ensemble towards emotionally resonant and artistically satisfying
stage pictures.

Those are the basic principles of ACTIVE ANALYSIS, with an
overview of some of the necessary rehearsal conditions. Let's
now go into more depth.

This is where the toolkit becomes intricate, as we're really
getting to the heart of Stanislavsky's legacy. We'll begin by
examining the actual nuts-and-bolts of ACTIVE ANALYSIS
which involve a series of ÉTUDE REHEARSALS based on the
sequence of: (1) read a scene, (2) discuss the scene, (3) improvise the scene, (4) discuss the improvisation, and (5) return to
the text. And to kick-start that process, you need six tools:

- events

- grasp

- connection

- 'here, today, now'

- justification

- adaptation

The first of these tools, EVENTS, focuses both on Step 1 (the
reading of the scene) and Step 2 (the analysis of the scene,
during which you locate the main EVENT around which you'll
then improvise).

You need the next three tools, GRASP, CONNECTION and
'HERE, TODAY, NOW' as you start to improvise the scene (Step
3) when your early ÉTUDES are entirely *silent*.

As Step 4 kicks in and you discuss the improvisation, the
next two tools come into play (JUSTIFICATION and ADAP-
TATION): they're very handy, because the more you get to know
the script through your improvisations, the more you need to
assess your own connection with the text, and that means

'justifying' and 'adapting' your ACTIONS as you merge with the role.

We start by looking at how the details of a production emerge through a series of what Stanislavsky called ÉTUDE REHEARSALS.

Étude rehearsals

As I've said, there's something quite chaotic about ACTIVE ANALYSIS. And yet there's a kind of logic in the chaos, as all the choices you make, even in your earliest improvisations, are steeped in a certain amount of round-the-table MENTAL RECONNAISSANCE of the script – just as they are with the METHOD OF PHYSICAL ACTIONS. The ACTIONS, OBJECTIVES, GIVEN CIRCUMSTANCES, possible SUBTEXT, etc., are discussed (just as they always were), so you have a firm springboard from which to leap into the creative unknown – or into Mamet's 'terrifying unforeseen' – when you get up and start to improvise.

Before you make any attempt at an improvisation or ÉTUDE, an ÉTUDE REHEARSAL will begin with Step 1 (Read the scene) followed by Step 2 (Discuss the scene). Again, like the METHOD OF PHYSICAL ACTIONS, the main difference between this and Stanislavsky's previous rehearsal practices is that the period of discussion and MENTAL RECONNAISSANCE before each improvisation may only last ten minutes – maybe half an hour – but certainly not three weeks.

Knebel is quite clear about the function of MENTAL RECONNAISSANCE in ÉTUDE REHEARSALS: it's to put even the smallest amount of living tissue onto the skeleton of the play (i.e. those black-and-white words on the page) so that you've got something to work off in your first improvisation. That living tissue (however small initially) comes from clarifying certain key areas:

- What does my character do in the play? (ACTIONS and EVENTS.)

- What are my character's aspirations? (OBJECTIVES.)

- With whom am I struggling? (Which characters have COUNTER-OBJECTIVES to mine? Which characters create obstacles to the achievement of my OBJECTIVES)?

- With whom am I allied? (Which characters support my OBJECTIVES?)

- How do I relate to those characters with whom I'm neither struggling nor allied?

Having found some tentative and intuitive answers to those questions (you don't have to know all the details of the play to begin with), there's one more question you need to answer before your improvisations can proceed: 'What is the main EVENT of the scene?'

Events

An EVENT (also known as an 'effective fact') is a piece of action *without which the scene could not take place.*

EVENTS are a vital part of our daily lives. As Stanislavsky urges:

> Look back at some stage or other in your life and
> recall what 'event' was the major one in that segment,
> and then you will immediately understand how it was
> reflected in your behaviour, in your actions, in your
> thoughts and experiences, and your relationships with
> people.[157]

As soon as you start to look at your own life, you realise how it's been constantly punctuated by EVENTS – both major and minor – which absolutely change your destiny. Often these EVENTS affect how you react to everything else that happens throughout the rest of your life, as well as how you relate to the people surrounding you. You say 'yes' to that party invitation and suddenly meet the person whom you eventually marry. You say 'no' to that outing with your uncle and it's the day his car-brakes fail and he hits a tree. You accept a job. You fail an exam. A parent dies. A son is born. A book is published. A finger is broken. An EVENT can be a split-second MOMENT OF DECISION, and in that split second, the rest of the course of a life is altered. Or it can take months to burgeon.

A play or a film is a radically reduced 'lifetime' – usually only lasting two or three hours, even if a whole biography is covered. Yet in each scene there'll be an EVENT which pushes the script forward and changes the courses of the characters' lives. If you use your brief period of MENTAL RECONNAISSANCE on a scene to pinpoint the main EVENT, you can plunge headlong into its drama. As Stanislavsky maintains:

> The 'event' . . . involves the actor in the world of the play . . . by the shortest possible route.[158]

You know from a cursory analysis of your own life that, when you identify the big EVENTS, it doesn't take long to feel the potency of those EVENTS. At some point, you usually tell people about your EVENT, and in so doing you aim to connect them, by means of their empathy, to your experience of the world, your world view, your life path. We like telling our stories. We like unpacking the main EVENTS of our lives, because they are, after all, what makes us *who* we are. Human beings are natural story-tellers, and stories evolve from EVENTS.

To identify an EVENT in a scene, you just ask the questions: 'What has to happen for this scene to take place? Why did the writer write this scene? What unfolds in it to push the narrative forward?' It might be Maria dropping the letter for Malvolio. It might be Macbeth meeting the witches. It might be as simple as 'Character A has to enter': if Character A didn't enter the scene at that particular point, he wouldn't find his wife *in flagrante* with the butler and the rest of the plot wouldn't unfold. It might even be something as momentary as a kiss. Here's an extract from Mark Ravenhill's 1990s' hit, *Shopping and Fucking*, where we see that both a kiss and a non-kiss constitute two very important EVENTS in one scene. Mark has just returned from his sojourn in a rehab centre to visit his friend, Robbie (with whom he'd had a sexual relationship) and their flatmate, Lulu:

ROBBIE: So. They let you out.

MARK: Sort of.

Pause.

ROBBIE: Thought you said months. Did you miss me?

MARK: I missed you both.

ROBBIE: I missed you. So, I s'pose . . . I sort of hoped you'd miss me.

MARK: Yeah. Right.

ROBBIE *moves to* MARK. *They kiss.*

ROBBIE *moves to kiss* MARK *again.*

MARK: No.

ROBBIE: No?

MARK: Sorry.

ROBBIE: No. That's OK.[159]

In those two EVENTS (the kiss and the non-kiss) – and indeed in the momentary PAUSE which must certainly exist between those two EVENTS – Robbie and Mark's lives change. EVENTS and how we respond to them are the keys to deep psychological understanding. As Stanislavsky suggested to his students:

> The basic task for the initial period of rehearsal is to understand the basic events, not becoming distracted by trivia which may lead one off to one side, to understand what the *action* and *counter-action* are, i.e. to define the dramaturgical conflict stemming from our deep analysis.[160]

In the incident with Robbie and Mark, Robbie's ACTION of the first kiss is greeted by Mark's COUNTER-ACTION of reciprocating the kiss. In his ACTION of the second kiss, he's greeted by Mark's COUNTER-ACTION of rejecting the second kiss. If you (as Robbie) were to actively analyse with another actor (as Mark) the EVENTS surrounding the two kisses, you'd be able to 'define the dramaturgical conflict' by experiencing what exactly unfolds between you as you improvise the encounter. And for any two actors, the nuances would subtly change.

In many ways, there may seem to be similarities between EVENTS and PRESSING ISSUES (see BITS above), and yet there's an important difference. An EVENT is a happening without which the scene cannot unfurl. The PRESSING ISSUE is an off-stage occurrence which serves almost to heat the scene like a Bunsen burner. So, for example, the PRESSING ISSUE in *A Doll's House* could be considered to be the fact that Nora has forged her husband's signature. We don't see that occurrence, but it sits like a smouldering coal beneath the cauldron of her life. An EVENT takes place when a letter arrives from Krogstad in which he reveals the forgery, and suddenly Nora's whole mode of behaviour radically shifts. In this encounter from *Shopping and Fucking*, Mark's PRESSING ISSUE is that he broke rehab rules and had a sexual liaison with a fellow patient: this is what he needs to disclose to Robbie, hence his inability to reciprocate the kiss.

Sometimes in a scene, the EVENT doesn't even take place. Let's look at the little interchange between Varya and Lopakhin in Act 4 of *The Cherry Orchard*, when Ranevskaya has sent Varya into the living room to be proposed to by Lopakhin. The imminent PRESSING ISSUE is the recent sale of the estate and everyone's departure; the scene is set up so that the EVENT we're expecting is a proposal of marriage:

A pause. Offstage, stifled laughter and whispering. VARYA *finally enters.*

VARYA (*inspects the luggage at some length*): That's strange, I can't find it anywhere . . .

LOPAKHIN: What are you looking for?

VARYA: I packed these myself, and now I can't remember.

Pause.

LOPAKHIN: So where are you off to now, Miss Varvara?

VARYA: Me? I'm going to the Ragulins. I've agreed to look after
the house for them . . . I'll be a sort of housekeeper.

LOPAKHIN: And that's in Yashnevo? That'll be about fifty miles
from here.

A pause.

So, life in this house is over now.

VARYA (*examining the luggage*): Where on earth is it? . . . Maybe I
packed it away in the trunk . . . Yes, life's finished in this
house . . . there'll be nothing left . . .

LOPAKHIN: And I'm off to Kharkov now . . . by the same train.
I've a lot of business on hand. I'm leaving Yepikhodov here to
look after the place. I've taken him on.

VARYA: Not really!

LOPAKHIN: This time last year we'd already had snow, if you
remember, and now it's so mild and sunny. It's cold
nonetheless . . . three degrees below.

VARYA: I haven't looked.

A pause.

Our thermometer's broken anyway . . .

A pause.

Someone calls through the door from outside: 'Mr Lopakhin!'

LOPAKHIN (*as if he had been waiting for this call*): Just coming!
(*Hurriedly exits.*)

VARYA *is sitting on the floor, lays her head on a bundle of dresses,
and begins quietly sobbing. The door opens, and* RANEVSKAYA
tentatively enters.

RANEVSKAYA: Well?

A pause.

We have to go.[161]

This beautiful and delicate interchange is based entirely on an EVENT which doesn't take place: Lopakhin doesn't propose. Chekhov cleverly juxtaposes the characters' inciting ACTIONS and COUNTER-ACTIONS. From one PERSPECTIVE, we could say that Varya's inciting ACTION is to find the OBJECT that she claims she's looking for (after all, she starts the scene by swooping in with a vast amount of energy). Lopakhin's COUNTER-ACTION is to ask her to marry him. Chekhov provides two big pauses in which Varya's inciting ACTION stops, but Lopakhin's COUNTER-ACTION doesn't kick in: Lopakhin simply hasn't got the bottle to propose.

From another PERSPECTIVE, we could say that Lopakhin's inciting ACTION is to propose, but the force of Varya's feigned COUNTER-ACTION of looking for the lost OBJECT takes the wind out of his sails and he never quite finds the impetus again. Either way, the cleverness of the scene is that it's built around a 'non-EVENT', and yet it holds the audience's rapt attention.

*

So far in this exploration of ACTIVE ANALYSIS, we've read the scene (Step 1) and we've done some basic MENTAL RECON-NAISSANCE including identifying the main EVENT and possibly locating the PRESSING ISSUE which might be underlying the main EVENT (Step 2). That's enough discussion. It's time to start improvising, and that requires the actors – through a series of SILENT ÉTUDES – to get each other in each other's GRASP.

Silent *études* and Grasp

As we saw with the METHOD OF PHYSICAL ACTIONS, the first stage of improvising isn't too scary as you don't have to say anything: it involves SILENT ÉTUDES.

What exactly does a SILENT ÉTUDE entail?

A number of things – and, at the same time, nothing.

During the course of his investigations into acting, Stanis-lavsky tried all sorts of SILENT ÉTUDES, some of which can sound pretty wacky if you read them cold. When he was rehearsing Turgenev's *A Month in the Country* in 1909, he had his actors moving through a scene either in utter silence or mouthing their lines silently, and sometimes communicating with nothing but the looks in their eyes. Sometimes only the key words of a scene were spoken. Sometimes the actors were encouraged to 'radiate' their mental states to each other, while sitting on their hands to stop them from gesticulating what they really wanted to say. There were all manner of experiments, from the esoteric to the downright weird. But at the core of most of them was a very important idea: that we communicate masses of information simply through our eyes. As Stanislavsky said to his actors towards the end of his life:

> Trust your eyes and you will guarantee audience
> attention. Be most aware of each other. Observe each
> other constantly and you will always guess when one
> finishes a sentence or completes a thought, although
> he never speaks it aloud.[162]

He understood that when actors work beyond the spoken word, they can tap into a deeper level of communication. The crux of a SILENT ÉTUDE is what Stanislavsky called 'communion' or 'radiation' (see below), allied to which is something called GRASP.

GRASP is a term embedded in Chapter 10 of *An Actor Prepares* entitled 'Communion', and I'd read the book nine times before I really noticed the term, let alone fully understood its impact and usability as a tool. I was already familiar with 'communion' and 'radiation', which cover similar territory, but both words were rather alienating and inaccessible. GRASP, on the other hand, seemed far more immediate and understandable. As Stanislavsky puts it, GRASP

> is what a bull-dog has in his jaw. We actors must have
> that same power to seize with our eyes, ears and all
> our senses. If an actor is to listen, let him do it
> intently. If he is called upon to smell, let him smell

hard. If he is to look at something, let him really use his eyes. But of course this must all be done without unnecessary muscular tension.[163]

At the heart of GRASP is the idea that you don't just communicate through words and gestures, but also through 'invisible radiations of will, vibrations which flow back and forth between two souls':[164]

> You experience an emotional state and you can make others, with whom you are in communion, do the same.

> A great and inveterate mistake made by actors is to believe that only what is visible and audible to the public, in the wide expanse of the theatre building, is of scenic quality.[165]

Real ACTIVE ANALYSIS goes beyond the audible and deep into the visual, as it plunges into the heart of ensemble interaction. In a SILENT ÉTUDE, you read every tiny detail of information that your partner gives you through their eyes, nostrils, eyebrows, breathing pattern, small step towards you, flinch away from you, tremor of the little finger, flutter of the left hand. It's a kind of litmus test of the scene, finding out exactly what's going on *between* two people – both actors and characters – and what's happening *under* the text. To be that tuned in to your partner requires immense focus and willing vulnerability, but it also requires a desire to take from your partner all the information they're offering both consciously and unconsciously. That means actually exchanging energies with them and getting them in your GRASP.

There's nothing esoteric or weird in this idea. We've all experienced how powerful a performance can be when two exciting actors are genuinely interacting on stage or in front of the camera – the electricity is tangible. When they're in each other's GRASP, they really listen, they really respond, they catch every nuance, they sense every movement. They are playful, alert, open in a childlike way, and up for the adventure of performance. They don't care about 'getting it right' (whatever that might mean) – because in exciting performances, there is only one way to get it right, and that's to respond to what's happening here and now, right in the moment of interaction.

These actors are also in their *own* GRASP. They're responding to their own inner impulses and breathing patterns, the pumping of their own adrenalin, their delight at being in front of a live audience or a mesmerised camera. GRASP is intoxicating and effortless, it's dangerous and creative, it's aesthetic and anarchic. But that anarchy isn't disruptive, it's collaborative and sexy. And it's truly absorbing. For Stanislavsky:

> Grasp does not in any way signify unusual physical exertion, it means greater inner activity.

> An actor must learn to become absorbed in some interesting, creative problem on the stage. If he can devote all his attention and creative faculties to that he will achieve true grasp.[166]

Getting yourself in your own GRASP and then magnetising your partner into that GRASP isn't hard work; it appeals to what Michael Chekhov called 'quality of ease'. The contact is intense but effortless, as really you're in nothing more than a natural state of creative curiosity and play. And if the script is good, the process is even more effortless:

> The main inner current of a play produces a state of inner grasp and power in which actors can develop all the intricacies and then come to a clear conclusion as to its underlying fundamental purpose.[167]

In other words, it's a two-way street. With a good sense of GRASP in ACTIVE ANALYSIS, you can uncover all sorts of intricacies about the play. And if the play is full of all sorts of intricacies, then your sense of GRASP will be all the more powerful.

In summing up the three most important features of the creative process, Stanislavsky cited GRASP as number one, followed by the THROUGH-LINE OF ACTION and the SUPER-OBJECTIVE. Since the references to GRASP come right in the middle of the chapter in *An Actor Prepares* on 'communion', we need to look at 'communion' or CONNECTION in relation to GRASP, and understand how the two tools interdepend.

Connection (see Preface)

Stanislavsky describes GRASP in quite robust terminology, whereas his description of CONNECTION is rather more esoteric. CONNECTION (like GRASP) is dependent on

> those impressions which you get from direct, personal intercourse with other human beings. This material is difficult to obtain because in large part it is intangible, indefinable . . . To be sure, many invisible, spiritual experiences are reflected in our facial expression, in our eyes, voice, speech, gestures, but even so it is no easy thing to sense another's inmost being, because people do not often open the doors of their souls and allow others to see them as they really are.[168]

Yet that's what you've got to do: open yourself up for your partner to really see you, and *vice versa*. It's a very intimate dialogue with your fellow actors. As Stanislavsky says, when we're in CONNECTION, we use our eyes, faces, vocal timbres, hands and fingers, our whole bodies are drawn into the exchange. Personally, I'd say it's almost as good as fine love-making! And this vibrant exchange of energies continues beyond your own lines in the script, so that it exists throughout your whole performance; between you and your fellow actors, there should be an unbroken dialogue, albeit partly silent.

Despite its sex appeal, it's curious that so few actors genuinely commit to establishing real CONNECTION between each other. Probably because it's actually quite hard work, and going through the 'theatrical motions' can be much easier. As Stanislavsky opines:

> We are supposed to use the feelings and thoughts
> created by the playwright. It is more difficult to
> absorb this spiritual material than to play at external
> forms of non-existing passions in the good old
> theatrical way.
>
> It is much harder truly to commune with your partner
> than to *represent* yourself as being in relation to him.
> Actors love to follow the line of least resistance, so
> they gladly replace real communion by ordinary
> imitations of it.[169]

Though it's not always the actor's fault. Even one hundred
years later, very little conventional actor-training seems to
focus on developing a sense of 'communion' or CONNECTION
between actors. If you haven't had the opportunity to
experience it in your training, how can you do otherwise in
your professional practice than 'replace real communion by
ordinary imitations of it'?

So how can we help ourselves?

First of all, through eye contact – which, as we've seen with
GRASP, is a vital starting point.

Then through the word itself. And the word is very powerful
(as we'll see with VERBAL ACTION below). Once a word has been
emitted into the ethersphere, there's no retrieving it. The late-
night phone call. The urgent text message. The invidious email.
The impassioned letter. The whispered promise. The shouted
threat. The loaded question. The drunken confession. Make
any one of these communications and the course of events can
change beyond expectation.

You see, the word is immeasurably powerful. And yet how
often as actors do we utter our lines with scant regard for the
true impact of what we're actually saying? Or, indeed, how
often do we hear our acting partners' words and *pretend* it's the
first time we've heard them, but without really absorbing on a
psycho-physical level the weight of what has just been said?
CONNECTION is mighty, whether it comes via the spoken word
or the silent exchange of energies. As a result, it requires a high

level of attention, and the words you speak have to fly like arrows:

> When you speak to the person who is playing opposite
> you, learn to follow through until you are certain your
> thoughts have penetrated his consciousness. Only
> after you are convinced of this and have added with
> your eyes what could not be put into words, should
> you continue to say the rest of your lines. In turn, you
> must learn to take in, each time afresh, the words and
> thoughts of your partner. You must be aware today of
> his lines even though you have heard them repeated
> many times in rehearsals and performances. This
> connection must be made each time you act together,
> and this requires a great deal of concentrated
> attention, technique, and artistic discipline.[170]

You might argue that Stanislavsky makes it sound rather like hard work, but it isn't really. As we saw in Chapter 1, 'artistic discipline' and 'concentrated attention' go hand in hand with a burning desire to tell this particular story in front of this particular audience (live or camera) in dialogue with these particular actors and playing these particular OBJECTIVES. When you love your work, DISCIPLINE, CONCENTRATION AND ATTENTION, and certainly CONNECTION are no big deal.

In fact, when there's no genuine CONNECTION going on between yourself and your partner, it can be almost painful and creatively debilitating. Stanislavsky recognised these situations only too well:

> What torture to play opposite an actor who looks at
> you and yet sees someone else, who constantly adjusts
> himself to that other person and not to you. Such
> actors are separated from the very persons with whom
> they should be in closest relationship. They cannot
> take in your words, your intonations, or anything else.
> Their eyes are veiled as they look at you. Do avoid

this dangerous and deadening method. It eats into you
and is so difficult to eradicate![171]

One of the easiest ways to eradicate 'dis-connection' is
through ACTIVE ANALYSIS. Because the rehearsal process
begins with *improvisation*, there is only one way in which you
can go about an ÉTUDE – silent or otherwise – and that's by
absolutely listening to all your fellow actors. After all, you
really don't have any idea what they might do or say next.
When you're improvising, CONNECTION becomes unavoidable,
because – like a game of chess – you're constantly penetrating
your partner's next move. The result is that 'a parallel interchange of currents' (as Stanislavsky calls it) exists beneath
the words:

> It is like an underground river, which flows continuously
> under the surface of both words and silences and
> forms an invisible bond between subject and object.[172]

Like a river, that 'interchange of energies' endlessly adjusts in
order to negotiate the various obstacles which might be thrown
up by your fellow actors in the course of your improvisation.
And the way to preserve your sense of TRUTH is to go with
whatever's happening 'HERE, TODAY, NOW'.

'Here, today, now'

The basis of your improvisations in ACTIVE ANALYSIS is that
you needn't be afraid of just getting up and giving the scene a
go. It doesn't matter how much or how little information from
the script you've retained in your memory at each stage in the
rehearsal process; anything really goes.

However . . .

To be this free and confident, there has to be an atmosphere
of immense liberation and experimentation in the rehearsal
room. I know from my own experience the icy chill of fear that
can percolate your innards when you're asked to get up and
improvise a scene in your own words. And yet, there's a sure-

fire way of dispelling that fear: you just have to be entirely assured that whatever you have in your imagination and intuition 'HERE, TODAY, NOW' is all that you need to actively analyse the scene.

This is the crux of 'starting from yourself' and 'merging with the character'. The character isn't 'out there' somewhere – meaning that, until you've acquired all the information, you won't be able to play it. 'HERE, TODAY, NOW' you have all you require to fuel your process. You don't have to know the play inside out, you don't have to carry reams of research in your head when you walk onto the rehearsal-room floor, you don't even have to know any of the lines. You begin with yourself, and from there you allow your IMAGINATION to do the rest of the work for you. You place yourself in the GIVEN CIRCUM-STANCES. You ask yourself what *you* would do 'if' . . . and from that transference of *self* into *circumstance*, you turn your ATTEN-TION towards your partner. Simply focus your ATTENTION on your onstage partner and open yourself to the limitless nuances of that exchange. Your partner is your main resource, not your own memory of the script. And if you're both mutu-ally relying on each other to keep the improvisation going, then true dialogue and real listening can't help but evolve.

But the process isn't wayward. As with the METHOD OF PHYSICAL ACTIONS, don't forget the key Steps (4) and (5): after each improvisation, you return to the script and check the discoveries you made in the ÉTUDE against the contents of the writer's words by discussing your improvisation and then re-reading the scene. Through this constant checking and re-reading, you can surreptitiously mutate your 'HERE, TODAY, NOW' knowledge step by step into the life of the character.

As ever, the LOGIC AND SEQUENCE of the exchange with your partner is very important, but that LOGIC AND SEQUENCE comes from your attentive interaction with them. So don't consciously make life easy for each other. Just because you may know parts of the scene and therefore know what ought to happen next, don't resort to trusty formulae and 'make-believe truth'. If your partner doesn't do what they need to do in order for the scene-as-written to proceed, you can only go with what they offer you 'HERE, TODAY, NOW'. If you genuinely respond to what they do, that genuine response will provide the LOGIC AND SEQUENCE of *this* particular encounter. Such a quality of listening and responding is far more important in the early stages of ACTIVE ANALYSIS than any accuracy arising from pure memory. Little by little, you'll work your way as part of an ensemble towards the most logical and sequential MISE-EN-SCÈNE for the scene by constantly returning to the table – and the script – after each impro- visation to discuss what unfurled. And these steps (Step 4: Discuss the impro, and Step 5: Return to the script) are absolutely vital in order to

> think through everything that [the actors] have
> discovered, to check exactly how they have fulfilled
> the dramatist's idea, to share their living experience
> acquired in the process of the work, to receive replies
> from the director to the questions that have arisen in
> their minds, to think through the author's text with
> still greater depth, noting that which was not true
> once again, to seek through action a fusion with the
> role.[173]

You'll even find that returning to the table after each impro- visation begins to create its own irresistible energy. As you realise how close you're coming to the actual structure and scenario of the scene, you'll be bursting to get up and give the scene another go. You'll want to take all the new information that you've gleaned from the script 'HERE, TODAY, NOW' and feed it into a new improvisation.

As your 'HERE, TODAY, NOW' comes closer to the writer's text, you can start to fine-tune your merger with the role. And this is where two more tools from the kit come in particularly handy: JUSTIFICATION and ADAPTATION.

Justification and Adaptation

All along we've stressed that everything you do in your performance is for a purpose. And that purpose can be subtle. Let's take Varya and Lopakhin in Act 4 of *The Cherry Orchard*: Varya comes into the room supposedly looking for something that she has lost. She knows that really she's distracting herself from Lopakhin's proposal, so she has to find a JUSTIFICATION which will also convince him that she's here on a mission and that she hasn't just been sent in by her mother in order to be proposed to. Chekhov has given a very specific physical activity to the character, thereby giving her a sense of purpose in an otherwise embarrassing situation and enabling her to 'justify' her presence in the room.

ADAPTATION (sometimes called 'adjustment') is similar to JUSTIFICATION but subtly different. ADAPTATION could be re-termed 'a constant state of improvisation'. Even when he required his actors to find an accurate and *repeatable* 'score of physical actions' with the METHOD OF PHYSICAL ACTIONS, Stanislavsky constantly invited his actors to be as spontaneous as appropriate in performance:

> Don't fix anything before the scene. This is the surest way to deaden the scene and your parts. The true adjustment will come on the stage as a result of the correct state of the actor in the character, from his desire to fulfil the problems of the part in the given circumstances.[174]

This hearkens back to the tool of the SIX FUNDAMENTAL QUESTIONS and the way in which the 'How?' doesn't need to be fixed. It's your right – no, your art – to adapt the 'How?'s each night to the nuances of your fellow actors and the audience. The degree of improvisation that we're talking about here is minimal: just like the constant adjustments you make to the steering wheel when you're driving. If you can dare to not fix the 'How?' beforehand, you leave a wonderful gap for the 'unexpected' and the SUBCONSCIOUS to slip in. And ADAPTATION is a useful coping strategy: a prop is missing . . . Who cares? Your onstage partner forgets his lines . . . So what? The pause you usually expect is three times as long as normal . . . Fantastic! Simply adapt to whatever is happening 'HERE, TODAY, NOW' and the 'unexpectedness of the incident will excite you and your nature will rush forward'.[175] And lo and behold! You've crossed the threshold of the SUBCONSCIOUS.

There are in fact three very subtle ways of using ADAPTATIONS.

1. You make constant adjustments to your own self, 'because we must necessarily make allowances for the state of mind we are in at any given moment'.[176] 'HERE, TODAY, NOW' – that's your starting point. So you feel vulnerable? Then use that feeling to uncover the vulnerability in your character. You feel confused? Find the way in which your character expresses confusion. You feel elated? That creative excitement may well elucidate something about the character that you hadn't thought of before. Anything does go. Like a child at play.

2. If you allow yourself room for these constant ADAPTATIONS, you can put your fellow actors in an appropriate mood to respond to you. You 'can transmit certain invisible messages, which can only be felt and not put into words',[177] thereby 'infecting' your partner with your own creative desire to be up for the adventure of improvising.

3. You can adapt your 'How?' response, as we've said, to the nuanced adjustments that you'll note in your partners' performances each time you enact the scene.

So these are the ways to use ADAPTATION: you listen to yourself; you 'infect' your partner; and you listen to your partner.

You take all the minor ADAPTATIONS of 'HERE, TODAY, NOW', and regardless of what you're given, you adapt to it and go with it, and turn it into something unexpected and creative.

That's the art of true listening, which the process of ACTIVE ANALYSIS encourages and which we talked about right at the start of *The Toolkit*. ACTIVE ANALYSIS develops your ability to listen to your self, to your onstage partner, and ultimately – when you reach the time of performance – to the audience, to the camera, and to the creative excitement aroused by the actual experience of acting itself. In the process of rehearsal, your ADAPTATIONS will never be random, because after each improvisation, you return to the script (Step 5), and thus you draw your discoveries incrementally closer to the words and actions that the writer provided.

*

By now, our improvisations (through the repeated sequence of Read / Discuss / Improvise / Discuss / Return to the script) will be picking up momentum. We've identified the EVENTS, we're in each other's GRASP, there's some good CONNECTION going on between us, our improvisational skills are developing through responding to the 'HERE, TODAY, NOW' and to our moment-by-moment JUSTIFICATIONS and ADAPTATIONS.

We can start to put more detail into our work by contemplating some of the specifics from the writer's text to build our sense of flow and dimension. This involves the tools of the SUPER-OBJECTIVE and its corresponding THROUGH-LINE OF ACTION. They in turn lead onto VERBAL ACTION and the PAUSE.

Super-objective and Through-line of action

The idea of ACTIVE ANALYSIS is that through the repeated sequence of read / discuss / improvise / discuss / return to the script, you come closer and closer to the actual words of the text in your improvisations. And the SUPER-OBJECTIVE is arguably the portal through which you can enter the writer's psyche.

The SUPER-OBJECTIVE is the ruling idea of the script. It forges a link between writer, director, actor and eventually audience. If you can identify the SUPER-OBJECTIVE, you can clarify the motivating force behind why the writer wrote the script in the first place:

> Just as a plant grows out of a seed, so too in exactly
> the same way does the writer's work grow out of his
> independent thought and feeling. The thoughts,
> feelings and dreams of the writer, with which his life
> is filled and which agitate his heart, put him onto the
> path of creativity. They become the basis of the play.
> It is for them that the writer writes his literary work.
> All of his life experience, his joys, his griefs, which he
> himself has borne and observed in his life, become the
> basis of the dramatic work. It is for the sake of them
> that he takes up his pen.[178]

If you can clarify what the writer's SUPER-OBJECTIVE may be, you and the director can begin to unify all the fragmented BITS of action and small OBJECTIVES throughout the script into one coherent whole. Identifying the writer's SUPER-OBJECTIVE prevents you concentrating exclusively on your own role: instead, you start to see the bigger picture, as well as the context in which your character exists, so that you have a concept of every character's function and journey. In this way, you're opening your improvisations out from one particular scene to understanding how those scenes fit together to create the arc of the script. As with an OBJECTIVE, the SUPER-OBJECTIVE is usually expressed as 'I want to . . .': it simply has greater magnitude than a scene-by-scene OBJECTIVE.

Personally, I have ambivalent feelings about the SUPER-OBJECTIVE. In my experience as an actor and director, I've never found it's something we've touched on in rehearsals. In fact, I've actually found that when it comes to theatre, a play's SUPER-OBJECTIVE doesn't really emerge until you put the production in front of a live audience. Their responses reflect back to you the dominant drive of the play and how the cumulative effect of the various actions shapes their overall experience. In terms of television, the SUPER-OBJECTIVE is even less easy to fathom. With soaps, series and serials, there's a host of writers, and their shared SUPER-OBJECTIVE may well be, 'We want to keep the audience tuned in'.

Whatever complexities it presents us with today, the SUPER-OBJECTIVE was one of the tools that Stanislavsky insisted that his actors used. In the final years of his experimentation, he even upheld the belief that anything an actor did on stage which *didn't* lead to the SUPER-OBJECTIVE was unnecessary.[179] For Stanislavsky, identifying the SUPER-OBJECTIVE unified the actors and director in their understanding of a play. It also unified all the acting processes within the actor: Stanislavsky maintained that if the actor pursued the SUPER-OBJECTIVE through a coherent line of ACTIONS, all the harvest of his acting 'system' would 'be brought about subconsciously, miraculously, by nature'.[180]

So how do you identify the SUPER-OBJECTIVE?

If the writer is still alive – why not ask him or her what their SUPER-OBJECTIVE was in writing the script in the first place? This is exactly what I did with David Hare and *The Permanent Way*. As Hare put it:

> For me, there are two axes in [*The Permament Way*] which became very interesting for me: one is the question of honour and dishonour – what it means to behave honourably and what it means to behave dishonourably, and the excitement of the contrast between the two is what animates the play.
>
> The other is suffering: it's the degree to which human beings distinguish . . . between suffering that's avoidable and suffering that's unavoidable, and what

they should be doing about suffering that's avoidable.
I wanted to study how these [rail] accidents could have
been avoided, and how people dealt with the results of
these accidents. And once those two ideas became clear
to me as the subjects of the play, then I was away. The
'super-objective' is quite simply: to express the anger
of people who have suffered unnecessarily and been
humiliated basically by the way they've been treated.[181]

As an actor, this was remarkably useful for me to know. I took
Hare's SUPER-OBJECTIVE idea of anger, and I related it to the
story told by my character, the Second Bereaved Mother. The
tool became particularly significant for me in a scene which
re-enacted Lord Cullen's Public Inquiry into the 1999
Paddington crash. Both Hare and the director, Max Stafford-
Clark, had impressed upon me that the Cullen Inquiry was the
Second Bereaved Mother's chance to express her anger without censorship. She could use the formal inquiry to channel
her private anger about the death of her son into public
outrage at the incompetence of those involved in the rail priva-
tisation. I therefore took the energy of Hare's SUPER-
OBJECTIVE and injected it into the choices I made for my
moment-by-moment ACTIONS.

If the writer isn't at hand to ask, then Stanislavsky suggests
you look at what the protagonist does. To a large extent, he or
she will be the 'principal mouthpiece of the play's ideas'.[182]
Having located it, you then need to be sure the emphasis of the
SUPER-OBJECTIVE is correct. Stanislavsky gives the example of
Molière's *The Hypochondriac* to illustrate what he means. If the
SUPER-OBJECTIVE of the principal character, Argan, is expressed as 'I want to be ill', the production becomes tragic. On
the other hand, if the SUPER-OBJECTIVE is expressed as 'I want
to be considered to be ill' then the play should fulfil its comic
potential.

Although the protagonist will give you a big clue as to the
overriding SUPER-OBJECTIVE of the play, of course each character has his or her own SUPER-OBJECTIVE, which will usually

relate to that of the protagonist in some way. And that's what you have to pursue through your moment-by-moment ACTIONS.

Whether you appeal directly to the writer or you look at the protagonist's actions, labelling the SUPER-OBJECTIVE mustn't be a dry, intellectual activity. Stanislavsky wards off directors who 'know the game' and can quickly come up with some clever label, which they then download on to the actors:

> An actor cannot be fattened like a capon. His own
> appetite must be tempted.[183]

The SUPER-OBJECTIVE should be 'irresistible', inciting and exciting all three INNER PSYCHOLOGICAL DRIVES, so that it's thought-provoking, *emotionally* charged, and it passionately propels you into *action*. In Stanislavsky's words:

> Defining the super-objective is a profound penetration
> into the writer's spiritual world, into his idea, into
> those motivating principles which have moved the
> author's pen. The super-objective must be conscious,
> emerging from the mind, from the actor's artistic
> *thought*. It must be *emotional*, provoking the whole of
> his human nature and finally it must be *strong-willed*,
> emerging from his mental and physical essence. The
> super-objective must awaken the artistic imagination
> of the artist, must arouse his belief, must arouse the
> whole of his psychic life . . . Without the subjective
> experiences of the person creating it, it is dry, dead.
> It is essential to seek responses in the artist's soul in
> order that the super-objective and the role should
> become living, quivering, shining with all the colours
> of authentic human life.[184]

The SUPER-OBJECTIVE provokes 'complete surrender, passionate desire, unequivocal action',[185] and just like an OBJECTIVE – but on a magnified scale – pursuing it is about wanting something so badly that you can't resist the desire to get up and act upon it.

To help this ardent pursuit of the SUPER-OBJECTIVE, we have the THROUGH-LINE OF ACTION (sometimes translated as 'through action'). As Stanislavsky puts it:

> For the actor, the through action is the *active attainment of the super-objective*. Thus the super-objective and the through action represent *creative goal* and *creative action*, which contain in themselves all the thousands of separate, fragmentary objectives, ['bits'], actions in a role.

> The super-objective is the quintessence of the play. The through-line of action is the leitmotif which runs through the entire work. Together they guide the creativeness and strivings of the actor.[186]

There's no script without a SUPER-OBJECTIVE (after all, that's what gave birth to the script in the first place). And there's no achievement of the SUPER-OBJECTIVE without a THROUGH-LINE OF ACTION. Given these two facts, it's fair to say the whole acting experience (certainly in theatre) is based on these two tools. Together, the SUPER-OBJECTIVE and the THROUGH-LINE OF ACTION are the fundamental components which 'inspire an actor to act'.[187] By means of the THROUGH-LINE OF ACTION, you manifest externally your inner, psychologically driven SUPER-OBJECTIVE. It

> totally unifies all the elements. It goes right through them like a thread through separate beads, and it directs them towards the general super-objective. If the actor does not thread together all his actions into the unified core of the through-line of action, which is leading him towards the super-objective, then the role will never be played in such as way that people talk about it as a serious artistic victory. More often than not the actor is confronted by artistic defeat when he replaces the through-line of action with more trivial inessential actions.[188]

And this is where the ÉTUDE REHEARSALS of ACTIVE ANALYSIS really come into their own. Through the process of improvisation, you test out various THROUGH-LINES OF ACTION (a little like the 'score of physical actions' in the METHOD OF PHYSICAL ACTIONS) and you find the one which most logically and coherently helps you to achieve your character's OBJECTIVES. You ditch the trivial and you harbour the essential. Your decisions aren't made cerebrally: this is a visceral, experiential and intensely psycho-physical voyage of discovery that you're making.

In brief:

- The SUPER-OBJECTIVE links the writer, director, actors and audience.

- The SUPER-OBJECTIVE is essentially the reason why the writer wrote the script in the first place.

- The SUPER-OBJECTIVE can usually be identified by analysing the protagonist's actions.

- The SUPER-OBJECTIVE often doesn't become entirely clear until you put the play in front of an audience.

- The SUPER-OBJECTIVE unifies all the components of Stanislavsky's 'system'.

- The SUPER-OBJECTIVE must be mentally stimulating, emotionally charged and able to propel you into ACTION.

(All these could apply just as equally to TV and film.)

In brief:

- The THROUGH-LINE OF ACTION is the means by which you physically manifest the SUPER-OBJECTIVE.

- The THROUGH-LINE OF ACTION unifies all the smaller BITS and OBJECTIVES throughout a script.

- By means of the improvisations which comprise ACTIVE ANALYSIS, you discover the THROUGH-LINE OF ACTION and test its validity.

(A THROUGH-LINE OF ACTION also applies to TV and film – and it can be especially useful if scenes are filmed out of sequence. If you've charted your THROUGH-LINE OF ACTION, you can fathom the emotional pitch that your character has reached in every scene. Then it won't bother you in what order the scenes are filmed, you can just drop into that 'pitch'.)

Finding an appropriate THROUGH-LINE OF ACTION to manifest a script's SUPER-OBJECTIVE shouldn't be too troublesome if you attentively apply the process of ACTIVE ANALYSIS. All the necessary discoveries will arise out of your improvisations if you really do work with whatever you have 'HERE, TODAY, NOW'. Of course, those discoveries are not just dependent on what you do physically. All along we've talked about 'listening' and 'creating the living word', so time now to turn to the power of VERBAL ACTION.

Verbal action

First things first: VERBAL ACTION always depends on physical ACTION. VERBAL ACTION is as potent as physical ACTION. And for Stanislavsky the fundamental basis of dramatic art was how to present through the bodies of the actors the ideas of the writer's TEXT.

As I mentioned in Chapter 1, the question of how to make words sound 'truthful' had been occupying the greatest minds of the international theatre for many, many years. Stanislavsky's own contribution to the debate was that learning the lines by rote actually *obscured* the meaning of the words, rather than bringing actor and audience *closer* to their meaning.

He was also canny enough to realise that if a script is very well written, it instantly ignites your creative journey as an actor, so there's a tendency with a good script to think that all you have to do is learn the lines and the play will stand up by itself. And, actually, when you look at Shakespeare or a play of such rapid rhythmic genius as a David Mamet masterpiece, you wonder what more you *need* to do other than learn the lines and let the play stand up by itself.

For Stanislavsky, it was all quite simple: words and ACTIONS served exactly the same purpose – to enable a performer to fulfil their character's OBJECTIVE. And that was only possible if the actors approached the rehearsal process with their whole bodies, their vibrant imaginations and their quivering viscera: in other words, they didn't leave all the work to their heads. Hence his emphasis on ACTIVE ANALYSIS.

Let's just recap the improvisation process so far, so we can see how VERBAL ACTION kicks into play.

Beginning with the tools of THE MAGIC 'IF' and 'HERE, TODAY, NOW' – i.e. 'What would I do *here, today, now* if I were in these circumstances?' – you read the scene and discuss it (Steps 1 – 2). You then start to improvise the text (Step 3).

At first there may be very little language, as you save your words until your inner impulse is so strong the only way forward is to express verbally what you want in the GIVEN CIRCUMSTANCES. Your own words might feel clumsy at first: but don't worry, and try not to censor yourself. You're the explorer of a character, not the author of a script. If you work from the premise that in life we usually speak for some productive, expedient purpose, then as long as you apply the same premise to your improvisations, your awkwardness as an actor should be fairly transitory.

Each time you improvise the scene, you draw closer and closer to the text as written. But this knowledge doesn't come from a cerebral learning process, it percolates through you on an holistic and experiential level, as you discuss the impro (Step 4) and return to the scene (Step 5).

If in any improvisation you find that one actor is much closer to the actual words of the text than the other, that's fine. As long as you all work in the 'HERE, TODAY, NOW' and simply respond to each moment as it arises, there shouldn't be a problem. Nor does it matter if one of you introduces a piece of text from a different scene. This mis-positioning of text can often illuminate a particular preoccupation or undercurrent within the character, one that you might not have uncovered otherwise. The 'HERE, TODAY, NOW' gives you the opportunity for all kinds of unexpected discoveries as you explore the script's VERBAL ACTION through the improvisations.

Once again, THE ROLE OF THE DIRECTOR is incredibly important. All the time, he has to ensure your improvised text doesn't become *learnt* text. Each new improvisation should bring you one step closer to the actual words, rather than embedding in your memory your own approximation of the written script. As Knebel says:

> Sometimes you encounter a particular phenomenon
> which puts a break on the work. After repeating the
> *étude* two or three times, the actor begins to fix his
> improvised text. It is essential to struggle against this.
> As soon as the *étude* becomes a repetition, not a search
> for a new and more profound sense of the image, it is
> vital to cut off immediately these attempts, which lead
> him down a false path.[189]

One thing we should be very clear about: the process of ÉTUDE REHEARSALS and the journey towards VERBAL ACTION in no way diminishes the need to be dead-letter-perfect. (I discussed this with the METHOD OF PHYSICAL ACTIONS.) Part of the discussion that goes on after each improvisation (i.e. Step 4) addresses questions such as: 'How did my language differ from or mirror the way in which the character speaks? What choices does the character make in terms of sentence structure, words, images? How did my use of language reflect that? Am I too formal at the moment? Am I too colloquial?' This issue arose when we looked at the way in which round-the-table discussions are concerned with the *choices of words* as much as with ACTIONS: these are vital GIVEN CIRCUMSTANCES. (See the 'literary plane' in reference to GIVEN CIRCUMSTANCES.) The energy that underpins a Shakespeare play or a verse drama is quite different from the energy of an episode of *Midsomer Murders*. The poetic mood and the VERBAL ACTION, which drive a character to speak in verse and not prose, give us significant clues into the character's psycho-physical make-up and the world in which the author has set the play. Your improvisations with ACTIVE ANALYSIS shouldn't reduce everything to a realistic ease. Form, genre, style are all part of the character: these elements aren't imposed on a script, they're deeply embedded as an active part of the action's landscape.

It doesn't mean that you're suddenly going to start improvising in iambic pentameters. And that wouldn't be the point anyway. Every reading of the text will bring more and more of the imagery and the TEMPO-RHYTHM of the language into both your conscious and your subliminal realms; they'll affect and influence the choices that you go on to make in each ensuing improvisation. The closer you draw to merging with the character, the more you'll find the writer's words are the most succinct and accurate means – the *only* means – of expressing what your character wants. Before long, you'll actually reach the point when you find yourself using the author's words with complete precision. This won't necessarily be an indication of your memory, but rather a revelation of how far you've progressed in mastering the character's (i.e. the author's) complex thoughts.

When you do reach this point in the course of your ÉTUDES, the director's attention to the detail of the VERBAL ACTION has to be absolutely rigorous. Maria Knebel calls the director to arms:

> All the actor's work in the process of mental
> reconnaissance all the complex process of coming to
> know the play through étude analysis is assisted by

returning to the play in the post-étude investigations, delving deeply into the role of the play . . . and creating an illustrated subtext for the play. All this will lead the actor to imperceptibly make the author's text his own. At the point where the collective has made the transition to the author's actual text, it is vital for the director to keep track of the accuracy of the delivery with total strictness and demand. He must wage a pitiless struggle against the 'approximate' text, against 'ad-libbing' which sometimes occurs with the actor. He must demand of the performer, not the mechanical assimilation of the text, but a profound and conscious knowledge of it, the full observation of the character with the author's intonation, as expressed by the whole structure of the phrase right down to the interjections and punctuation marks.[190]

VERBAL ACTION is precise. The exact rhythm, syntax, genre and style are all part of the way in which the character expresses him or herself. Any approximation will take you away from the character, not towards it. It'll render your VERBAL ACTIONS imprecise, and then they'll miss their target, leaving your performance generalised – whereas we want razor-sharp.

There's one final, crucial point to be made about VERBAL ACTION. There may well come a point when you're actually *ready to learn the lines.* In other words, the improvisations don't have to go on *ad infinitum*: once you've unlocked the inner workings of a scene, you're free to go away and learn the script. This isn't a contradiction of the 'don't learn by rote' dictum: it's simply that, if you've fully understood on a psycho-physical level the inner mechanism of a scene, then there's no point in improvising any more. The goal of improvisations is simply to get inside the part. If you've done that, then learning the lines will be effortless, and you'll find yourself grabbing greedily at the author's words.

There's no hard-and-fast rule about knowing when you've reached that moment: Stanislavsky suggests it's up to the director to sense it. And from my own experience of directing with ACTIVE ANALYSIS, it's usually very evident when the actors are ready to learn the text. They have a palpable sense of interaction, they're feeding off each other, and they clearly understand the essence of the scene. It might take only two or three ÉTUDE REHEARSALS to get to that degree of understanding: during my time of training in Russia, we performed an extract from Harold Pinter's *The Lover* after two rehearsals and a very effortless learning of the lines. My fellow actor, Mark D'Aughton, and I quickly seemed to catch the essence of the scene, and at that point, our director, Albert Filozov, whose heritage is in ACTIVE ANALYSIS, curtailed the rehearsal time and told us to go away and learn the text.

Of course, when you approach a text, there are not only the words through which you can convey your inner ACTION and VERBAL ACTION; you also have the glorious PAUSE.

The pause

There are certain tools which leap out of the kit as vital, 'Don't-Leave-Home-Without-Them' tools: the PAUSE (or 'zone of silence') is one of them. It's at the heart of ACTIVE ANALYSIS; it's essential for the 'creation of the living word', and it's the means by which you can truly listen to what's being said. It's the root of genuine onstage CONNECTION and the provoker of authentic EMOTION. As Knebel writes:

> The life of the actor in the zones of silence [i.e. 'pauses'] is directly and organically connected with inner monologues, the subtext, the 'burden' as Nemirovich-Danchenko termed it.[191]

(See below for INNER MONOLOGUES.) Unless you allow yourself some 'zones of silence' – or active PAUSES – you start to short-circuit the life-giving sequence of Action – Reaction – Decision. Stanislavsky insisted on the PAUSE because:

> The actor always cheats you during moments of surging temperament. To really measure the power of

the actor's excitement, we must direct our attention to
how he takes in the facts and events, how he evaluates
the thoughts of his partner; we must watch him during
his moments of absorption . . .[192]

Replacing 'surging temperament' with 'moments of absorption' requires you to hear *yourself* as much as your partner. It's
back to the basics of PSYCHO-PHYSICALITY, listening to your
own words, thoughts and body, as much as those of your fellow
performers. And the PAUSES give you the time to hear that
information. There should almost be the sense that when you
do speak the words of the text, they've risen up out of your
silence until the point at which you just can't hold back your
thoughts any longer. All the ideas that you need to express
pour out through your spoken words.

For Stanislavsky, there are two kinds of PAUSES: the 'logical
pause' and the 'psychological pause'.

The 'logical pause' is predominantly a technical PAUSE. It
shapes the measures of the text's phrases; in other words, it's
the means of making sense of the speech. It usually comes at
the end of a line or a stanza, and you need it to make literary
sense of a text and render it intelligible.

The 'psychological pause' adds life to the thoughts. It
manifests the SUBTEXT: it's an 'eloquent silence': [193]

If speech without the logical pause is unintelligible,
without the psychological pause it is lifeless.[194]

A 'psychological pause' can come anywhere, as long as it's
necessary and breathes life into the text.

Often a 'logical pause' coincides with a 'psychological pause',
but in either case, a PAUSE is never empty. As Nemirovich-
Danchenko put it, the function of the PAUSE is

to manifest the completion of an immediately
experienced perturbation, to prepare the outburst of
an approaching emotion, or to imply a silence charged
with intensity.[195]

It's the silent, inner continuation of one ACTION, or the preparation for a new ACTION, or even both. But one thing's for sure: it's never static. When you're rehearsing with ACTIVE ANALYSIS, you can really fathom the nature of the PAUSES. They reveal *your own character's* SUBTEXT, as well as giving you the chance to decode *the other character's* SUBTEXT. It's an intricate dialogue.

*

In our consideration of ACTIVE ANALYSIS so far, we've moved from early SILENT ÉTUDES to well-established ÉTUDE REHEARSALS; we've progressed from improvised text to absorbing the writer's script. Before we conclude our 'Approaches to Rehearsal', we'll look at a series of tools for really developing the three-dimensionality of a role through ACTIVE ANALYSIS.

Two of the tools are imagination-orientated:

- the second level
- inner monologue

And two of the tools are partner-based:

- envisaging
- the moment of orientation

All four are incredibly useful for creating the finer details in a dialogue and putting the real polish on a character.

The second level

Once the role starts to mature for you through the process of ACTIVE ANALYSIS, you can begin to develop the SECOND LEVEL. This consists of building the volume and substance of the character, ensuring it has an affecting and dynamic onstage life, which will resonate for the audience beyond the duration of the performance. In other words, the emphasis of *The Toolkit* is slightly shifting from the discoveries you make holistically about the character, towards how the actual performance of that character may eventually impact on an audience.

It was Stanislavsky's co-director, Vladimir Nemirovich-Danchenko who mainly experimented with the SECOND LEVEL, and it works very closely both with the FUNDAMENTAL QUESTION 'For what reason?' and with SUBTEXT, as well as with the idea of the PRESSING ISSUE. As Knebel describes it:

> Very often we do not reveal even strong impulses, experiences and thoughts to the gaze of outsiders. Nemirovich-Danchenko tried to reach a point where the actor would be able to make this inner line, these unexpressed thoughts, the property of the audience, not by means of external action, but by means of that internal psycho-technique that he called the 'second level' of the scenic image.

> In Nemirovich-Danchenko's understanding, the second level is the inner, spiritual 'baggage' of the character, with which the latter comes into the play. It is formed from the whole sum total of the character's impressions of life, from all the circumstances of his personal fate, and it embraces all shades of his sensations, his perceptions, thoughts and feelings.

> The presence of the well worked out 'second level' renders all the reactions of the character to the events of the play more precise, makes them more vivid and significant. It clarifies, brings out, the motives of his behaviour. It saturates the words he utters with profound meaning.[196]

Stanislavsky gives a very vivid example of what was meant by the SECOND LEVEL from Chekhov's short story, *Melancholy* in which an old Petersburg hansom cab driver, Yola, has buried his son just three days earlier:

In this ordinary cabby, people perceive only what
throws itself directly into their eyes. His cap sprinkled
with snow, his hands with large limbs mechanically
holding up the reins. It doesn't enter anyone's head
that inside Yola's bosom there is 'an enormous
sadness which knows no boundaries'. If you were to
split open Yola's chest, and if the sadness were to
pour out of it, then it would seem as if it had flooded
the whole world. But nevertheless you can't see it. It's
managed to contain itself in such an insignificant shell
that you wouldn't see it by day with a light. So what
the majority of people do not perceive, a great artist
[Chekhov] has seen, and he has led us into that world
with such expressive power, that we sense Yola's grief
almost physically . . .

The actor would have to fantasise all of Yola's life
which gave birth to this boundless, all-consuming
melancholy. This would be Yola's 'second level', and
yet externally his life would proceed modestly,
unnoticed.[197]

Both Nemirovich-Danchenko and Stanislavsky believed that it
was through the creation of a SECOND LEVEL that an actor
could create a piece of work which could affect the audience on
a profound level, stirring them, educating them, even transforming them. Of course it's perfectly possible for a spectator
to enjoy a well-articulated characterisation without a SECOND
LEVEL – you may laugh and cry with the character at various
stages on their journey. But as Nemirovich-Danchenko put it,
if an actor

succeeds in creating a deep human character, the
audience senses a deep second level, and then the
audience will say to itself, 'Aha! I've sussed it!' It is
this divination, behind the external behaviour which
makes the actor live, that is the most valuable thing in
the actor's art . . .[198]

Creating a SECOND LEVEL is about creating a breadth of experience, a volume of expression for your character. As with the FUNDAMENTAL QUESTION 'For what reason?', the SECOND LEVEL can liberate you as an actor because it allows your IMAGINATION to go in any direction you fancy. It accesses a sense of authorship and ownership of the part: it enables you to 'be a creator, not a mere narrator'. As we discussed with 'For what reason?', the audience will be oblivious to the details of your imaginative journey. But it doesn't matter. There'll be a sense of CONNECTION with your audience, a sense of some kind of life or secret existing for your character beyond the limits of the text.

Let's take the characters in *Three Sisters*. Nemirovich-Danchenko said:

> Each character bears within itself something unspoken, some concealed drama, concealed dream, concealed experience. The whole big life is not expressed in words. At some point it will suddenly burst through in some phrase in some scene, and that's when that high artistic joy which constitutes theatre will arrive.[199]

And, indeed, they do 'burst through': Solyony loves Irina and suddenly lets it out in Act 2. Chebutykin is in despair about his life and work, and suddenly lets it out by smashing the clock in Act 3. Andrey knows that his sisters despise his wife, Natasha, and he has to let it out in Act 3. We already know Natasha's 'concealed drama': she's having an affair with Protopopov.

The SECOND LEVEL works quite provocatively with the 'HERE, TODAY, NOW' in the sense that while you're making moment-by-moment ADAPTATIONS to whatever's happening onstage, you also have a sense of a future for your character. There's a dream which spurs your 'HERE, TODAY, NOW' existence. Irina's thoughts are always on the prospect of Moscow. Masha's mind becomes increasingly fixated on an imaginary future with Vershinin. Thus, the SECOND LEVEL and the 'HERE, TODAY, NOW' work together to create a power-ful and resonant dialogue between present-tense and future.

Developing the SECOND LEVEL involves acquiring a certain amount of 'inner' or 'spiritual cargo' for your character, and there are a number of tools for doing this, not least of which is the INNER MONOLOGUE.

Inner monologue

The INNER MONOLOGUE is a powerful way of linking the 'creation of the living word' with your limitless attention to your partner. Like the SECOND LEVEL, it's also very closely connected with the notion of SUBTEXT. And it's exactly what it says it is: a silent, INNER MONOLOGUE to yourself, expanding, justifying, debating, deflecting whatever's going on externally.

The INNER MONOLOGUE grew from Stanislavsky's belief that it was inappropriate for actors to limit themselves to the words proposed by the author. Just as we do in everyday life, we should be listening to our performance partners and mentally arguing or agreeing with what's being said. It's back to the notion that we only really vocalise 10% of what we think, the other 90% remains unspoken. The INNER MONOLOGUE is a means of provoking all those things we leave unsaid and really getting inside every phrase that we do choose to speak. As Knebel puts it:

> The more compressed the phrase which is evoked by
> large thoughts, the more saturated and the more
> powerful it is.[200]

When you create an INNER MONOLOGUE, you relate to your character not as literature, but as a 'living person'. For Nemirovich-Danchenko, the INNER MONOLOGUE stops actors simply staring at each other when they're waiting for their cue, because the only way you can evolve a truthful INNER MONO-LOGUE is by absolutely listening to the words of your perfor-mance partner, evaluating them, and finding an appropriate, heartfelt response. If *what* you say depends on the text, *how* you say it depends on your INNER MONOLOGUE, and if you're truly responding to your character's GIVEN CIRCUMSTANCES as you listen to your partner, then an appropriate INNER MONOLOGUE cannot fail to manifest itself. With an appropriate INNER MONOLOGUE, you should then find yourself *thinking* in the same way as the character, adopting their world view and desiring to persuade other people of that world view. In invisible ways, the INNER MONOLOGUE lures you more and more intimately towards the character's world.

For Stanislavsky, the INNER MONOLOGUE

> is the basis of any role for an actor. When this inner monologue – inaudible to an audience, but observable on the actor's face, in his behaviour, and his form of expression – has become part of the actor's consciousness, then the role is ready.[201]

If the INNER MONOLOGUE is a stream of thoughts fuelling the SUBTEXT, then parallel to it runs an inner show-reel of images, which Stanislavsky calls a series of ENVISAGINGS. Both of them vibrantly inform the spoken word and activate the potency of VERBAL ACTION.

Envisaging

As actors, we're a bit like a bout of malaria: our job is to 'infect' others – the audience and our partners, the camera and the spectator. As Stanislavsky puts it:

> Infect your partner! Infect the person you are concentrating on! Insinuate yourself into his very soul, and you will find yourself the more infected for doing so.[202]

We 'infect' through our words, and one way to keep our words infectious is to fuel them with vibrant images within our own heads, which we then strive to project into our listeners' heads.

Knebel's encapsulation of Stanislavsky's ideas about ENVISAGINGS is very useful:

> The more actively the actor is capable of seeing the living phenomena of reality behind the authorial word, of invoking inside himself a conception of the things that are being talked about, the more powerful will be his impact on the audience. When the actor himself can *see* what it is he needs to talk about and what he needs to convince his partner of on the stage, he succeeds in grabbing the audience's attention with his visions, his convictions, his beliefs and his feelings. The audience's response – that whole sphere of images and associations which may rise in its mind – also depends totally on what is put into the word, in what stands behind the word in the artist's conception and on how the word is spoken.[203]

Knebel goes on:

> When we are talking about something we have experienced in life, we always strive to make the listener see the picture which has left an impression in our consciousness. We always want the picture which we're conveying to be similar to the original. That is, similar to those visions which were evoked by one or other event in our lives. The task of every actor is to achieve the same vividness of visions on the stage.[204]

My own experiment with the tool of ENVISAGING was startlingly revealing, and again it was with reference to my performance of the Second Bereaved Mother in *The Permanent Way*. In the script, I had the lines, 'My son was totally literally destroyed': the fire had been so fierce at the train crash that nothing remained of the woman's son, not even the gold ring on his finger. As I described in THE MAGIC 'IF', I decided to go along to the memorial site at Ladbroke Grove, and, as I looked at the landscape in the bright October sun, the experience was potently provocative and extremely evocative. I had a palpable sense of what the mother must be going through. The result of my impressions was that, whenever in the course of the ten-month run I spoke the words, 'My son was totally literally destroyed', I had in my mind's eye the cold steel glint of the tracks and the bare trees, with the young man's soul or spirit or energy among them somewhere. By conjuring up that image, I endeavoured to plant in my audience's head a conception – however fleeting – of the 'total literal' destruction caused by the terrifying train crash. I felt that psycho-physically I was executing an ACTION on the audience, even though all I was doing was sitting and recounting my tale.

ENVISAGINGS have a powerful energy attached to them: you appeal to your audience's *inner eye* as much as to their *physical ear*. You want your ENVISAGINGS to be so powerful that the listener is compelled to see the world from your PERSPECTIVE. As Stanislavsky says:

> If you have this inner goal sitting inside you, then you will act with words. If you don't have this, then things won't go well. You will inevitably speak the words of the role for the sake of the words, and then the words will be bound to hit or fall upon the muscles of the tongue.[205]

We know how hard it is in everyday life to get someone to see the world through *our* eyes: how much harder is it then with words which aren't our own? Stanislavsky was firmly of the belief that if you could train your IMAGINATION to accumulate powerful images – which can be done in non-rehearsal time, just as I did with the visit to the crash site – then you can create the appropriate inner cargo for your role which is then expressed through your individual, living features.

In many ways, ENVISAGINGS and INNER MONOLOGUE, along with SUBTEXT and PAUSES, inextricably interweave, as you 'in-fect' your listener with your words, thoughts and feelings. And this artistic 'infection' should begin from the very first encounter between two charcters, using what is arguably one of the most significant – and yet frequently overlooked – of Stanislavsky's tools: the MOMENT OF ORIENTATION.

The moment of orientation

I'm sitting in the dentist's waiting room. In comes the dental assistant. Looking round the room, she asks, 'Bella Merlin?' She orientates herself to the room, even though it's a room she knows very well, and she orientates herself to me, whom she doesn't really know at all. She also orientates herself to the rest of the patients – her audience – who acknowledge her presence, await her words with bated breath, and relax when they hear that it's not their name being called. Each orientation takes but a moment, yet onstage or in front of a camera how vital those moments can be!

Chiding one of his actors as he came bounding on stage to deliver his first line, Stanislavsky declared:

> You begin with the dialogue right away, leaving out the most interesting moment – the moment of orientation, the moment they become acquainted with each other.[206]

Although a MOMENT OF ORIENTATION may be very short and barely perceptible, it marks the difference between a formal actor who's going through the motions of a choreographed MISE-EN-SCÈNE and an actor who's listening to his partner on a fully psycho-physical level. It exists in the silence and it exists in the words. It's a vital moment for seeding your character's OBJECTIVE while simultaneously trying to understand what your partner's COUNTER-OBJECTIVE might be: you really have to figure out what you want from your partner and what your partner wants from you. In the words of Stanislavsky:

> The moment of orientation, the feeling out of each other, does not end invariably when the partners enter into conversation . . . They continue to feel each other out in order to have greater influence on each other.[207]

The MOMENT OF ORIENTATION is also a means of connecting with your audience – like the dental assistant and the waiting-room people. And this is very important. Actor Miles Anderson recounted to me an experience he'd had working with the Norwegian actor Espen Skjønberg, in Ibsen's *Rosmersholm* at the Manchester Royal Exchange – the auditorium of which is built in-the-round. As Skjønberg came on for each entrance, Anderson described how there was just a tiny beat before he spoke, during which he orientated himself to the whole 360° audience, as well as to the onstage actors, with the result that everyone was lured mesmerically and instantaneously into his performance.

The MOMENT OF ORIENTATION is a wonderful tool, and launches you straight into the LOGIC AND SEQUENCE of a scene. It's a little, bitty tool, like a bradawl or a pair of tweezers – and it's just as invaluable.

*

Overview

In our 'Approaches to Rehearsal', we've acknowledged THE ROLE OF THE DIRECTOR and his or her responsibility for constructing an aesthetic and coherent MISE-EN-SCÈNE.

We've looked at the basic principles underlying the holistic processes of the METHOD OF PHYSICAL ACTIONS and ACTIVE ANALYSIS. These principles have included the gradual movement from 'self' to character through ÉTUDE REHEARSALS, including SILENT ÉTUDES. The first stages of these ÉTUDE REHEARSALS require us to:

- locate the vital EVENTS of a scene;

- get the other actors in our GRASP;

- develop a powerful sense of CONNECTION through our eyes, faces and bodies;

- allow whatever information exists in the 'HERE, TODAY, NOW' to be sufficient to kick-start our creative process;

- JUSTIFY the decisions made in the 'HERE, TODAY, NOW' of the ÉTUDE;

- ADAPT to the nuanced changes of the ÉTUDE.

Once we've laid down those vital foundations, the merger between self and character can accelerate as we:

- identify the SUPER-OBJECTIVE of the author and our character;

- discover an appropriate THROUGH-LINE OF ACTION to bring that SUPER-OBJECTIVE into being;

- realise the potency of our character's VERBAL ACTION as we come closer and closer to the author's script;

- fill the inner machinations of that script with ACTION through our PAUSES, both logical and psychological.

We've then started to add dimension and textures to our characters as our improvisations have matured, as we:

- develop a SECOND LEVEL for our character;

- substantiate the writer's script with the impulses of our INNER MONOLOGUE;

- add power to the spoken word by investing it with our ENVISAGINGS;

- ensure that every aspect of all the work so far is put into place from the very first MOMENT OF ORIENTATION.

We're now at the end of the rehearsal period. As the stages of ACTIVE ANALYSIS develop, more and more of the tools become completely interdependent and unusable without the others. As our own processes develop, our merger with the character becomes seamless, our absorption of the writer's TEXT becomes effortless, our 'embodiment' reverberates with a vivid SECOND LEVEL and an open-pored quality of listening to the nuances of the 'HERE, TODAY, NOW'. With such an open heart and a playful mind, it's time to step out in front of the audience.

3

Performance Practices

3

Performance Practices

And . . . 'Action!'

Y ou've gone through the training.
You've found a character through rehearsal.

Now it's time to get out onto that set and perform.

At this stage, it's important to remember that Stanislavsky never promised his 'system' would guarantee INSPIRATION. All he was trying to do was find some conscious means to prepare the ground in which your INSPIRATION and your SUBCONSCIOUS might appear. And that's no mean feat. Acting is a kind of work unlike any other:

> Very often the actor has to do the impossible for an ordinary man, he is defenceless before the injustice of the press and the public. He has ideals in art and makes great sacrifices to it.

> If an actor loves his work, he loves it selflessly and disinterestedly. And that calls for respect . . . Human talent, pure human aspirations, and human nerves should be handled with greater care.[208]

And that means it's the actors themselves who should be handling the 'human talent' with greater care. Stanislavsky had two pet hates. The first was actors of 'genius', who assumed that no technique was required. The second – at the opposite pole – was actors who followed a method (especially his) purely for its own sake. He believed that the blind pursuit of a 'system' was as harmful to INSPIRATION and CREATIVE INDIVIDUALITY as the nonchalance of the untrainable 'genius'.

He also means in the above quotation that the actors' 'human nerves should be handled with greater care' by the public – especially the critics. And yet we can't monitor or censor the audience's response to our work. All we can do is deliver our performances with integrity, artistry and a sense of play. It's up to them to do what they will with the results of our creative endeavours.

In this chapter, we're going to look at some tools from the kit which can serve an actor in performance. As with everything we've covered in *The Toolkit* so far, the divisions are somewhat artificial and we inevitably cross back into the realms of training and rehearsal in various respects. Which is great, because the more we can see the 'system' as holistic, the easier it is to use.

That said, there is one tool, or rather one aspect of the acting process, which can't be appreciated fully until the actual performance itself, and that of course is the AUDIENCE.

TRAY 14

PERFORMANCE COMPONENTS

The audience

Most aspects of this tool are applicable to live, rather than recorded performances; nonetheless, one or two ideas are perfectly transferable. It may seem strange to call the AUDIENCE a 'tool', and yet the way in which it can access and magnify the meaning behind a performance is as tangible as anything else in *The Toolkit*. And to some extent, the camera lens, camerawoman, film-director, and indeed everyone else on the set can be your AUDIENCE, as much as a host of spectators in a darkened auditorium.

One thing's for sure: Stanislavsky loved audiences. He didn't really mind what 'system' you used, as long as you were *never* indifferent to the AUDIENCE, as they are *always* an active part of the live performance.

So why did he build the invisible 'fourth wall' between the stage and the auditorium? Wasn't that to shut the AUDIENCE out?

No. Let's return once more to the nineteenth-century Russian theatre and those celebrities who courted the audience's approval.

Stanislavsky had grown up in an environment where the actor felt duty bound to win the crowd's fancy and to be a success whatever the cost, and he came to the conclusion that this kind of performance ultimately disempowered the actor:

> This dependence on the crowd makes [the actor] feel
> helpless, lost, stiff, tense, frightened, unnerved,
> absent-minded, and he wants to pander to the crowd
> by playing for effect. All this puts him in an unnatural
> state which we shall call an *actor's self-consciousness*. It
> is the principal obstacle to nature's creative
> freedom.[209]

The 'fourth wall' wasn't necessarily conjured up to push the AUDIENCE out: it was there to preserve 'nature's creative freedom' by reconnecting actors with a more useful onstage OBJECTIVE. That OBJECTIVE need no longer be, 'I want to impress the audience'; it could be 'I want to win Juliet's love' or 'I want to be Thane of Cawdor' or 'I want to woo Orsino'. As Stanislavsky realised from his own performance experience, the more an actor tries *to entertain the spectator* rather than *engage his onstage partner*, the more the spectator will

> sit back like a lord and wait to be entertained without
> making the slightest effort to take part in the creative
> work that is taking place before him; but . . . as soon
> as the actor stops paying any attention to him, the

spectator will begin to show an interest in him, especially
if the actor himself is interested in something on the
stage that the audience, too, finds important.[210]

It's back to the tool of GRASP: if as actors you can draw each
other into each other's GRASP, then the AUDIENCE will in turn
be magnetised towards whatever's going on on the stage. (It's a
little different on screen, as often you might find yourself
playing your close-up to the First Assistant or even to an
upturned waste-paper bin if your fellow actor has already been
broken because their shots are finished. How much stronger an
IMAGINATION do you need to create a sense of GRASP with an
upturned waste-paper bin rather than a flesh-and-blood actor?)

Yet Stanislavsky's relationship with an AUDIENCE was very
textured. For all his emphasis on the necessity of onstage GRASP
and the invention of the 'fourth wall', he put the audience right
at the fore of theatre's ability to transform people. We have a
tendency to plonk Stanislavsky and his ideas at one end of the
spectrum and Brecht and his ideas at the other, stressing that
one was into empathy and realistic psychology, the other was
into 'alienation' and political comment. In fact Stanislavsky's
social and moral conscience was extremely well-developed, and
his directives to his actors were surprisingly inflammatory:

> You should love your art because it makes it possible
> to talk to the spectator about the things he cares most
> for in life, and to make him a more useful member of
> society by embodying certain definite ideas on the
> stage in artistically creative characters. If the spectator
> obtains an answer to what is engaging his thoughts, he
> will grow fond of the theatre and will learn to look on
> it as a necessity. But if all we do in the theatre is to
> entertain him, he will come and have a look at us and
> then go away.[211]

You can't help but wonder whether one hundred years later,
we've really taken this on board. Of course, theatre now has to

compete with TV and film. But if there were always something dramatically exciting – some real GRASP between living people happening on the stage – wouldn't audiences flock to the theatre? For a performance to be 'resonant', you have to start by 'infecting' your partner. Unless you can 'infect' your partner, you make it almost impossible to touch the restless spectator sitting in the dark on K15.

Alexei Popov, one of Stanislavsky's acolytes, stresses exactly what this exchange between actor and audience is about:

> We the dramatists, directors, actors have forgotten
> that the performance is a friendly intimate talk (in the
> dark) with the spectator about life's deepest, most
> sacred and crucial problems . . .[212]

What this means in practical terms is that you've actually got two dialogues going on at any one moment in performance time: the dialogue between the characters on stage, and the dialogue between the actor and the AUDIENCE. Stanislavsky summed it up by saying:

> We are in relation with our partner and simultaneously
> with the spectator. With the former our contact is
> direct and conscious, with the latter it is indirect, and
> unconscious. The remarkable thing is that with both
> our relation is mutual.[213]

These mutual and simultaneous dialogues – the exchange of live currents between actor and actor, and between actor and AUDIENCE – are at the heart of exciting performance. And they're gloriously sexy, because they're real and unpredictable.

However . . .

If you're really going to juggle these two dialogues, you need a certain connection with your own acting process: one in which there are two key things:

- dual consciousness

- perspective

Once we've looked at these two tools, we'll consider three others for developing performance awareness:

- creative individuality
- the inner creative mood
- scenic speech

TRAY 15

FIVE TOOLS FOR DEVELOPING
PERFORMANCE AWARENESS

Dual consciousness and Perspective

At the tender age of 24, Stanislavsky described in his acting journal his performance of *The Miserly Knight*, saying:

> It's strange, when you feel you are right inside it, audience reaction is not so good; when you are in control of yourself and don't let the part take you over, it is better.[214]

Who knows how often an actor is really 'taken over' by a part? There are tales of the acclaimed British actors Jonathan Pryce and Daniel Day-Lewis both seeing their dead fathers when they were playing Hamlet. And I myself have worked with actors whose in-the-wings prep has involved all kinds of Method-manifestations – some quite magical, some quite mad. But I do believe that most actors have an inbuilt DUAL CONSCIOUSNESS, whether they're aware of it or not.

There's undoubtedly a very delicate balance between immersing yourself in the onstage action and having an inner eye and ear open to what's going on in the auditorium, the wings, the flies and the sound-booth. This balance becomes even more delicate in film acting, where the technical demands are a hundred times more complex. Obviously, with screen acting, the *visual* texture of your performance is far more important than any tangible exchange of energies between you and the audience *per se*, as your performance and the consumption of that performance don't take place at the same time. While your audience is sitting in the dark of the cinema watching you act your heart out, you're basking in the Bahamas or making your next movie or sitting at home waiting for your agent to call! At the moment of filming, however, you're looking to fix here and now a performance which will reverberate forever across cinemas and televisions without you having any 'in-the-moment' 'energetic' exchange with your spectator. Your sense of DUAL CONSCIOUSNESS has quite a different quality, but is no less vital, as you negotiate the technical challenges and keep your performance alive in bite-size morsels.

DUAL CONSCIOUSNESS actually develops long before the performance, as you analyse your own behaviour to assess what's appropriate for the character and the script. As we saw with DISCIPLINE, this process begins right at the start of actor-training. It continues into rehearsal as you build your character while simultaneously creating a natural and coherent MISE-EN-SCÈNE: one inner eye is on your process, the other inner eye is on the production. Even in performance, you never completely lose the sense of 'being yourself' on stage or in front of the camera. After all, you have nothing but your own body, imagination, emotional repertoire and voice, so how *can* you actually 'lose yourself'? It's nonsense. That said, we shouldn't deny the immense creative pleasure you can take in 'transforming' your everyday self into your character.

And that transformation is an important part of the fun of acting. Adopting the semi-fictional voice of the student Kostya in *Building a Character*, Stanislavsky describes his split focus between self and transformed being, when he played the role of the Critic in an acting exercise:

> Actually I was my own observer at the same time that another part of me was being a fault-finding, critical creature . . .

I divided myself, as it were, into two personalities.
One continued as an actor, the other was an observer.

Strangely enough, this duality not only did not
impede, it actually promoted my creative work. It
encouraged and lent impetus to it.[215]

The important note here is that the duality did not *impede*, but
rather *improved* his incarnation of the character. And that's
exactly how it should be.

So how can this duality exist? How can you utterly commit
to what you're doing and yet at the same time retain enough
detachment to 'manage' your own performance?

By immediately drawing upon two tools: one that we already
know (THE MAGIC 'IF') and a new one (PERSPECTIVE). Let's take
THE MAGIC 'IF' first.

As we know, Stanislavsky never asked his actors to *believe* in
the reality of what was going on on the stage: he actually asked
them to believe in the *possibility* of that reality. 'What would
happen *if* this was my reality? How would I behave and react
if I were to find myself in these circumstances?' The result is
that throughout the performance, the audience doesn't see a
man who *becomes* Hamlet: they see a man who places himself *in
Hamlet's* GIVEN CIRCUMSTANCES. And this is where the second
tool comes in, as it's about PERSPECTIVE.

Because you've committed yourself to the possibility of the
onstage action with such conviction, the audience can immerse
themselves wholly in what they're watching, yet you won't end
up on the psychiatrist's couch having become irredeemably
stuck inside your character. Your inner stage-manager ensures
that you're constantly monitoring the appropriate choices: that
you have a PERSPECTIVE on what you're doing.

PERSPECTIVE was very important for Stanislavsky: it's a
technical tool to be applied to all aspects of a performance. It's
really a kind of subtle 'sub-tool' of DUAL CONSCIOUSNESS: it's
the end bit that you add to your adjustable screwdriver. Every
gesture, word, thought, feeling, every exit and entrance –

however straightforward – has to carry its appropriate PER-
SPECTIVE in terms of the play as a whole.

And PERSPECTIVE has two aspects.

> The one is related to the character portrayed, the
> other to the actor. Actually Hamlet, as a figure in a
> play, has no idea of perspective, he knows nothing of
> what the future has in store for him, whereas the actor
> who plays the part must bear this constantly in mind,
> he is obliged to keep in perspective . . .

> His own perspective, as the person playing the role, is
> necessary to him so that at every given moment while
> he is on the stage he will be in a position to assess his
> inner creative powers and ability to express them in
> external terms, to apportion them and make reasonable
> use of the material he has amassed for his part.[216]

This is why you need to develop a finely tuned psycho-physical
instrument – through your actor-training and your rehearsal
processes. Then you can maintain the healthy balance between
being the *creator of your role* and the *observer of your performance* once you're out there in front of the audience.

Yet again *The Permanent Way* proved very useful for me in
understanding DUAL CONSCIOUSNESS and PERSPECTIVE. Although our rehearsal time was dedicated to everyone finding an
authentic and true-sounding connection with some very
emotional material, director Max Stafford-Clark referred to
our role *in performance* as being 'sheep-dogs'. We were there to
herd the audience gently towards particular responses. We still
laughed full-belliedly or wept real tears: everything had to have
a genuine base and a committed manifestation. But ultimately
it was the AUDIENCE who were to cry the tears and experience
the anger; we were there to 'get out of the way' and tell the
story with a narrative clarity and an artistic PERSPECTIVE.

Actually, I have my own sense of DUAL CONSCIOUSNESS and
PERSPECTIVE. There's a phrase going around academic circles
which strikes chords for some actors and alienates others: it's

'bodymind'. Quite what constitutes 'bodymind' seems up for debate. For me, the phrase *mind-body* is more useful. My 'mind-body' is a kind of imaginary inner membrane beneath my skin and over my bones. Through this membrane, I can sense whether what I'm doing in performance feels too much, too little, too forced, too relaxed. In fact, it's not dissimilar to Miles Anderson's 'thin skin'. In effect, it's my DUAL CON-SCIOUSNESS, but rather than placing it in my brain (which the word 'consciousness' implies), I experience it as a psycho-physical sensation. Did that moment *feel* right? Did those words *resonate* truly? My 'mind-body' is a kind of porous filter, the core of which sits just beneath my solar plexus, around my 'emotion-centre', and it serves as a subtle monitor of what I'm doing in performance. In effect, it's closely allied to my inner sounding-board of TRUTH which Stanislavsky advocated that actors should develop.

This leads us on to the next tool in the kit, as, through my 'mind-body', I can begin to sense when my own personality is too evident and when my character's CREATIVE INDIVIDUALITY comes to the fore.

Creative individuality

CREATIVE INDIVIDUALITY is closely connected to DUAL CON-SCIOUSNESS. It's a key word in Michael Chekhov's technique, though Stanislavsky's definition is subtly different. Chekhov's definition implies that your CREATIVE INDIVIDUALITY is a part of you which comes into the creative process and guides you towards the threshold of the SUBCONSCIOUS. While this defi-nition certainly resonates with Stanislavsky's ideas, his inter-pretation is arguably more hands-on. Right at the end of *An Actor Prepares*, Stanislavsky describes what he means by CREA-TIVE INDIVIDUALITY:

> *Our type of creativeness is the conception and birth of a
> new being – the person in the part. It is a natural act
> similar to the birth of a human being . . .* In the creative

process there is the father, the author of the play; the mother, the actor pregnant with the part; and the child, the role to be born.[217]

The 'person in the part' is your CREATIVE INDIVIDUALITY. It's comprised of your own personality. (Indeed, how could it be otherwise, when it's *your* body, emotions and imagination manifesting the role in front of the audience's eyes or the camera's lens?) Yet it's not just you playing yourself. It's the merger of your personality with the circumstances of the character to create *a new being*. Stanislavsky's portrayal of Dr Stockmann in Ibsen's *Enemy of the People* was a prime example of experiencing CREATIVE INDIVIDUALITY:

> The image and the passions of the part became my own organic ones, or rather the reverse was true: my own feelings were transformed into Stockmann's, and in the process I experienced the greatest joy an actor can ever experience, namely, the ability of speaking the thoughts of another man on the stage, of putting yourself entirely at the service of someone else's passions, and of reproducing someone else's actions as if they were your own.[218]

So how do you step into this state of CREATIVE INDIVIDUALITY?

We've already seen how to achieve it through the process of rehearsals. First of all – as is so often the case throughout *The Toolkit* – you take the MAGIC 'IF':

> From the moment of the appearance of [the Magic] *If* the actor passes from the plane of actual reality into the plane of another life, created and imagined by him.[219]

Secondly, you find the appropriate ACTIONS arising from that MAGIC 'IF', and your combination of ACTIONS (call it a 'score' or a THROUGH-LINE) enables you to move beyond your everyday self into the character as created by the writer, through the process of re-styling your inner building blocks from a chapel to a chalet, or from a mosque to a mansion.

Obviously there's an inbuilt paradox in CREATIVE INDIVIDU-ALITY. While you can't completely change your stature or features in performance despite all manner of prosthetics and make-up, you can seemingly change the composition of your personality to create this new 'person in the part'. As Stanislavsky points out, you don't *lose* your sense of individuality or personality, but rather you *find* a deeper sense of your humanity as drawn out by the writer's material.

And how does CREATIVE INDIVIDUALITY impact on performance?

If you're truly relaxed and truly listening to yourself and your fellow actors, with the total bestowal of all your playful energy on the 'HERE, TODAY, NOW', you have the chance – and you give the audience that chance – to discover and understand new things about yourself and the human condition. Real people are seen to negotiate an infinite number of life situations, using their own human raw materials as the starting point and the writer's text as the finishing point. And this is why acting can be so exciting: it's an ongoing discovery of self and human nature. If you're talking about live performance, then the longer the run, the more opportunities you have through the endless nuances of each performance to penetrate those human depths. If your involvement is in the recorded media, you have the unique chance to bring a whole range of human experiences right into the living rooms of millions of people. Each part you incarnate has the potential to take you and your audience deeper into the human psyche. For Stanislavsky:

> There is no end to the work on a part or to the actor's ability to bring it to perfection, as there is no standing still in it, if the man's own life is spent in obtaining an understanding of himself as one who reflects the whole of life in his parts.[220]

The paradox is delicious. You're playing yourself in an un-limited combination of circumstances, smelted in the furnace of your own life experiences and the collective unconscious of human kind – but you're 'becoming' someone else. This is CREATIVE INDIVIDUALITY. This is the work of the SUBCON-SCIOUS in the moment of performance. And these are wonder-ful, healthy and artistic moments of creative flight. And it's most likely to flourish at its most profound, if you're in the appropriate INNER CREATIVE MOOD.

The inner creative mood

The INNER CREATIVE MOOD evolves when you're physically relaxed and imaginatively alert, when you're mentally obser-vant and can harbour a belief in the *possibility* of what's going on onstage or on screen. If you can place yourself in the appro-priate INNER CREATIVE MOOD, then you can adapt to all the 'capricious mutations',[221] which take place in every moment of performance. And that's when acting is exciting. You're ready and willing and delighted to respond to all those changing subtleties between you and your fellow actors, across the footlights to the audience, or in response to the film director's instructions.

The INNER CREATIVE MOOD is more or less the performance equivalent of the INNER CREATIVE STATE. If the INNER CREATIVE STATE allows you to respond to your rehearsal discoveries, your INNER CREATIVE MOOD ensures you can put those discoveries across in performance.

For Stanislavsky, the INNER CREATIVE MOOD was an entirely normal state and yet at the same time a better than normal state, and he was very clear about how to create it (as I outline here – with some adaptations):

1. Arrive two hours ahead of your first entrance onto the stage (or the film-set): in this way, you can give yourself plenty of time to knead your emotional clay, to shape it as

you wish, or warm up your psycho-physical instrument so you can test its keys, pedals and stops.

2. Relax your muscles so you can rid yourself of any physical tension.

3. *Warm up your* IMAGINATION by contemplating a particular OBJECT – maybe a prop you use in the play – and seeing what new ideas your fantasy comes up with.

4. *Warm up your* CONCENTRATION AND ATTENTION by focusing on the largest 'circle of attention' which might include the furthest seat in the gods or the whole of the film-set, then reducing it to the smallest CIRCLE OF ATTENTION such as the hand-held prop or the close-up on your face.

5. *Warm up your psychology* by thinking through your various OBJECTIVES and inventing a few new imaginative fictions for your character.

6. *Warm up your physical body* by going through a few simple ACTIONS, which you execute as part of your character's MISE-EN-SCÈNE to be sure there's a sense of TRUTH in what you're doing. Indeed, British actor Michael Caine apparently spends hours in his caravan working through his moves again and again, before going onto the set to film them.

This sequence is very comprehensive. Though I can't say I've personally been as rigorous in a psycho-physical warm-up as to go through all these particular stages, I know plenty of actors, including myself, who do arrive two hours before their first appearance. After all, we each have our own way of preparing ourselves before a performance, and just being in the atmosphere of the building – theatre or film studio – can be hugely beneficial in terms of shifting the body and psyche away from the detritus of your daily life into the realm of your creative IMAGINATION.

So we're opened ourselves to our AUDIENCE, we've tapped into our DUAL CONSCIOUSNESS and our sense of PERSPECTIVE, we've allowed ourselves to evolve into a CREATIVE INDIVIDUALITY, and we've acknowledged that all of these processes are facilitated when we're in the appropriate INNER CREATIVE MOOD. In many respects, the tools in this chapter on 'Performance Practices' are quite esoteric. Before we complete our investigation of *The Complete Stanislavsky Toolkit*, we're going to turn to one final aspect of performance, which is hands-on and technical: SCENIC SPEECH. Although in previous chapters, we've considered PUNCTUATION and we've looked at VERBAL ACTION, let's just consider how the voice might work once we're in performance.

Scenic speech

Stanislavsky was known for quoting the great tragic actor, Salvini, who said there are three things an actor needs in order to be a tragedian: voice, voice and more voice. The SCENIC SPEECH department took first place at the Moscow Art Theatre, and Stanislavsky paid particular attention to the correction of sibilance, whistling, over-resonance, speech impediments and poor diction.

Of course, you have to be able to control your sounds as an actor in order to express the inner life of your character. So, for all our concern with psychology and emotions, we're going to close *The Toolkit* with something technical.

We know that despite Stanislavsky's emphasis on improvisation in ACTIVE ANALYSIS, he considered that a character's vocal patterns, rhythms, syntax and choice of vocabulary were crucial. He believed the more complex a character's inner life, the more artistic your SCENIC SPEECH should be, and the more subtle, direct, and simple should be your vocal embodiment of the script. Speaking simply and beautifully is a science in its own right with particular, immutable laws, based on *diction*, PUNCTUATION and *stressing*.

With *diction*, Stanislavsky suggested that you think of the consonants like the banks of a river through which the vowels may flow. If your consonants are weak, the banks will burst and your flow of speech will be incoherent and inarticulate. Diction is the ultimate means of conveying your performance to an audience: if they don't know what you're saying, then you might as well not say it. But more than that. On a psycho-physical level, diction and words are messages to your own inner landscape, as much as to your receiving audience or your acting partners: the very feel of the words in your mouth can give you huge amounts of visceral, sensual and psychological information. So – literally – eat your words! Chew them around your mouth, and see just how they feel. Then when you get into performance, you'll know their vibrancy and muscularity – that in turn will fuel your sense of their irreversible power.

We've seen Stanislavsky's concern in rehearsal with PUNC-TUATION as a means of gleaning information from a text. When it comes to performance, of course, PUNCTUATION con-tinues to be vital. This became particularly clear to me working with Max Stafford-Clark on *The Permanent Way*. After a num-ber of performances, Stafford-Clark noticed that all of us as actors had begun to insert full-stops in places where Hare hadn't put any in the original script. It seems to be a frequent problem in long runs of a play, and Stafford-Clark's assess-ment of the phenomenon was:

> If you put false full-stops in, then you heat up one bit of text, but at the expense of the rest, and then people stop listening. It's an actor's tendency after a while to add extra false stops in order to 'microwave' their parts. They think: a quick flick of the microwave and it'll seem boiling hot. And in fact it does, but then everything else around it gets dried up, and then the audience are being asked to respond on so many different lines that they become wary – particularly in a script as dense as *The Permanent Way*.[222]

Lesson to be learnt: don't over-punctuate!

When it comes to *stressing*, Stafford-Clark and Stanislavsky also sing from the same hymn sheet: don't overstress! It's all too easy with a piece of text to feel you should emphasise every vital image. But as with 'microwaving' full-stops, you simply end up bombarding your audience's ears with so much information they can't tell what's important and what's supplementary, so they stop listening properly. As Stanislavsky says:

> Actors often forget that the main purpose of the word is the conveying of thought, of feeling, of a conception, an image, a concept and so on. And this greatly depends on correctly distributed stresses, on the marking out of the main words. The more clearly the actor sees what he wants to say, the more miserly will be his placing of stresses. Miserliness in the placing of stresses, especially in the case of a long, difficult text with big clauses, helps the actor to convey the basic thoughts . . . An actor who does not know how to pick out a stressed word correctly will not be able to convey the precise meaning of a phrase which is a link in the chain of the development of the meaning of the text.[223]

The Permanent Way is based on verbatim accounts, so much of the language is very colloquial. As Stafford-Clark pointed out, the speeches are often padded with extraneous phrases, yet if you took those phrases away, the speech would be too bald. Their presence creates a musicality, a naturalness and a fluidity to the speeches. That said, they are only padding. Like the anacrusis in music, they're the upbeat before the next bar starts; if you give them too much weight, you pull the speech out of shape. With all written scripts, we need to dare to lightly 'throw away' certain phrases, in order to give the important pieces of text more validity.

So the advice here is: when it comes to SCENIC SPEECH in performance, be abstemious with punctuation and stresses, and you keep your audience listening.

Which brings us full circle back to where we first began: the art of true listening, and the art of great acting.

'Truthful' acting can flourish when you listen psycho-physically to yourself, to your partner, to the script, to the performance space, and to your audience. Once you're really listening, you need the liveliness of your heart to understand all the information you've heard. Then you need the expressiveness of your body to communicate all that information to your audience. This is what *The Toolkit* is for: assisting you in 'the creation of the living word' – through your body, your psyche and your soul.

The art of the word in performance is complex and textured. Because at the heart of the word lies action. Word and action. Verbal action. Physical action. Psychological action.

To create the 'living word', the active word, the reactive word: that's your challenge as an actor. From the moment you pick up the writer's script to the final curtain and the ultimate 'Cut!'

4

*An Overview of
the Toolkit and Exercises*

4

An Overview of the Toolkit and Exercises

This final chapter takes a look at everything we've got in *The Toolkit* and offers some hands-on strategies for putting them to use. Owing to the nature of some of the individual tools, as well as the holistic nature of the toolkit as a whole, there isn't necessarily an exercise for every tool. The invitation is for you to invent your own.

Level 1: Actor Training

TRAY I

THREE 'ATTITUDES'
TOWARDS THE ART OF ACTING

- Psycho-physicality
- Discipline
- Stage ethics

TRAY 2

FOUR BASIC TOOLS
FOR PREPARING THE 'BLANK CANVAS'

- Relaxation
- Breathing
- Concentration and attention

Relaxation Exercises

There's a whole host of RELAXATION exercises which you could use, from the tensing and relaxing of all your muscles to the picturing of a ball of honey gliding through your limbs. I propose developing some of the ideas in Stanislavsky's 'system', which Soviet censorship prevented him from expounding himself.

Along with his reading of Hindu philosophies, Stanislavsky's experiences with the acting tutor, Leopold Sulerzhitsky, a colourful character who worked in his studio laboratories for some years, opened him to various Yogic practices. As a result, he began to use the term *prana*, referring to the energy centre located below the solar plexus. The following RELAXATION exercise expands the idea of *prana*, by drawing upon the Seven Chakra energy centres located along the spine. It does require a certain amount of IMAGINATION and connection with the notion of inner energy centres, which some actors may feel is too 'mystical' and intangible. If that's the case, then simply return to the physical tensing and releasing of specific muscle groups, and that should activate quite simply and effectively your awareness of where you're most relaxed or tight. That said, I use the following exercise a lot in workshops, and even the most sceptical of practitioners usually find they can benefit significantly from it.

- Find a comfortable place on the floor. Close your eyes and take a moment to still your thoughts.

- Picture yourself lying on a warm beach, where the sand is soft enough to take the imprint of your body, yet firm enough to give you a sense of support.

- Allow your head to sink into the sand and feel the warmth radiate through your body – across your shoulders, down your back, along your arms with your elbows relaxed and your hands lying loosely on the sand. Feel the warmth support your butt (which is one of your biggest, strongest muscles, so allow yourself to relax it), down your legs so that your calves lie easily on the sand, your heels make a delicate imprint, and your toes are relaxed.

- Lie there for a few moments just paying attention to your breathing. You don't have to alter your breathing pattern in any way, just be aware of the breath entering your body and leaving your body in a natural, easy wave motion.

- Take your attention to the base of your spine – to your coccyx – and picture a vibrant red globe of energy gently rotating there. This is your Root or Base Chakra: it's your connection with the earth, it's how you manifest yourself on this planet, it's your sense of identity or personality. This is a vital centre for the actor as it's through our corporeal presence on the earth that we can begin to physicalise characters and manifest in a concrete way the inner life within us. Through our physical bodies, we can communicate our emotional landscape and our imaginative realm to the audience. Spend some moments injecting that red globe with colour and vitality. Feel your increasing sense of 'self' as you do so.

- Bring your attention up to your lower abdomen, and picture a bright globe of orange energy rotating there. This is your Creative centre, your sexual centre, the root of your desire to create on this planet. Obviously this is a vital centre for actors, as by virtue of our profession we're inherently creative beings. When you find yourself struggling with a character or you're blocked in your creativity, it may help to infuse this globe of vibrant orange with a sense of vital energy and just see what happens in your IMAGINATION and EMOTIONS. Spend some moments now just paying attention to this centre and feeling your desire to create percolating through your body.

- Now take your attention up your body to your solar plexus. The solar plexus is a knot of nerve endings between the stomach and the spine, and it houses (metaphorically) the Emotion centre. This centre is coloured a magnificent yellow, so picture that swirling globe of yellow energy massaging your solar plexus. As we know, the Emotion centre is a complex centre, as it holds the whole gamut of feelings which comprise our personality. Our jealousy, hate, anger, joy, excitement, frustration, vulnerability, passion, mischief. We know this is the root of our emotions because we feel it. When we fall in love, we feel it in our stomach area (we even lose our appetites). When we're angry, we feel that knot in the pit of our stomach. When we're excited or nervous, we talk about 'butterflies in the stomach'. Of course, it's a vital centre for actors because we need to have at our finger-tips the palette of emotions which colour and texture our performances. Spend some moments now infusing the Emotion centre with a vibrant yellow colour. Enjoy the kind of inner massage, which can ease out any muscular tensions you might have and consequently alleviate any emotional tensions.

- Coming up the body, take your attention to the centre of your chest. This is your Heart centre; it's not located in the left of your chest where your anatomical heart is, but right in the middle of your rib cage. This centre is coloured a vibrant emerald green, so picture the swirling globe of emerald green energy residing in your chest and emanating out of your body. This centre is vital for us as actors: we have to be able to love – without coyness or whimsy – every aspect of our work. We have to love the character we're playing, even if it's the Butler and not the Lead. We have to love our fellow actors: if we can be open to their creative processes, then our own creative journey will be far richer and more textured. We have to love the director's vision of the play and his approach to rehearsal: if we find ourselves shutting down on the basic premise of a production or the way in which we're being directed, then we simply curtail our own creative discoveries. We have to love the camera or the audience, to radiate out to them the nuances of the script. Allied to love, of course, is trust, and if we can trust in the creative environment – including our own creative journey, the director's approach and that of our fellow actors – we can further unblock the realms of our fantasy and PSYCHO-PHYSICALITY. Spend some moments now infusing the Heart centre with vibrant green light and feel that light radiating out of your body, engendering your sense of creative pleasure.

- Take your attention up to your throat: this is your Communication centre, and once again it's vital for an actor. Blockages in our creative process often manifest themselves as blockages in our vocal cords: the words don't sound right, we find it hard to learn the lines, sometimes we even develop laryngitis. If you find you develop any of these vocally orientated problems, take your attention to the Communication centre and imaginatively allow it to open. It's coloured a vibrant sky-blue, so picture for a moment that sky-blue swirling energy centre gently massaging your vocal cords and opening up for you a direct channel between the writer's script and your own inner mechanism. If you can open this centre, you'll begin to understand exactly how the text should be spoken and how those words resonate in your IMAGINATION. Spend a few moments now injecting your Communication centre with a sky-blue energy, and feel that expansion in your throat.

- Now move up the body to your forehead. In the centre of your forehead is your Third Eye, your centre for clairvoyance. If, as actors, we can open this centre so that we put ourselves in a powerful, instinctive place in the classroom, rehearsal space, stage or film studio, we can develop a sense of alertness in which we're almost *ahead* of the moment. We can sense when our fellow-actor is going to do or say something unusual, we can feel the woman on the fifth row about to have a coughing fit, we're tuned into the tracking movement of the camera or the sudden decision of the director to try something new. We're like cats: serene and still, but able to pounce at any moment. This centre is incredibly powerful: it's one step away from our SUBCONSCIOUS, underlining Stanislavsky's repeated claim that his 'system' provided a *conscious* means of preparing the ground for *subconscious* creativity. The centre is coloured a vibrant violet colour; so spend some moments now investing that centre with violet energy and feel the frown lines begin to fade away as your imagination and mind become relaxed and expanded.

- Finally, take your attention to the top of your head, to your Crown chakra, and allow yourself to feel as if the top of your head is opening up, letting a stream of light come pouring in. There's a good deal of discussion in Stanislavsky's writings about the SUBCONSCIOUS (see above) and, in many ways, by opening the Crown chakra, we're putting ourselves in a strong position to access it. This centre is infused with ultraviolet light and it's our connection with the universe: if the Base chakra is our connection with the earth, the Crown chakra is our con-nection with the cosmos.

- Imagine that the stream of light is cascading down through your opened Crown chakra and passing through your body. As it descends, it ignites the violet light of the Third Eye in the middle of the forehead, passing the sky-blue Communication centre in the throat, through the emerald green centre of the Heart and lighting it up as it passes down to the Emotion centre in the solar plexus, which resonates with yellow energy, then down to the Creative centre in the lower abdomen igniting the orange globe, and finally down to the coccyx, where the red globe in the Base chakra grounds us and connects all our energy centres right the way up the spine.

- Take a moment to feel that utter sense of *who you are* – your personality, your creative energy, your emotions, your capacity for love, your ability to communicate, your spontaneous response to sound and action, and your higher consciousness which keeps everything integrated and open.

- When you're ready, gradually bring yourself back to the warm beach and the imprint of your body in the sand. Finally bring yourself back to your breathing, noting how the quality of your breath may have altered as a result of opening up the energy centres along your spine.

- Slowly, to end, roll onto your right side and slowly come up to sitting or standing.

One of the reasons I use the Chakra sequence as a RELAXATION exercise is that it's very energising. It's important not to think of RELAXATION as something you do before you go to sleep. Somehow, by imagining the cascading energy through the various centres along your spine, you should conclude the exercise feeling both physically relaxed and imaginatively switched on. You should be raring to go, and not ready for bed.

Breathing Exercises

The following BREATHING exercises are adopted from Yogic practices and are aimed at opening up (1) the upper breathing cavities and (2) the lower breathing cavities, and then (3) combining the two areas of the body into a unified breathing pattern. They were taught to me by Vladimir Ananyev, my Scenic Movement teacher in Moscow.

Exercise 1
Upper body breathing

- Stand with your arms relaxed by your sides and your feet together in sixth position (i.e. in parallel), and with your knees soft (i.e. not rigidly straight, but not consciously bent: it's a sensation as much as a physical positioning). Sense your contact with the floor through the soles of your feet and gently release any extraneous breath from your lungs.

- As you *inhale*, your arms cross the front of your groin in opposition to each other as they begin to describe a large arc in front of your body;

- both arms continue their respective arcs, passing right across your body and above your head, where their oppositional paths separate and your left arm descends to the left as your right arm descends to the right;

- as your outstretched arms come level with your shoulders (parallel to the floor), tuck your thumbs into the sides of your body just below your armpits with your palms facing the floor, so your hands are at right angles to your body, your fingers pointing forwards.

- As you *exhale*, push the palms of your hands downwards towards the floor, with the heels of your hands sliding down the sides of your torso as if you were brushing the air out of your body.

- The finishing position is the same as that with which you began.

- Repeat this sequence twice more.

Exercise 2
Lower body breathing

- Stand with your legs a little more than shoulder distance apart, your feet in parallel pointing forwards, your knees slightly bent, and your hands lightly placed over your belly.

- As you *inhale*, the palms of your hands stroke outwards across the belly from the centre towards your sides, as you simultaneously thrust your chest forwards and your bottom backwards like a strutting cockerel.

- In the *pause* between your inhalation and your exhalation, you cross your arms in front of your body so that your elbows meet just in front of your belly and your forearms curl round your belly.

- As you *exhale,* you draw your elbows away from your belly towards the sides of your body, clenching your fists as if you're drawing weights across you; you simultaneously curl your pelvis underneath your body, and your neck and torso curve gently forwards.

- In the *pause* between your exhalation and the next inhalation, bring your body back to the neutral starting position, with the spine straight and the hands lightly placed on the belly.

- Repeat this sequence twice more.

Basically, the *inhalation* curves your spine outwards from the belly, so your tailbone is thrust backwards and your chest is thrust out. The *exhalation* reverses that curve, so your tailbone is tucked under and your head is curled towards the chest. The impulse to move on both inhalation and exhalation is from your belly, so your lower breathing cavities get a really good work-out.

Exercise 3
Combined upper and lower breathing

- Stand with your legs fairly wide apart, your feet in a comfortable second position and your knees bent in a deep *plié*. Your arms are held in front of your body like a Native American 'How!' sign, with your left arm horizontally across the torso and your left palm facing the floor, and your right forearm at 90° to it, right elbow balancing on left finger tips and right palm facing forward.

- As you *inhale*, your right forearm rotates from your elbow and starts to describe an arc towards the elbow of your bent left arm, and in so doing the right palm inevitably turns 90° from its forward-pointing position toward the bent left elbow;

- the right forearm continues the circle, passing in between your bent left arm and your upper body, at which point your bent left arm begins to straighten upwards in an arc rotating from your shoulder away from your body;

- as your right arm arc passes across your torso down towards your legs, your right upper arm and shoulder join in the movement so that the entire right arm passes across the 6 o'clock position in front of the pelvis;

- at the same time as your right arm reaches the 6 o'clock position, the arc of your left arm reaches the 12 o'clock position, so that your left arm is pointing skywards as your right arm is pointing earthwards;

- both arms continue carving their respective arcs in counterpoint – your right arm to the right, your left arm to the left, so that your left arm reaches the 9 o'clock position just as your right arm reaches the 3 o'clock position;

- both arms continue on their journeys for another 90° so that the right arm reaches 12 o'clock as the left arm reaches 6 o'clock. By the end of the *inhalation*, you're still standing in a deep *plié* with your right arm vertically above your head and your left arm streaming to the ground. (The fact this movement all takes place within one *inhalation* indicates the speed and indeed the energy with which you're executing the arms' circles.)

- As you *exhale*, you concertina your two arms together (the right arm vertically downwards and the left arm vertically upwards) to bring the heels of the two hands to meet just in front of your solar plexus. At the same time, you contract the front of your torso very slightly to coincide with the meeting of your hands as if you're pressing the breath out of your body.

- In the *pause* between the first *exhalation* and the second *inhalation,* you resume the opening 'How!' position, but this time in reverse with the right arm horizontally in front of your body and your left forearm at right angles to it with your left palm facing forwards.

- You repeat the entire sequence with your left arm initiating the action, and then once again with your right arm initiating it, as it did the first time round.

If you follow each of these three exercises through, and execute each one three times, you should feel a sense of real energy coursing through your body as stimulated by your breath. As with the RELAXATION exercise, you're preparing yourself for some exciting creative work, rather than lulling yourself into a meditative, sleepy state.

Concentration and Attention Exercises

I offer two exercises here: one features CONCENTRATION AND ATTENTION and the second is an adaptation of what Stanislavsky called CIRCLES OF ATTENTION. Both help towards warming up your IMAGINATION.

Exercise I
Concentration and Attention

- Find a comfortable place to sit or lie down, close your eyes, and gently let your train of thought settle.

- Turn your ATTENTION to a role you would love to play, but haven't yet done so.

- Appealing to whatever knowledge you have of the play (however great or little that knowledge is), note what it is that *lures* you towards the character.

- Find a phrase or statement that sums up that 'lure' or trigger (e.g. the character's humour).

- Word that phrase in such a way that it can become an OBJECTIVE: i.e. formulate it into a phrase which begins, 'I want to . . .' (e.g. 'I want to delight everybody').

- As you CONCENTRATE YOUR ATTENTION on the OBJECTIVE and whichever details you know of the character so far, allow your IMAGINATION to visit various scenes in the play, meet with various characters in the drama, and maybe interact with various props or OBJECTS in your imaginary setting. (It really doesn't matter how well or how little you know the play: you're warming up your IMAGINATION, not sitting a Theatre Studies exam.)

- As you imagine various scenarios from the play, test the way in which you adjust your OBJECTIVE according to the details that your CONCENTRATED ATTENTION conjures up for you.

- Change the character.

- Change the play. Focus your ATTENTION on different materials with which to play imaginatively.

Exercise 2
Circles of Attention

In Chapter 5 of *An Actor Prepares*, Stanislavsky illustrates the vagaries of an actor's ATTENTION by setting up a mini light-show. During this light-show, a beam of light darts all over the theatre. Sometimes it lingers as a very bright spotlight over an imaginary Severe Dramatic Critic in the auditorium. Sometimes it hovers as a very dim flicker over the onstage partner. From this light-show comes what he calls the CIRCLES OF ATTENTION. These are illustrated by a Small Circle of Attention (focusing on the actor's head and hands, creating a sense of 'solitude in public'), a Medium Circle (which is harder to focus on, as it's much less clearly defined and usually incorporates just one or two other actors), a Large Circle of Attention (filling the whole stage), and the Very Largest Circle (which lights up the entire auditorium).

The following exercise is an adaptation of this Circles of Attention light-show:

- Lie on the floor or sit in a comfortable position, and close your eyes.

- Focus your ATTENTION on the smallest possible circle – i.e. yourself and your BREATHING. There's no need to change your breathing pattern, just note the incoming and outgoing breath, along with the rhythms and sounds that your body makes as it breathes. Allow your ATTENTION to sit in your body: if you cough or sneeze or your tummy rumbles or your bones creak, attend to those sounds. Let them be part of your focus of ATTENTION.

- Gradually expand your ATTENTION to incorporate the room you're in. If there are other people doing the exercise, listen to their sounds. Note the gurgling of the radiators or the buzz of the aircon. Simply allow your ATTENTION to take in the whole of the room. If your mind wanders, gently bring it back to the sounds in the room. Begin to let your IMAGINATION join in the exercise so it's not just a meditational task. If the pipes are bubbling, imagine what's going on inside the radiator. If someone coughs, let your ATTENTION go to them and imagine, for example, what clothes they're wearing or where you think they're lying in the room.

- Expand the CIRCLE OF ATTENTION to include the rest of the building. Hear doors slamming, lifts whirring, telephone con-versations in offices, footsteps in the corridors. Again allow your IMAGINATION to work: Whose footsteps are they? Which floor is the lift going to? What's being said by the unheard voice on the other end of the telephone in the room next door? What document is being printed off the computer in the office?

- Now make the circle even larger and hear the sounds in the immediate neighbourhood. Cars. Pedestrian traffic lights. Cash tills. Dogs barking. Sirens wailing. Even if you can't hear all the noises, imagine the details of the cashier in the post office, the barman in the pub, the paramedics in the ambulance.

- Expand the CIRCLE OF ATTENTION even further until the sounds of the whole town are in your awareness. By now, of course, your IMAGINATION is doing most of the work, rather than your ear. Be aware of how each sound in the distance creates a narrative in your head. Give your IMAGINATION free rein.

- Little by little, reduce the circles. Come back to the immediate environment, the building, the room, until you're simply residing with yourself and your own BREATHING. As you return to your own, intimate circle of ATTENTION, be aware of how your PERSPECTIVE on yourself has subtly shifted by virtue of the imaginative and aural journey that you've just undertaken.

TRAY 3

FOUR 'CONDITIONS' OF ACTING PRACTICE

- Inspiration
- Spirituality
- Inner creative state
- Creative atmosphere

Level 2: Rehearsal Processes

1: Mining the Text

TRAY 4

FOUR GENERAL TOOLS
FOR BEGINNING TEXTUAL ANALYSIS

- The first reading
- The text
- Mental reconnaissance
- Given circumstances

Exercise combining the first reading
+ the text + mental reconnaissance
+ given circumstances

- At random, pick any script off the shelf, ideally one with which you are totally unfamiliar.

- At random, pick any character from the *dramatis personae*, large or small, male or female.

- Prepare yourself for your FIRST READING – whatever that might entail for you – putting yourself in the strongest INNER CREATIVE STATE to receive all the intuitive impressions from the script. [Personally, I like to have a big pot of tea or a glass of red wine, a pen or pencil for making spontaneous scribblings in the margin or a notebook; I like to be sure I won't be disturbed, so I'll switch off my mobile phone or find a time when I'm least likely to be interrupted.]

- Read the script.

- As you read, note how the script's atmosphere affects you, note how evident its rhythm is, note your initial response to the character you've selected – even if they end up not saying very much or you don't particularly like them or it's highly unlikely that you'd ever be cast in the part anyway.

- Having read the script once, scribble down some immediate responses, using the seven 'planes' of the text to guide you. You might ask yourself questions such as:

1.   *What's the script's overall structure?* (4 acts? 96 scenes? One extended act?) *How does that structure dictate its* TEMPO-RHYTHM?

2.   *What are the main* EVENTS *of the script?*

3.   *How do the main* EVENTS *determine what the script is really about? i.e. is it about fathers and daughters? Betrayal? Unrequited love? Social reform? Manic depression? The state of the Latvian government? Avian bird flu?*

4.   *What is the dominant dramatic form or genre? Is it Comedy? Tragedy? Epic? Tragi-comedy? Ghost story? Love story? Heist? Science fiction? Thriller?*

5.   *What social milieu do the characters operate within?*

6.   *What is their nationality?*

7.   *What era are we in?*

8. *What style of writing does the author predominantly use? Poetry? Prose? Realism? A mixture? Metaphor? Myth? Allegory? Are there lots of overlapping speeches? Unfinished sentences? What does the* PUNCTUATION *look like on the page? What does that tell us about the style of writing?*

9. *How does the language of the character you've chosen distinguish them from the other characters in terms of their* TEMPO-RHYTHM, *vocabulary, and syntax?*

10. *What kind of theatrical devices are used? What kind of atmosphere do those devices create?*

11. *What scenic choices are inherent in the writer's directions? Are there any coups de théâtre? If so, what are they and how do they affect the overall atmosphere of the piece?*

12. *What's your gut reaction to the character you've chosen in terms of their inner drives or* OBJECTIVES? *Their inner* ACTIONS? *Their underlying feelings?*

13. *What kinds of physical activities are specified by the writer? What physical attributes has the writer given your character? What sort of physical activities do you imagine them undertaking?*

- Now consider the rock-solid GIVEN CIRCUMSTANCES of the script which haven't already emerged from your consideration of the seven 'planes'. Your character's age, gender, EMPLOI, family network, hobbies, domestic situation, social environment, etc. Make as many lists as you want that haven't already been covered by the various 'planes': story, epoch, facts, time and place of action, conditions of life, costume, props – personal or general – etc.

- Gradually move your work from the cerebral trawling of facts to the imaginative shaping of those facts. In your IMAGINATION, begin to conjure up a past and a future for your chosen character: what might be his or her ambitions or dreams for the future? How have those ambitions or dreams been shaped by his or her past?

- Read the play again, and note how the accumulation of the various GIVEN CIRCUMSTANCES, as well as your own intuitive reaction, is altered or amplified through your second encounter with the script.

TRAY 5

FIVE TOOLS FOR BREAKING DOWN
THE STRUCTURE OF A SCENE

- Bits
- Objectives and counter-objectives
- Subtext
- Punctuation
- The Six Fundamental Questions

Subtext Exercises

Here are three extracts from plays in which the writers use SUBTEXT to entirely different ends. Look at them carefully and fathom the resonance between what's said and what's done, what the audience knows and what the other onstage characters don't. Read each extract out loud and sense the inner energy of everything that remains unspoken:

Extract 1

Act IV, Scene iii, *The Country Wife* by William Wycherley

This is the famous china scene, which makes delicious subtextual use of *double entendre*. Lady Fidget and Horner emerge from an ante-room, where we assume they've been having adulterous sex. Clutching a piece of china, they then conduct the following conversation in front of Lady Fidget's cuckolded husband and her exasperated competitor-in-love, Mrs Squeamish:

> LADY FIDGET: And I have been toiling and moiling for the prettiest piece of china, my dear.
>
> HORNER: Nay, she has been too hard for me, do what I could.
>
> MRS SQUEAMISH: O lord, I'll have some china too. Good Mr Horner, don't you think to give other people china, and me none. Come in with me too.
>
> HORNER: Upon my honour, I have none left now.
>
> MRS SQUEAMISH: Nay, nay, I have known you deny your china before now, but you shan't put me off so. Come.
>
> HORNER: This lady had the last there.
>
> LADY FIDGET: Yes indeed, madam, to my certain knowledge he has no more left.
>
> MRS SQUEAMISH: Oh, but it may be he may have some you could not find.
>
> LADY FIDGET: What, d'ye think if he had had any left, I would not have had it too? For we women of quality never think we have china enough.
>
> HORNER: Do not take it ill, I cannot make china for you all, but I will have a roll-waggon for you too, another time.
>
> MRS SQUEAMISH: Thank you, dear toad.[224]

For the audience, the pleasure in this scene stems from the knowledge they have of the SUBTEXT, and from working out the 'code' the characters are using. For the actors, the pleasure arises from the complicity between themselves and the audience. SUBTEXT creates tensions – which can be performatively highly sexy for us as actors, even if the characters we're playing are at odds with each other.

Extract 2
The Lover by Harold Pinter

Here Pinter exploits to the full the sense of play inherent in lively SUBTEXT as you sound out each other and uncover what each other wants. We see in this extract that as much information is transmitted *between* the lines as *through* the lines. Husband Richard and wife Sarah are indulging in a fantasy role-play scenario in the middle of the afternoon in their suburban living room, in which Richard takes on the character of 'Max':

MAX: Excuse me.

> SARAH *glances at him and away.*

Excuse me, have you got a light?

> *She does not respond.*

Do you happen to have a light?

SARAH: Do you mind leaving me alone?

MAX: Why?

> *Pause.*

I'm merely asking if you can give me a light.

> *She moves from him and looks up and down the room. He follows to her shoulder. She turns back.*

SARAH: Excuse me.

> *She moves past him. Close, his body follows. She stops.*

I don't like being followed.

MAX: Just give me a light and I won't bother you. That's all I want.

SARAH (*through her teeth*): Please go away. I'm waiting for someone.

MAX: Who?

SARAH: My husband.

MAX: Why are you so shy? Eh? Where's your lighter?

He touches her body. An indrawn breath from her.

Here?

Pause.

Where is it?

He touches her body. A gasp from her.

Here?

She wrenches herself away. He traps her in the corner.

SARAH (*hissing*): What do you think you're doing?

MAX: I'm dying for a puff.

SARAH: I'm waiting for my husband!

MAX: Let me get a light from yours.

They struggle silently.

She breaks away to wall.

Silence.

He approaches.

Are you all right, miss? I've just got rid of that . . . gentleman. Did he hurt you in any way?

SARAH: Oh, how wonderful of you. No, no, I'm all right. Thank you.

MAX: Very lucky I happened to be passing. You wouldn't believe that could happen in such a beautiful park.

SARAH: No, you wouldn't.

MAX: Still, you've come to no harm.

SARAH: I can never thank you enough. I'm terribly grateful, I really am.

MAX: Why don't you sit down a second and calm yourself.

SARAH: Oh, I'm quite calm – but . . . yes, thank you. You're so kind. Where shall we sit?

MAX: Well, we can't sit out. It's raining. What about that park-keeper's hut?

SARAH: Do you think we should? I mean, what about the park-keeper?

MAX: I am the park-keeper.[225]

The whole play of *The Lover* is based on games, the rules for which keep changing, and this provokes a fantastic amount of SUBTEXT, as, through the characters, you have to work out the changing rules of each game and what exactly the other character really wants from you and the situation.

Extract 3
Act I, Scene iii, *Othello*

The content of Iago's speech is rather different. He reveals to us everything that's going on in his head and his heart. However, the knock-on effect is that, in his subsequent scenes with Othello, we as an audience are patently aware of Iago's SUBTEXT, although Othello remains entirely oblivious to it. See how the words offer up all the elements of what will later be Iago's complex SUBTEXT:

IAGO: Thus do I ever make my fool my purse;
　　For I mine own gain'd knowledge should profane,
　　If I would time expend with such a snipe,
　　But for my sport and profit. I hate the Moor;
　　And it is thought abroad, that twixt my sheets
　　He has done my office: I know not if't be true;
　　But I, for mere suspicion in that kind,
　　Will do as if for surety. He holds me well;

The better shall my purpose work on him.
Cassio's a proper man: let me see now:
To get his place and to plume up my will
In double knavery – How, how? – Let's see.
After some time, to abuse Othello's ears
That he is too familiar with his wife.
He hath a person and a smooth dispose
To be suspected, fram'd to make women false.
The Moor is of a free and open nature,
That thinks men honest that but seem to be so,
And will as tenderly be led by the nose
As asses are.
I have't. It is engender'd. Hell and night
Must bring this monstrous birth to the world's light.

Punctuation Exercises

Taking the following two extracts, compare the way the writers use PUNCTUATION, and note the way in which it informs the SUBTEXT of the piece and fuels the characters' emotional pitch:

Extract 1
Scene 3, *Shopping and Fucking* by Mark Ravenhill

MARK: Are you dealing?

ROBBIE: Fuck. You made me – How long have you - ?

MARK: Just now. Are you dealing?

ROBBIE: That doesn't . . .

Pause.

So. They let you out.

MARK: Sort of.

Pause.

ROBBIE: Thought you said months. Did you miss me?

MARK: I missed you both.

ROBBIE: I missed you. So, I s'pose . . . I sort of hoped you'd miss me.

MARK: Yeah. Right.

ROBBIE *moves to* MARK. *They kiss.*
ROBBIE *moves to kiss* MARK *again.*

MARK: No.

ROBBIE: No?

MARK: Sorry.

ROBBIE: No. That's OK.

MARK: No, sorry. I mean it. Because actually I'd decided I wasn't going to do that. I didn't really want that to happen, you know? Commit myself so quickly to . . . intimacy.

ROBBIE: OK.

MARK: Just something I'm trying to work through.

ROBBIE: . . . Work through? [226]

Extract 2
Act 1, *American Buffalo* by David Mamet

TEACH: [. . .] Everyone, they're sitting at the table and then Grace is going to walk around . . . fetch an ashtray . . . go for coffee . . . this . . . and everybody's all they aren't going to hide their cards, and they're going to make a show how they don't hunch over, and like that. I don't give a shit. I say the broad's her fucking partner, and she walks in back of me I'm going to hide my hand.

DON: Yeah.

TEACH: And I say anybody doesn't's out of their mind.

Pause.

We're talking about money for Chrissake, huh? We're talking about cards. Friendship is friendship, and a wonderful thing, and I'm all for it. I have never said different, and you know me on this point.

Okay.

But let's just keep it separate huh, let's just keep the two apart, and maybe we can deal with each other like some human beings.

Pause.

This is all I'm saying, Don. I know you got a soft spot in your heart for Ruthie . . .

DON: . . . yeah?

TEACH: I know you like the broad and Grace and, Bob, I know he likes 'em too.

DON: (He likes 'em.)

TEACH: And I like 'em too. (I know, I know.) I'm not averse to this. I'm not averse to sitting down. (I know we will sit down.) These things happen. I'm not saying that they don't . . . and yeah, yeah, yeah, I know I lost a bundle at the game and blah blah blah.

Pause.

But all I ever ask (and I would say this to her face) is only she remembers who is who and not go around with her or Gracie either with this attitude. 'The Past is Past, and this is Now, so Fuck You.'

You see?[227]

Just note that even from the lay-out on the page – let alone the PUNCTUATION – the TEMPO-RHYTHM, SUBTEXT and thought processes can be discerned. Mamet even writes at the start of some of his plays:

Some portions of the dialogue appear in parentheses, which serve to mark a slight change of outlook on the part of the speaker – perhaps a momentary change to a more introspective regard.[228]

Exercises for the Six Fundamental Questions

Exercise I

- Pick any scene from any play that you know reasonably well and compile four lists – 'Who?', 'Where?', 'When?' and 'Why?'

- Now allow your IMAGINATION free rein to conjure up a future for your character and from there, think up some long-term goals behind the character's ACTIONS which could answer the question 'For what reason?'

- Line by line, find ACTIONS for the text. These ACTIONS are in effect your 'hows'. Stafford-Clark tends to use a very particular and quite small range of verbs, which can be seen as the primary colours or basic raw materials. His list has been expanded by Marina Caldarone and Maggie Lloyd-Williams in their book *Actions: The Actor's Thesaurus*,[229] which can serve as a useful guide and stimulant to your IMAGINATION. Though be warned: Stafford-Clark upholds that the more metaphorical your ACTIONS become, the less easy they are to play accurately and truthfully. E.g. 'I kick you', 'I press you', 'I stroke you' might work initially, but after a while they'll be less razor-sharp than 'I provoke you', 'I threaten you', ' I charm you', etc.

Exercise 2

- Taking the piece from *Anna Karenina*, make lists of 'Who?', 'Where?', 'When?', 'Why?', and 'For what reason?'

- Add some line-by-line ACTIONS to offer a series of 'Hows?'. Then colour those 'Hows?' with appropriate adverbs. Here are some suggestions:

ANNA (*probes lightly*): You met him?

VRONSKY (*reprimands lightly*): Yes. At the door.

ANNA (*chastises petulantly*): It serves you right for being late.

VRONSKY (*reproaches seriously*): Your note said he would be at the Council; I would never have come otherwise.

ANNA (*challenges aggressively*): Where have you been, Alexei?

VRONSKY (*diverts apologetically*): I'm sorry, my darling. It's been a busy week.

ANNA (*tests tauntingly*): Really? Busy? (*Straightens goadingly.*) Betsy came to see me this morning. I heard all about your Athenian evening. (*Dismisses lightly.*) How disgusting.

VRONSKY (*deflects disinterestedly*): It was disgusting but I had to go. The Colonel asked me to entertain a foreign dignitary.

ANNA (*tests knowingly*): Oh – you mean that little French girl you used to see. I believe she was there.

VRONSKY (*corrects directly*): Anna, you don't understand . . .

ANNA (*attacks vulnerably*): No, I don't. What do I know – a woman who can't even share your life? (*Challenges provocatively.*) I only know what you tell me and how do I know whether you tell me the truth?

VRONSKY (*arrests openly*): Anna, don't you trust me?

ANNA: (*reassures impulsively*): Yes, yes. (*Enlightens passionately.*) You just don't understand what it's like for me. How can I go out like this and with the way people are talking? (*Reassures haltingly.*) I don't think I'm jealous, I'm not jealous – I trust you when you're here but when you're away leading your own life . . . (*redirects vehemently*) oh, I believe you, I do believe you. (*Reassures insistently.*) Alexei, I've stopped now. The demon has gone.

VRONSKY (*castigates sombrely*): I don't enjoy that kind of life any more. I thought you understood that.

ANNA (*reassures determinedly*): I do, I do. I'm sorry. (*Embraces questioningly.*)

She kisses him.[230]

I offer these ACTIONS and adverbs – these 'Hows?' – just as suggestions to illustrate the way in which your chosen adverb can sometimes be at odds with your verb; the disjuncture between the two will add all sorts of nuances to how you might play these moments. You might also find you play the same ACTION several times, such as 'reassures' in the example above, but the adverb will give a slightly different emphasis each time, as the character strives to impress their point of view upon the other characters through a series of shifting tactics.

Exercise 3

- Working with a partner, read the text again, but without predetermining the ACTIONS or adverbs. After each line, the actor listening describes what they heard or felt. For example, the actor playing Vronsky might say after Anna's first line, 'It felt as if you were mocking me dangerously', etc. In this way, you can detect whether or not what you think you played as 'How?' impacted on your listener in the way you intended.

Level 2: Rehearsal Processes

2: Embodying the Role

TRAY 6

THE TOOL WHICH UNDERPINS OUR
CREATIVE WORK ON A ROLE

• Truth

TRAY 7

THREE BASIC TOOLS
FOR BUILDING A SENSE OF TRUTH

• Imagination

• Observation

• The Magic 'If'

**Exercise combining truth +
imagination + observation**

• Take five random OBJECTS and place them on a table.

• Now go out into the street and for about ten to fifteen
minutes, observe someone in the outside world. You may sit
in a café or go into a shop and find someone to observe;
perhaps the person you observe is homeless and lying in a

doorway or selling the *Big Issue;* perhaps they're on a train or a bus; perhaps you simply follow them down the street. During the allotted time, try to be sure they don't know you're observing them, so that they don't consciously alter their behaviour – or have you arrested!

- Note their body language, their carriage, their posture, their clothing. Are they alone or in company? Do they look as if they're waiting for someone? Are they talking? Are they listening?

- What can you glean about their inner TEMPO-RHYTHM? Does there seem to be a synchrony or a fracture between their inner TEMPO-RHYTHM and their outer TEMPO-RHYTHM? How can you tell? What physical details reveal their TEMPO-RHYTHM – tapping feet, twirling hair round fingers, etc?

- At the end of the allotted time, return to your own space, whether it's your home, a rehearsal room or studio, and simply sit on a chair. Gradually let the body of the person you observed begin to percolate your own physicality: allow the process to be subtle and precise, rather than slapping the new physicality on your own body like someone else's overcoat.

- Note whether your body shrinks to fit theirs, or expands to fill theirs. Be sure that you're embodying them, not *imitating* them. The idea is that you're merging your own body with that of the person observed in order to understand the *psychological* implications of the transformation as much as the *physical* alterations.

- How does this new body alter your inner sensations psycho-physically? How does their posture affect you? How does their TEMPO-RHYTHM – both inner and outer sit with you? Do you find it comfortable inhabiting their body? Is it strange? Do *they* seem comfortable inhabiting their particular physicality?

- Imagine the person is sitting alone in their room. Why are they alone? What do they do? Are they happy just sitting? Conjure up some imaginative GIVEN CIRCUMSTANCES to JUSTIFY why they might be sitting there alone in their room.

- Now imagine they're sitting on a crowded underground train. How do they respond to these new GIVEN CIRCUMSTANCES?

- Now imagine they're sitting in a hospital waiting room. Are they ill or injured? Or are they waiting for someone? Who? How do they respond to their environment?

- Look at the five random OBJECTS that you assembled at the beginning of the exercise, and consider what significance each of these OBJECTS has in the person's life. Allow your IMAGINATION to conjure up stories surrounding each OBJECT; you may find the stories interlink all the OBJECTS or they remain entirely separate.

- Choose one of the OBJECTS and decide why this is the most important OBJECT for the person whom you observed.

- Throughout the exercise, let the new person's body dictate to you the images, movements, OBSERVATIONS and OBJECTIVES, rather than feeling that you have to impose them upon the person.

- As your imaginative journey comes to a conclusion, picture a stopcock in your right heel. Slowly open it and allow the character's body to flow out of you, gradually leaving you alone in your own body once again. This is an important step because, I repeat, this exercise is not about impersonation, but embodiment. We're not talking about physical accuracy in your portrayal of the person, but psycho-physical rever- beration: how you felt when that person's body inhabited yours, what kind of images and sensations were conjured up.

The more subtly you move from self to character, and then back from character to self, the more precisely you'll feel the psycho-physical nuances of the physical embodiment, as well as the muscular specifics.

The Magic 'If' Exercise

- This exercise starts by considering the same person whose body and TEMPO-RHYTHM you just inhabited, but this time the creative process is a little different.

- Ask yourself the following questions:

    1. What would I do if I was shopping / sitting in the café / waiting at the bus stop (or whatever activity your person was initially engaged in)?

    2. What would I do if I had this person's outer TEMPO-RHYTHM?

    3. What would I do if I had this person's inner TEMPO-RHYTHM?

    4. What would I do if I was wearing this person's clothes / shoes?

- Remember all the activities your person undertook during the fifteen minutes when you watched them, and ask yourself: 'How would I justify that sequence of movements?' 'What would my inner JUSTIFICATION be?'

- Implicit within your answers to the questions 'What would I do if . . . ?' are various psycho-physical sensations which accompany the ACTIONS. Note what feelings and sensations arise for you. It's important to ask yourself 'What would I do if . . . ?' rather than 'How would I feel if . . . ?', as it's often not until we've done something that we can sense what the true feelings arising from that ACTION are.

You'll note in this exercise that the sensations are subtly different from the first exercise involving OBSERVATION. With a truly psycho-physical process, you can work just as readily from the inside out or the outside in. The first exercise in which your OBSERVATION of the person's body leads to a physical embodiment, you're working very gently from the *outside in*. N.B. You are not *impersonating*, you are *embodying*: the subtle difference is that if you try too hard to *impersonate* the person, you're in danger of becoming deaf to the various psycho-physical nuances which accompany the physical tasks. If, on the other hand, you *embody* the character, you're inviting the person's body to inhabit yours, so you remain in touch with all the psychological, emotional, and sensate changes, as well as the physical shifts in balance, energy, posture and TEMPO-RHYTHM, etc.

With THE MAGIC 'IF' exercise, you're working from the *inside out*. By asking yourself 'What would *I* do if . . . ?', you begin much more directly from yourself, noting how your own responses colour your attitude to the person whom you're embodying. Either sequence is equally valid – inside out or outside in – but it's important to alert yourself to the different nuances of each exercise so you can feel the subtle shifts in your own approach to embodying a role.

TRAY 8

FOUR TOOLS FOR BUILDING
PSYCHO-PHYSICAL CO-ORDINATION WITH A CHARACTER

- Action
- Tempo-rhythm
- Emotion memory
- Emotions

Tempo-Rhythm Exercises

This exercise is one of Stanislavsky's own from *Building a Character*[231] (and I quote it myself in *Konstantin Stanislavsky*):[232]

- Place a number of OBJECTS on a tray and set a metronome beating.

- To the set beat of the metronome, carry the tray and start to distribute the OBJECTS to others in the room.

- As the beat of the metronome dictates to you the TEMPO-RHYTHM at which you distribute the OBJECTS, allow your IMAGINATION to come up with some GIVEN CIRCUMSTANCES which JUSTIFY your ACTIONS. In *Building a Character*, the imaginary student, Kostya, pretends that he's the president of a sports club, distributing prizes.

- Increase the TEMPO-RHYTHM of the metronome, and see how the increased speed affects the ACTIONS. Repeat this a few times, each time noting how your IMAGINATION responds to the increased TEMPO-RHYTHM. In *Building a Character*, Kostya imagines he's a butler handing out champagne. When the TEMPO-RHYTHM is increased again, he imagines he's a waiter on a train trying to serve everyone before the next station. When it's increased for a final time, Kostya feels like he's the clumsy, clownish Epikhodov in *The Cherry Orchard*.

- Find another simple physical activity. Set the metronome at varying speeds. From acting out the ACTIONS at the different TEMPO-RHYTHMS, note what images and sensations come to you.

Emotion Memory and Emotion Exercises

It's very important that you feel you can contact your EMOTIONS without any unnecessary coercion. To this end, I offer the following exercise, which I've used many times, both with professional actors and acting students, and it always produces some great results. It's a very simple exercise, though it does take some preparation on the workshop leader's part. Because it's so simple, actors often find themselves tapping into all sorts of memories and EMOTIONS that they haven't contacted for a long time. It's very liberating.

The exercise involves the simple stimulation of each of the five senses to see what kind of EMOTION MEMORIES they provoke.

We begin with *touch*.

- Sit in a circle, blindfolded. [I usually ask individuals to bring their own blindfolds, forewarned that they might be wearing them for some time, so the fabric should be comfortable.]

- A series of OBJECTS is placed on the floor, one in front of each participant. On the word of the instructor, pick up your OBJECT, feeling its texture and shape. Don't worry too much about identifying the OBJECT, just note what sensations you experience and what thoughts, memories, images, come flooding into your head. The workshop leader then asks two or three people to respond to their OBJECT *without identifying it*. This is important, so that when the OBJECTS are passed around the circle, you each have a 'virgin' experience. At regular intervals, the workshop leader instructs you to pass your OBJECT on to the next person in the circle. Each time, two or three people are asked to share their responses, images, memories. [OBJECTS I've used include a teddy bear, a velvet glove, a pumice stone, a rubber duck, a pebble, a feather boa, a scouring pad, a plastic toy, but you can use anything: the varying weights, textures and pliability offer a range of stimuli.]

Following touch, we have *smell*.

- With participants still wearing blindfolds, a series of plastic cups with various smelly things in them are passed around the group one by one, as with the OBJECTS. Again, you don't have to identify the smell, just respond to the sensations, images and memories it provokes. Do you like the smell? Does it remind you of some time or place or person? What images does the smell evoke? As with touch, two or three people are invited to share their thoughts or memories, before the cups are passed around the circle. A few minutes are spent with each one, before being passed on again to the next person, and so on. [I tend to prepare these the night before so that the smells have some hours in the cups, covered so they can marinate: I usually soak pieces of cotton wool in the substances to make them easily transportable. Smells might include bubble bath, wet earth or mown grass, stale beer and fag ends, coffee, and some sort of cleaning solution. Soya sauce is a good one: this has been described in the past as a range of things from prawn curry to smelly feet!]

Smell is followed by *taste*.

- With the participants still wearing blindfolds, a series of edibles are placed on cocktail sticks. Simultaneously, you all put the same edible into your mouths to ensure that everyone has the same experience as the same time. Again, two or three people are invited with each edible to share any thoughts, images or memories which come flooding into their heads. [I always check beforehand there are no food allergies, and I usually walk round the group putting the cocktail sticks between each person's extended forefinger and thumb, so the process of getting everyone to eat the same edible at the same time is easy. Food stuffs might include a grape, a silverskin pickled onion, a cheesy ball, a marshmallow, a chunk of bagel – items that can be easily skewered onto a cocktail stick. Of course, a certain amount of trust is needed in this part of the exercise, since it's bold asking people to put things into their mouth without seeing what the food stuffs are. Because of the slight 'danger' element, taste produces some great memories, as the participants are already in a heightened state.]

Taste is followed by *sound*.

- This can take a variety of forms. Perhaps four or five pieces of music or soundscapes are played to the group, which you can respond to physically if you wish. (Your blindfolds are still on at this point, so just be careful if you do move or dance, as there are X number of other blindfolded people in the room.) Or you can simply lie on the floor and let each sound or music piece influence you imaginatively and emotionally.

Finally, the blindfolds can come off and *sight* is considered.

- A series of pictures are placed in the centre of the circle and the group are invited to respond. [Sometimes I provide the pictures, sometimes I ask each of the group to bring in a picture, at which point they briefly explain why that image attracted them, as the pictures are passed around the circle. Images might include those from newspapers or magazines, family photographs, abstract paintings, visual illusions (like those by Escher or Kitaoka) in which the eye is invited to see first one image and then another, etc. The idea is to provide a variety of visual stimuli, just to draw the group's attention to the amount of information which is taken in by the eye and assimilated at every moment of our waking lives.]

TRAY 9

FOUR TOOLS FOR TEXTURING A CHARACTER

- Inner psychological drives
- Heroic tension
- *Emploi*
- Objects

Inner Psychological Drives Exercises

Exercise I

- Imagine that whichever room you're in – studio, bedroom, rehearsal room, church hall – is in fact a modern art gallery, so any OBJECT around you might be a work of art.

- Take your attention to your *head*, your 'thought-centre'. Wander round the art gallery letting your head lead your travels. Note what inner sensations occur when your 'thought-centre' dominates. What's your attitude to the OBJECTS? How does the rest of your body respond when your 'thought-centre' leads? What's your TEMPO-RHYTHM – inner and outer?

- Take your attention to your *chest*, your 'emotion-centre', and do the same. What do you notice now? How does your response to the OBJECTS change? What about the rest of your body? Your TEMPO-RHYTHM?

- Take your attention to your *pelvic area*, your 'action-centre', and do the same. Again notice the changes in your attitude, body, and TEMPO-RHYTHM.

Exercise 2

- Imagine you're sitting in a hospital waiting room. Someone very close to you has just been knocked off a motorbike and you're waiting to hear if they're going to survive or not. Take your attention to your *head*, your 'thought-centre', and just note how you respond to the GIVEN CIRCUMSTANCES. Don't force anything, just note what thoughts, memories, fantasies go through your head, and where your CONCENTRATION AND ATTENTION are focused.

- Now shift your ATTENTION to your *chest*, your 'emotion-centre'. You don't have to do anything other than open your chest, and note the changes in your response to the GIVEN CIRCUMSTANCES. What sensations arise? How does the rest of your body respond?

- Now shift your ATTENTION to your *pelvic area*, your 'action-centre'. Note how you respond to the GIVEN CIRCUMSTANCES now. Does your body stay sitting in the chair? Where are your CONCENTRATION AND ATTENTION focused now?

- Now change the GIVEN CIRCUMSTANCES and run through each of the INNER PSYCHOLOGICAL DRIVES again, but this time it was *you* who knocked the person off their motorbike, and you're waiting to hear whether they've survived or not. Again, note the shifts in your ATTENTION, and how the different centres respond to the change of the GIVEN CIRCUMSTANCES.

- Now change the GIVEN CIRCUMSTANCES again: this time you're waiting to hear whether your girlfriend, wife, or sister has just given birth to a baby boy or a baby girl. As you shift through your centres, again note how the change in the GIVEN CIRCUMSTANCES affects your body on an inner and outer level. Just note the state of development of your inner-outer psycho-physical co-ordination.

Heroic Tension Exercises

Exercise 1

- Take any character from any play (e.g. Masha in *Three Sisters*) and think of any three adjectives which sum up your intuitive response to that character. The adjectives for Masha, for example, could be 'passionate' (as revealed in her love affair with Vershinin), 'brooding' (as revealed in Act 1 when she sits reading her book and whistling distractedly) and 'challenging' (as revealed in Act 3 when she incites her sisters to address the issue of Andrey and his mortgaging of their house).

- Now think of the opposites of those adjectives, which in the case of 'passionate', 'brooding' and 'challenging' might be 'self-contained', 'light-hearted' and 'accepting'.

- Think of moments from anywhere in the script where the character displays the opposite adjectives of those which initially sprung to mind. It can be a tiny moment: it's all up for grabs in your interpretation. So Masha, for example, could be considered to be 'self-contained' at the beginning of Act 3 when Natasha chastises Anfisa the old servant, and Masha simply walks out clasping her pillow. In Act 3, we also see her being 'light-hearted' when she hums her little love-tune in response to Vershinin. At the end of the play, she is remarkably 'accepting', both of her husband and the situation in which the sisters find themselves after the departure of the soldiers.

- Try the same with any other characters from any other plays.

Exercise 2

• Again, take a monologue by a character from a play you know well and decide whether that character is a 'thinking', 'feeling' or 'doing' type character; i.e. what's their predominant INNER PSYCHOLOGICAL DRIVE? So for example, Chebutykin in Act 3 of *Three Sisters* delivers an alcohol-induced confession of his 'killing' of a patient. The dominant INNER PSYCHOLOGICAL DRIVE here would arguably be the 'emotion-centre'.

• Now find a physicality for the character, letting the dominant centre (head, chest, pelvis) initially lead the emerging 'embodiment'. So the chest would be the leading centre with an embodiment of Chebutykin at this moment.

• Now, speak the monologue with the dominant INNER PSYCHOLOGICAL DRIVE guiding you, noting how the opening of the relevant physical centre affects the emphasis of the text.

• Then work through the other two INNER PSYCHOLOGICAL DRIVES, noting how the shift in focus from (for example) thought to feeling to action alters the character's physicality and psychology. What happens if the emphasis of Chebutykin's monologue becomes the rationalisation of his life ('thought-centre')? What happens if the emphasis of Chebutykin's monologue becomes his attempt to control his body which is uncoordinated by his drunken state ('action-centre')? This would certainly spur his smashing of the clock a few pages later, as we see his physical body is more dominant than his logical brain.

• Now go back to the dominant INNER PSYCHOLOGICAL DRIVE that you selected and, as you go through the monologue again, shift your physical centre so that in effect you're *hiding* the character's dominant centre or *transmuting* it into another part of your body. So with Chebutykin, for example, note what happens to your delivery of the monologue if you shift your attention to your head ('thought-centre') while keeping a sense of emotional openness. What happens when you shift your attention to your pelvis area ('action-centre') while keeping a sense of emotional openness? What do you notice when you start to explore the tensions between the character's natural disposition and how he or she might hide or change or disguise that? How does it affect (a) your delivery of the speech, and (b) your embodiment of the character?

Object Exercise

This exercise is borrowed from my Russian Scenic Movement teacher, Vladimir Ananyev. Every time I've used it either as workshop leader or actor, I've been fascinated by the range of experiences it provokes. It's best not to think about the exercise too much beforehand: as with many psycho-physical exercises, your body and imagination will make huge discoveries in the course of trying it out, so avoid letting your head come up with too many questions.

- Place an OBJECT on the floor in front of you. You can use any OBJECT you like: a notebook, a water bottle, a pencil.

- Imagine the OBJECT is extremely valuable to you (though you may not know at this stage why it is so important).

- For the duration of the exercise (which can last anything from twenty to forty minutes), you can come as close to your OBJECT or as far from your OBJECT as you like, but you mustn't touch it! However, important your OBJECT may be to you, your OBJECTIVE must be 'to prevent yourself from touching it'.

- 'This OBJECTIVE instantly establishes an inner contradiction: if you have to stop yourself from doing something, it suggests

that part of you wants to do it and part of you certainly
doesn't. There's a dynamic set up between attraction and
repulsion, between desire and denial.'[233]

- At the beginning of the exercise, you'll probably have no idea
  what you're going to do. Trust yourself: a host of images and
  JUSTIFICATIONS for why you can't touch the OBJECT will spring
  into your IMAGINATION.

- Indeed, you may find very quickly that your IMAGINATION
  transforms the OBJECT. So a notebook might become a tome
  holding the secrets of the universe. A bottle of water might
  become a vial of poison. A pencil might become a stiletto
  dagger. If the OBJECT does transform, only let it change once.
  So the pencil can't become a dagger, then a hypodermic
  needle, then the quill used by Shakespeare to write *King Lear*.
  Stick with the first image otherwise the exercise will become
  too fractured.

- If you play your OBJECTIVE whole-heartedly, you might find
  you love the OBJECT, then hate the OBJECT. You might want to
  hit it, stamp on it, embrace it, protect it. Just open your INNER
  PSYCHOLOGICAL DRIVES – your 'thought-centre', your
  'emotion-centre', your 'action centre'. Go with your impulses,
  and see what happens.

- You may even find that certain characters come to mind. Do
  you feel like Hamlet? Willy Loman? Stanley Kowalski? Jimmy
  Porter? Juliet? The Duchess of Malfi? Salome? Nora? You don't
  necessarily have to 'play' the character, just allow essences of
  character to filter into your psyche if they want to, and note
  how your relationship to the prop then alters. And here, if you
  find different characters do come to mind, go with them – as
  long as the OBJECT remains the same.

- After about twenty minutes, allow yourself to pick up the
  OBJECT. Notice how readily you want to. How easy is it to
  touch it? Which sensations are aroused in you when you have
  permission to pick it up? Explore the feelings without forcing
  them. How does your relationship with the OBJECT alter
  before and after the moment when you can actually pick it up?

Part of the reason you shouldn't think about the exercise too
much before hand is that you might start to premeditate
scenarios. Try not to. Just go with the 'HERE, TODAY, NOW'.
You'll usually find that the simplicity of the exercise 'stimulates a myriad of contradictory reactions and interconnections
between the actor and the object, while all the time there's an
unbroken line between inner (psychological) and outer (physical) action.'[234]

TRAY 10

THE MEAT OF THE TOOLKIT
AND THE 'SYSTEM'

- The subconscious

Level 2: Rehearsal Processes

3: Approaches to Rehearsal

TRAY 11

GENERAL PRINCIPLES
OF DIRECTING AND STAGING

- The role of the director
- *Mise-en-scène*

TRAY 12

REHEARSAL PROCESS 1:
THE METHOD OF PHYSICAL ACTIONS

- The Method of Physical Actions

TRAY 13

REHEARSAL PROCESS 2:
ACTIVE ANALYSIS AND ITS COMPONENTS

- Active Analysis
- Étude rehearsals
- Events
- Grasp

- Connection

- 'Here, today, now'

- Justification

- Adaptation

- Super-objectives

- Through-line of action

- Verbal action

- Pauses

- The second level

- Inner monologue

- Envisaging

- Moment of orientation

Active Analysis Exercise incorporating grasp + connection + 'here, today, now' + justification + adaptation

---

[This exercise moves from a SILENT ÉTUDE to an improvisation of a scene.]

My own experience of actor-training in Russia was heavily influenced by my acting tutor, Katya Kamotskaya,[235] who combined her own understanding of Stanislavsky with training received at Grotowski's Teatr Laboratorium. She has developed a simple SILENT ÉTUDE which I in turn have evolved. I now use it to begin most of my actor-training workshops. It also forms the kernel of my rehearsing a production using ACTIVE ANALYSIS, as it's a simple and effective way of helping actors to get each other in each other's GRASP.

- Working with a partner, stand opposite each other about three metres apart.

- Establish eye-contact and imagine there's a coiled spring linking you both from solar plexus to solar plexus.

- Keeping on a straight line, you gradually make your way towards each other and see if you can find some sort of contact between each you. The contact might be an embrace, a handshake, a slap, a kiss, a stroke of the cheek, or – depending on the silent 'dialogue' between you and the nuances of your inciting ACTIONS and COUNTER-ACTIONS – you might find it doesn't happen at all.

N.B. It's not a game of chess in the sense that one actor takes one step, then the next actor has to move the next, and so on. Quite the opposite: you might find that one actor remains stock still, or even moves backwards as the fellow actor approaches. You don't have to predetermine anything: just get each other in each other's GRASP and absorb all the nuances of the person's face, energy, body language.

- Really sense the power of that invisible spring joining your solar plexuses. Feel the space expand, feel the space contract.

- To begin with, it's useful to remain on a straight line, keeping your body language as simple as possible. Try not to cross your arms or shove your hands in your pockets. Avoid adding any 'nudge-nudge-wink-winks' or superimposed characterisations. Although it's incredibly difficult to maintain this degree of utter simplicity, it really is the only way to ensure the purest ACTIVE ANALYSIS of the dialogue. The moment you start to muddy the waters with running your fingers through your hair or rubbing your nose or casting sideways glances, etc., you'll catapult yourself away from any true and exciting discoveries about the character. Any everyday, contemporary gestures – which ultimately only reveal how uncomfortable you are simply inhabiting your own body – form a kind of barrier between you and the character, let alone between you and your fellow-actor. They can project you back into your own habits and clichés, making it almost impossible to have a real, psychologically reverberant process of discovery about the scene.

- After some time, the director stops the SILENT ÉTUDE, and you discuss what kind of inner dialogue went on between you and your partner in the course of the exercise.

It's important to be sure that the improvisation doesn't stop at the point of contact: some of the most interesting discoveries occur once you've made contact and you're then trying to understand what kind of relationship exists between you beyond that moment.

Often, actors opt for the embrace as the point of contact: a kind of 'Phew, we got through that, didn't we?' Dare to really listen to what's going on between you and your partner. One of you might offer a point of contact which the other then rejects. Try not to censor yourself. That said, the embrace can sometimes be a relieving way of eliminating the gap, having been so open and connected to each other for such an intense time.

In effect there are three rules to this exercise:

- Block nothing: so if you have an impulse to do something, follow it.

- Force nothing: so don't feel you have to be entertaining or clever or inventive; just follow the moment and you'll 'hear' the appropriate impulse.

- Hurt no one, yourself included: so if your impulse is to punch your partner's lights out or crack your head against a brick wall – that might be an impulse worth blocking!

Initially, you work completely as yourselves. But this SILENT ÉTUDE can be the starting point of any ACTIVE ANALYSIS of a given scene; just keep the body language as simple as it was when you were just being yourself. The basic GIVEN CIRCUMSTANCES of the scene serve as a backdrop to the silent dialogue, but neither of you need indicate overtly which part of the scene is being enacted. Trust yourselves: you'll see it in each other's eyes if you're really listening to each other.

To make sure that your merger with the character is gentle, imagine that you're a flask of clear water, into which a couple of drops of character have been pipetted, just to give the flask a hint of colour, a hint of character. After each ÉTUDE discuss what you discovered, then return to the text and re-read it. Compare the discoveries you made in the SILENT ÉTUDE with what's in the text.

After one or two SILENT ÉTUDES on a scene, you can start to introduce words. The idea of improvising a script in your own words can be daunting at first and you don't have to go beyond one or two words or phrases initially. If words come into your head, just let them drop into your mouth. No doubt your early improvisations will seem clumsy and unliterary. The point of focus isn't the words you speak, it's the ACTIONS that you execute: there's no inseparability between tasks and ACTIONS.

This is pure ACTIVE ANALYSIS. If you can trust yourselves to be as simple as possible, the kind of discoveries that you might make about the characters – emotionally, psychologically, physically, imaginatively – can be extraordinary.

Pause Exercise

This is one area of ACTIVE ANALYSIS where an exercise comes in handy. It's a wonderfully simple combination of TEXT and experience, devised by one of my second-year students, Tracey Wills, on 'The Psycho-Physical Actor' module at Exeter University, 2006.

- In partners, take the following extract from Act 3 of *The Seagull* and play the dialogue three times.

- First of all, with no PAUSES.

- Secondly, marking the 'logical pauses'.

- Thirdly, marking the 'logical' and 'psychological pauses'.

- Note the change in pace, TEMPO-RHYTHM, intensity, SUBTEXT – not to mention the ADAPTATIONS to your body language, facial expressions, proximity to each other – and all manner of psycho-physical adjustments which occur once you include the 'psychological pauses'.

NINA (*holding out her clenched fist to* TRIGORIN): Odd or even?

TRIGORIN: Even.

NINA (*sighs*): Wrong. I've only one pea in my hand. I'm trying to decide whether I should go on the stage or not. If only someone would advise me.

TRIGORIN: Nobody can advise you about that.

A pause.

NINA: So, you're leaving . . . we probably won't see each other again. I'd like you to take this little medallion as a keepsake. I had your initials engraved on it, and the title of your book 'Days and Nights' on the other side.

TRIGORIN: How charming! (*Kisses the medallion.*) What a delightful present!

NINA: You'll think of me sometimes?

TRIGORIN: I shall indeed. I'll think of you just as you were that sunny day – you remember? – about a week ago, you were wearing a white dress, and we had a long talk . . . there was a white bird, a seagull, lying on the bench.

NINA (*thoughtfully*): Yes, the seagull . . .

A pause.

We'd better not say any more, someone's coming. Let me have two minutes with you, please, before you leave.

Exits left.[236]

Here's a suggested version: [L] = logical pause; [P] = psychological pause.

NINA (*holding out her clenched fist to* TRIGORIN): Odd or even? [P]

TRIGORIN: Even.

NINA (*sighs*): [P] Wrong. I've only one pea in my hand. [P] I'm trying to decide whether I should go on the stage or not. If only someone would advise me.

TRIGORIN: Nobody can advise you about that. [L] + [P]

A pause.

NINA: So, you're leaving . . . [P] we probably won't see each other again. I'd like you to take this little medallion as a keepsake. [P] I had your initials engraved on it, and the title of your book 'Days and Nights' on the other side.

TRIGORIN: How charming! [P] (*Kisses the medallion*) What a delightful present! [P] + [L]

NINA: You'll think of me sometimes?

TRIGORIN: I shall indeed. I'll think of you just as you were that sunny day – you remember? – about a week ago, you were wearing a white dress, [P] and we had a long talk . . . [P] there was a white bird, a seagull, lying on the bench.

NINA (*thoughtfully*): [P] Yes, the seagull . . .

A pause. [P] + [L]

We'd better not say any more, someone's coming. [P] + [L] Let me have two minutes with you, please, before you leave.

Exits left.

Without any PAUSES, you'll probably find the extract is all rather rushed, superficial and even nonsensical. The LOGICAL

PAUSES essentially mark a BIT of action: when you play only the 'logical pauses', the flow certainly feels more natural than with no PAUSES, but it can seem rather neat and tidy. Once you add the layer of the 'psychological pauses', you'll suddenly sense the addition of MOMENTS OF DECISION. A change of thought might just be a 'logical pause', but a moment of considered decision ('How will this person react if I decide to say this?') will definitely be a 'psychological pause'. It can feel much messier, which is good – and certainly more natural.

It's interesting to note what Stanislavsky himself did with the PAUSES in this scene in his production plan for *The Seagull*. Let's take the moment where Trigorin reminds Nina of the dead seagull: the following is a combination of Stanislavsky's specifics and my responses:

> After a moment's awkwardness, Nina jumps to her feet to leave the room, but Trigorin catches her hand to stop her. She stands with her back to him in silence, as Trigorin raises her caught hand to kiss it. Gently she withdraws her hand from his lips and moves to the stove, where . . . she traces something with her finger. This is a moment of decision for her. That tracing finger marks a resolution, [because she then] turns quickly to Trigorin to finish her speech and immediately exit.
>
> The details piled into that one 'pause' indicate a whole sequence of conflicts *between* the two characters as well as *within* each of the two characters. Their emotions battle with their thoughts, their desires battle with their sense of duty. The vividness of Stanislavsky's imagination has jam-packed that one moment with a complexity of realistic human responses, full of varying 'tempo-rhythms' and life-changing decisions.[237]

Moment of Orientation Exercise

Take the first act of Arthur Miller's *The Crucible*.

- Think through all the GIVEN CIRCUMSTANCES: that the young girls have been out dancing in the woods; that they've been spotted naked; that the youngest, Betty – the Reverend Parris's daughter – has fallen into a dead faint; and that now the village is alive with talk of witchcraft. The scene takes place in the room in which Betty is lying unconscious.

- As each character comes in – starting with the Negro slave, Tituba, who was caught dancing naked, right through to Reverend Hale arriving 'loaded down with half a dozen heavy books' – contemplate the elements of their very first MOMENT OF ORIENTATION.

- *Do they know that Betty is in the room?*

- *Do they know where Betty is lying?*

- *Do they know that she's unconscious?*

- *Do they know who else is in the room?*

- *What's their relationship with others in the room?*

- *Who is suspicious of whom?*

- *Who is afraid of whom?*

- *Who is surprised to see whom?*

- *Who is relieved to see whom?*

- *How familiar is the room to them?* [Obviously Abigail and Reverend Parris have been in the room many times, but for Reverend Hale it's the first time. Where's the bed? Where's the window? Where's the table?]

- *How does John Proctor orientate himself to Abigail's presence, bearing in mind they've had an affair?* [Note Miller's stage directions around Proctor's entrance, each of which gives clues into the nature of the MOMENT OF ORIENTATION:

  Enter JOHN PROCTOR. *On seeing him,* MARY WARREN *leaps in fright* [. . .] MERCY LEWIS *both afraid of him and strangely titillated* [. . .] *Since* PROCTOR'S *entrance,* ABIGAIL *has stood as though on tiptoe, absorbing his presence, wide-eyed.*][238]

Level 3: Performance Practices

TRAY 14

PERFORMANCE COMPONENTS

- The audience

TRAY 15

FIVE TOOLS FOR DEVELOPING
PERFORMANCE AWARENESS

- Dual consciousness

- Perspective

- Creative individuality

- Inner creative mood

- Scenic speech

Scenic Speech Exercise

Take the following speech from the Bereaved Mother (played wonderfully by Flaminia Cinque in the original production by Out of Joint and the National Theatre, 2003) of *The Permanent Way*, and mark which phrases could be 'thrown away' *à la* Mamet:

> I was a supervisor at Marks and Spencers. My son Peter
> was 29, he worked at Freshfields, the solicitors, you know.

He was a hotshot lawyer, about to be made a partner. In the firm they couldn't believe how clever he was, coming from Essex. When I heard him on the phone, I used to think, he doesn't sound like my son, he sounds like a proper lawyer. Later, when I was running the Disaster Action Group, I would find myself saying things like, 'I put it to you.' It was like he was at my side. Peter was on my shoulder. We loved our son to bits. Very proud of him. Normal parents. On the night we were waiting to hear, we were standing in the dark, September – so the nights were getting dark already – making cups of tea and not drinking them – and we just stood in the kitchen. And I kept saying 'Well if he's gone, it's written', and I felt as if this was coming from somewhere – and my husband said to me and it was in the dark – and he's just made another cup of tea which he'd thrown away and he said, 'Maureen' – (*turning to husband*) You don't mind me saying this do you? He said, 'Maureen', and he was crying, and he said 'If Pete has gone you've got to forgive me'. And I said 'What do you mean?' And he said 'I'm not staying here, I'm going to go'. He was going to kill himself. [. . .]

We went to the mortuary. Pete was on a trolley. His nose had come off and they'd just put it back on. And they'd combed his hair into a fringe, he'd never had a fringe in his life, and he had this fringe. I didn't actually feel that I'd actually left my son there – because it wasn't him. His spirit had gone.

Below, I've marked the speech with where I'd put stresses (marked in **bold**) and where I'd throw away phrases (marked in [brackets]); it's just a suggestion but it's based on what Cinque did both intuitively and in response to Stafford-Clark's direction:

I was a supervisor at Marks and Spencers. My son **Peter** was 29, he worked at **Freshfields**, the **solicitors**, [you know]. He was a hotshot **lawyer**, about to be made a **partner**. In the firm they couldn't believe how clever he was, [coming from Essex.] When I heard him on the phone, I used to think, he doesn't sound like **my son**,

he sounds like a **proper lawyer**. Later, [when I was
running the Disaster Action Group, I would find myself
saying things like], '**I put it to you.**' It was like he was
at my side. Peter was **on my shoulder. We loved
our son to bits. Very proud of him. Normal
parents**. On the night we were waiting to hear, we were
standing in the dark, [September – so the nights were
getting dark already – making cups of tea and not
drinking them] – and we just stood in the kitchen. And
I kept saying '**Well if he's gone, it's written**', and I
felt as if this was **coming from somewhere** – and my
husband said to me [and it was in the dark – and he's
just made another cup of tea which he'd thrown away
and he said], '**Maureen**' – (*turning to husband*) You
don't mind me saying this do you? He said, '**Maureen**',
and he was **crying**, and he said '**If Pete has gone
you've got to forgive me**'. And I said 'What do you
mean?' And he said '**I'm not staying here, I'm going
to go**'. He was **going to kill himself.** [. . .]

We went to the mortuary. Pete was **on a trolley.** [His
nose had come off and they'd just put it back on.] And
they'd combed his hair into a **fringe, he'd never had a
fringe in his life**, and he had this **fringe**. I didn't
actually **feel** that I'd actually **left my son there** –
because **it wasn't him. His spirit had gone**.[239]

You don't have to bash out all the highlighted areas: it's really
just an indication of the phrases that might need some colour,
as opposed to the [bracketed] phrases which could be thrown
away. Note that one of the most important details in the
speech – 'His nose had come off and they'd just put it back on'
– could be said quite lightly, and be doubly effective and
affecting for the lightness of touch. (Which is exactly what
Flaminia Cinque did, to great and moving effect.) What we
had to remember when we were working on *The Permanent
Way* was that these were oft-recounted stories: the survivors
and bereaved had shared their experiences many times – they
were accomplished story tellers. What upset us as first-time

listeners had been processed by them on many complex levels: that's why it was important that the audience should be the emoters and not the actors.

Postscript

The terrific British actor John Lyons told me a delightful tale from his early days at drama school. He was a teenage actor, standing in the wings, waiting to go on for a scene in *Romeo and Juliet*, and he saw the young actress playing Juliet also standing in the backstage darkness, and in one hand she was clutching a copy of *An Actor Prepares* and in the other hand – an onion. She was clearly trying to decide which of the two objects would be the most inspirational tool for the emotional scene before her.

I'd be inclined to say to any young actor: try them both! See what the book does for you, and see what the onion does for you. The important thing about a good technique is that it's open to all possibilities and all provocations. *The Complete Stanislavsky Toolkit* is only another provocation among many. There will be ideas, exercises, and suggestions in here which have instantly appealed to you; there will be others with which you were already familiar; and there will be those tools which you can't immediately see how to implement. No doubt you'll find – as indeed I have in my own practice – that some tools will come to hand on numerous occasions for a very long time . . . until suddenly they don't seem to serve you any more. Others will lie forgotten at the bottom of the toolkit until one day you unearth them again and rediscover their practicability.

Particular favourites of mine – apart from ACTIONS, BITS and OBJECTIVES which I just can't do without – are MOMENTS OF DECISION and MOMENTS OF ORIENTATION, along with HEROIC TENSION and GRASP. Each role you play will provoke different challenges, as indeed will each director and every medium, demanding different inroads and different tools: use those which help, ditch those which hinder, loot the toolkit as and when necessary. And remain ever mindful of the fact that your instrument as an actor is constantly changing with each new day and each new experience. Just as I always stash my Leatherman penknife and a torch in the glove compartment of my car, so too do I always keep my acting manual to hand every time I embark on a new performance adventure. But Stanislavsky never wanted his words to be taken as gospel, and so we won't. Here's to the onion!

Index of Tools

Endnotes

Variant versions of Russian names appear in these endnotes due to authors choosing different, yet equally valid, transliteration systems.

1   Constantin Stanislavski, *An Actor Prepares*, translated by Elizabeth Reynolds Hapgood (London: Methuen 1980), pp. 67, 68
2   Stanislavsky, cited in Jean Benedetti's *Stanislavski: His Life and Art* (London: Methuen 1999), p. 23
3   Constant Coquelin, *The Art of the Actor*, translated by Elsie Fogerty (London: Allen and Unwin 1932), p. 81
4   Constantin Stanislavski, *Stanislavski's Legacy: A Collection of Comments on a Variety of Aspects of an Actor's Art and Life*, edited and translated by Elizabeth Reynolds Hapgood (New York: Theatre Arts, Routledge 1999), p. 52
5   David Mamet, *True and False: Heresy and Common Sense for the Actor* (London: Faber and Faber 1998), p. 30
6   Michael Chekhov, *To the Actor on the Technique of Acting* (London: Routledge 2002), p. 13
7   Jerzy Grotowski, *Towards a Poor Theatre* (London: Eyre Methuen 1976), p. 101
8   Constantin Stanislavski, *Creating a Role*, translated by Elizabeth Reynolds Hapgood (London: Methuen 2000), p. 26
9   Constantin Stanislavski, *Building a Character*, translated by Elizabeth Reynolds Hapgood (London: Methuen 2000), p. 292
10   *Creating a Role*, p. 237 (original emphasis)
11   *An Actor Prepares*, p. 16
12   Konstantin Stanislavsky, *On the Art of the Stage*, translated by David Magarshack (London: Faber and Faber 1973), p. 118
13   *Building a Character*, p. 276
14   Ibid., p. 265
15   Ibid., p. 250
16   Ibid., p. 258

17 Ibid., p. 255
18 *Stanislavski's Legacy*, p. 149
19 *On the Art of the Stage*, p. 98
20 Ibid., p. 168 (my emphasis)
21 Ibid., p. 169
22 David Magarshack, *Stanislavsky: A Life* (London: Faber and Faber 1986), p. 304
23 *An Actor Prepares*, p. 75
24 Ibid., p. 72
25 *True and False*, p. 94
26 Ibid., p. 95 (my emphasis)
27 Ibid., p. 96 (my emphasis)
28 *On the Art of the Stage*, p. 166
29 Constantin Stanislavski, *An Actor's Handbook*, edited and translated by Elizabeth Reynolds Hapgood (London: Routledge 2004), p. 134
30 William Shakespeare, *Richard III*, Act I, Scene ii
31 *On the Art of the Stage*, p. 178
32 Ibid., p. 122
33 *Stanislavsky: A Life*, p. 281
34 *An Actor's Handbook*, p. 149 (my emphasis)
35 *An Actor Prepares*, p. 280
36 *An Actor's Handbook*, p. 85
37 Ibid., p. 85
38 *An Actor Prepares*, p. 37
39 Ibid., p. 118
40 Ibid., p. 287
41 Ibid., p. 304
42 Stanislavsky, cited by Alexei Popov in 'Reminiscences and Reflections about the Theatre', *Stanislavski Today: Commentaries on K.S. Stanislavski*, compiled and edited by Sonia Moore (New York: American Center for Stanislavski Theater Art 1973) p. 86 (my emphasis)
43 Ibid., p 89
44 *An Actor's Handbook*, p. 44
45 Stanislavsky, cited by Popov, 'Reminiscences', p. 86 (my emphasis)
46 Stanislavsky, cited in *On the Active Analysis of Plays and Roles*, Maria Knebel, in unpublished translation by Mike Pushkin, 2003, p. 97
47 Ibid., pp. 99–100
48 *An Actor's Handbook*, pp. 64, 65
49 *Creating a Role*, p. 4

50 Ibid., p. 5
51 Ibid., p. 7
52 Konstantin Stanislavsky, *Selected Works*, compiled by Oksana Korneva, this chapter ('Report on Ten Years of the Moscow Art Theatre's Activity') translated by Olga Shartze (Moscow: Raduga 1984), p. 126 (my emphasis)
53 Stanislavsky, cited in Sonia Moore, *The Stanislavski System* (USA: Penguin USA 1984), p. 13
54 *On the Art of the Stage*, p. 128
55 *On the Active Analysis of Plays and Roles*, p. 8
56 Stanislavsky, cited in *On the Active Analysis of Plays and Roles*, p. 2
57 *Creating a Role*, p. 8 (original emphasis)
58 Ibid., p. 11
59 Anton Chekhov, *Three Sisters* in *Chekhov, Four Plays*, translated by Stephen Mulrine (London: Nick Hern Books 2005), p. 179
60 Bertolt Brecht, *Mother Courage and Her Children*, translated by John Willett (London, Methuen 1980), p. 21
61 This list is drawn from *An Actor Prepares*, p. 51
62 Ibid., p. 149
63 Stanislavsky, cited in *On the Active Analysis of Plays and Roles*, p. 15
64 Anton Chekhov, *The Seagull* in *Chekhov: Four Plays*, translated by Stephen Mulrine (London: Nick Hern Books 2005), p. 4
65 *An Actor Prepares*, p. 115
66 *Stanislavski's Legacy*, p. 156 (original emphasis)
67 *An Actor Prepares*, pp. 116–7
68 Ibid., pp. 121, 122
69 Ibid., p. 122 (my emphasis)
70 Ibid., p. 123 (original emphasis)
71 Ibid., p. 126
72 Helen Edmundson, *Anna Karenina* (London: Nick Hern Book 1996), pp. 48–9
73 *An Actor Prepares*, p. 310 (original emphasis)
74 *Building a Character*, p. 113
75 Stanislavsky, cited in *On the Active Analysis of Plays and Roles*, p. 95
76 *Building a Character*, p. 121
77 *Creating a Role*, p. 160 (my emphasis)
78 *Three Sisters*, pp. 205–6
79 *On the Active Analysis of Plays and Roles*, p. 88

80   Ibid., p. 83–4
81   C. P. Taylor, *Good*, Act 2, *Good & And a Nightingale Sang* . . .
     (London: Methuen 1990), p. 43
82   *An Actor Prepares*, p. 68
83   Max Stafford-Clark, *Letters to George: The Account of a
     Rehearsal* (London: Nick Hern Books 1997)
84   I detail my experience of working with Stafford-Clark on
     'actioning' with *The Permanent Way* in an essay entitled '*The
     Permanent Way* and the Impermanent Muse' in a special
     edition of *Contemporary Theatre Review*, entitled 'On Acting',
     Phillip B. Zarrilli and Bella Merlin (guest editors), Volume 17,
     No. 1 (January 2007), pp. 41–9
85   *An Actor Prepares*, p. 242, Logic and Coherence (See Preface)
86   Ibid., p. 156
87   Ibid., p. 128
88   Ibid.
89   Ibid., p. 158
90   *Stanislavsky's Legacy*, pp. 152–3 (original emphasis)
91   *An Actor Prepares*, p. 130
92   Ibid., p. 130
93   Jean Benedetti, *Stanislavski: An Introduction* (London:
     Methuen 1989), p. 43
94   *An Actor Prepares*, p. 149
95   Ibid., p. 54
96   S. D. Balukhaty (ed), *The Seagull, Produced by Stanislavsky*,
     translated by David Magarshack (London: Dobson 1952)
97   *Building a Character*, p. 126
98   *An Actor Prepares*, p. 57
99   *Creating a Role*, p. 40
100 *Stanislavski's Legacy*, p. 151
101 *An Actor's Handbook*, p. 76 (original emphasis)
102 Ibid., p. 78
103 *An Actor Prepares*, p. 49
104 *On the Art of the Stage*, p. 131
105 Stanislavsky, cited by Vasily Toporkov in *Stanislavski in
     Rehearsal: The Final Years*, translated by Christine Edwards
     (New York: Theatre Arts Books 1979), p. 215 (original
     emphasis)
106 *Creating a Role*, pp. 48, 49–50
107 *An Actor Prepares*, p. 149 (my emphasis)
108 Ibid., p. 141
109 *An Actor's Handbook*, pp. 140–41

110 Cited by Benedetti in *Stanislavski: A Biography*, p. 179 (my emphasis)
111 *My Life in Art*, pp. 561–62
112 Norris Houghton, *Moscow Rehearsals* (USA: Octagon Books 1975), p. 61
113 *Stanislavski in Rehearsal*, p. 62 (original emphasis)
114 *Building a Character*, p. 216
115 *Stanislavski in Rehearsal*, p. 170
116 *An Actor Prepares*, p. 189 (original emphasis)
117 *Stanislavsky Directs*, pp. 292–3
118 *An Actor Prepares*, p. 174 (original emphasis)
119 Cited by Christine Edwards in *The Stanislavsky Heritage* (London: Peter Owen 1966), p. 270
120 *Stanislavski's Legacy*, p. 151
121 *Stanislavsky Directs*, pp. 96–7
122 Ibid., p. 157
123 Interview with Miles Anderson, June 2006
124 *My Life in Art*, p. 194
125 *An Actor's Handbook*, p. 54
126 *Stanislavsky Directs*, p. 157
127 *An Actor Prepares*, p. 69
128 Ibid., p. 247 (original emphasis)
129 *On the Art of the Stage*, p. 195
130 *Creating a Role*, p. 69
131 *My Life in Art*, p. 183
132 Stanislavsky, cited in *Stanislavski in Rehearsal*, p. 205
133 *An Actor Prepares*, p. 76
134 Ibid., p. 89
135 *On the Art of the Stage*, p. 146
136 *An Actor Prepares*, p. 282 (original emphasis)
137 Antony Sher, *Primo Time* (London: Nick Hern Books, 2005)
138 *An Actor Prepares*, p. 293 (my emphasis)
139 *My Life in Art*, pp. 199, 308
140 Stanislavsky, cited in *Stanislavsky Directs*, p. 192
141 *Stanislavski in Rehearsal*, p. 152
142 *On the Art of the Stage*, p. 201 (my emphasis)
143 Stanislavsky, cited in *Stanislavsky: A Life*, pp. 390, 389
144 *My Life in Art*, p. 405–6
145 *An Actor Prepares*, p. 142
146 Sharon M. Carnicke, 'Stanislavsky's System' in *Twentieth Century Actor Training*, Alison Hodge (ed.), Chapter 1 (London: Routledge 2000), pp. 26–7

147 *Creating a Role*, p. 262
148 Stanislavsky, cited in *Stanislavsky Directs*, p. 120
149 *Creating a Role*, p. 95
150 Ibid., p. 95
151 Ibid., p. 141
152 Ibid., p. 207
153 Ibid., p. 208
154 Stanislavsky, cited in *Stanislavski in Rehearsal*, p. 170
155 Stanislavsky, cited in *Stanislavski: A Biography*, pp. 312–13
156 *On the Active Analysis of Plays and Roles*, p. 101
157 Stanislavsky, cited in *On the Active Analysis of Plays and Roles*, p. 20
158 Ibid., p. 20
159 Mark Ravenhill, *Shopping and Fucking* in *The Methuen Book of Modern Drama* (London: Methuen 2001), Scene 3, p. 286
160 Stanislavsky, cited in *On the Active Analysis of Plays and Roles*, p. 21
161 Anton Chekhov, *The Cherry Orchard*, translated by Stephen Mulrine (London: Nick Hern Books 2005), pp. 274–5
162 Stanislavsky, cited in *Stanislavsky Directs*, p. 316
163 *An Actor Prepares*, p. 217
164 *Creating a Role*, p. 29
165 Ibid., p. 106
166 *An Actor Prepares*, p. 218
167 Ibid., p. 273
168 Ibid., pp. 93–4
169 Ibid., p. 205 (original emphasis)
170 Ibid., pp. 201–2
171 Ibid., pp. 202–3
172 Ibid., p. 214
173 *On the Active Analysis of Plays and Roles*, p. 9
174 Stanislavsky, cited in *Stanislavsky Directs*, p. 94
175 *An Actor Prepares*, p. 294
176 Ibid., p. 225
177 Ibid., p. 224
178 Stanislavsky, cited in *On the Active Analysis of Plays and Roles*, p. 25
179 *Stanislavski in Rehearsal*, p. 90
180 *An Actor Prepares*, p. 307
181 Interview with David Hare, March 2004
182 *On the Active Analysis of Plays and Roles*, p. 27
183 *An Actor Prepares*, p. 303

184 Stanislavsky, cited in *On the Active Analysis of Plays and Roles*, pp. 25–6 (my emphasis)

185 *An Actor's Handbook*, p. 138

186 *Creating a Role*, pp. 78–9 (my emphasis)

187 Ibid., p. 78

188 Stanislavsky, cited in *On the Active Analysis of Plays and Roles*, p. 27

189 *On the Active Analysis of Plays and Roles*, p. 29

190 Ibid., pp. 76–7

191 Ibid., p. 93

192 Stanislavsky, cited in *On the Active Analysis of Plays and Roles*, p. 93

193 *Building a Character*, p. 138

194 Ibid., p. 138

195 Vladimir Nemirovich-Danchenko, *My Life in the Russian Theatre*, translated by John Cournos (Boston: Little, Brown & Co, 1936), p. 162

196 *On the Active Analysis of Plays and Roles*, p. 55

197 Ibid., p. 56

198 Nemirovich-Danchenko, cited in *On the Active Analysis of Plays and Roles*, pp. 56–7

199 Ibid., p. 59

200 *On the Active Analysis of Plays and Roles*, p. 62

201 Stanislavsky, cited in *Stanislavsky Directs*, p. 266

202 *Building a Character*, p. 123

203 *On the Active Analysis of Plays and Roles*, p. 65 (my emphasis)

204 Ibid., p. 65

205 Stanislavsky, cited in *On the Active Analysis of Plays and Roles*, p. 66

206 Stanislavsky, cited in *Stanislavski in Rehearsal*, p. 123

207 Ibid., p. 124

208 *Konstantin Stanislavsky: Selected Works*, p. 119

209 Ibid., p. 172 (original emphasis)

210 *On the Art of the Stage*, p. 21

211 Stanislavsky, cited in *Stanislavsky: A Life*, p. 372

212 Alexei Popov in 'Reminiscences and Reflections about Theatre', p. 90

213 *An Actor Prepares*, p. 203

214 Stanislavsky, cited in *Stanislavski: A Biography*, p. 32

215 *Building a Character*, p. 21

216 Ibid., pp. 179, 180–1

217 *An Actor Prepares*, p. 312

218 *On the Art of the Stage*, p. 16
219 *An Actor's Handbook*, p. 94 (original emphasis)
220 *On the Art of the Stage*, p. 230
221 *Stanislavski's Legacy*, p. 156
222 Interview with Max Stafford-Clark, March 2004
223 Stanislavsky, cited in *On the Active Analysis of Plays and Roles*, pp 80–7
224 William Wycherley, *The Country Wife* (London: Nick Hern Books Drama Classics 2001), pp. 108–9
225 Harold Pinter, *Plays: Two* including *The Lover* (London: Methuen 1981), pp. 176–8
226 *Shopping and Fucking*, p. 236
227 David Mamet, *Plays: 1* including *American Buffalo* (London: Methuen 1994), pp. 162–3
228 Ibid., p. 148
229 Marina Caldarone and Maggie Lloyd-Williams, *Actions: An Actor's Thesaurus* (London: Nick Hern Books 2004)
230 *Anna Karenina*, pp. 48–9
231 *Building a Character*, pp. 200–2
232 Bella Merlin, *Konstantin Stanislavsky*, Routledge Performance Practitioners (London: Routledge 2003), p. 151
233 Bella Merlin, *Beyond Stanislavsky: The Psycho-Physical Approach to Actor-Training* (London: Nick Hern Books 2001), p. 60
234 *Konstantin Stanislavsky*, p. 141
235 Kamotskaya trained as an actress as the Shchukin Institute, before working extensively in Russia. She spent time at Grotowski's Teatr Laboratorium, taught at the State Institute of Cinematography in Moscow, following which she took up a teaching post at the Royal Scottish Academy of Music and Drama in Glasgow in 1999. Full details of her work can be found in my account of the Russian training, *Beyond Stanislavsky*.
236 *The Seagull*, pp. 36–7
237 *Konstantin Stanislavsky*, pp. 105–6 (original emphasis)
238 Arthur Miller, *The Crucible*, Act 1 (London: Penguin 1962), pp. 27, 28
239 David Hare, *The Permanent Way* (London: Faber 2003), pp. 27, 28–9